The Story of the Goths

The Story of the Goths:
From the Earliest Times to the End of the Gothic Dominion in Spain

By

Henry Bradley

Enhanced Media
2016

The Story of the Goths, From the earliest times to the end of the Gothic dominion in Spain by Henry Bradley. First published in 1888.

This edition published by Enhanced Media.

Enhanced Media Publishing
Los Angeles, CA.

First Printing: 2016.

ISBN-13: 978-1523604524

ISBN-10: 1523604522

Contents

Preface 7
I: WHO WERE THE GOTHS? 8
II: FROM THE BALTIC TO THE DANUBE 15
III: FIRE AND SWORD IN ASIA AND GREECE 18
IV: HOW THE GOTHS FOUGHT WITH CONSTANTINE ... 22
V: THE GOTHIC ALEXANDER 25
VI: THE JUDGES OF THE VISIGOTHS 28
VII: THE APOSTLE OF THE GOTHS 31
VIII: FRITHIGERN AND VALENS—THE BATTLE OF HADRIANOPLE 35
IX: THE GOTHS AND THEODOSIUS 40
X: ALARIC THE BALTHING 43
XI: KING ATAWULF AND HIS ROMAN QUEEN 50
XII: THE KINGDOM OF TOULOUSE 53
XIII: HOW THE WESTERN EMPIRE CAME TO AN END 62
XIV: THE BOYHOOD OF THEODERIC 65
XV: THE RIVAL NAMESAKES 68
XVI: HOW THE OSTROGOTHS WON ITALY 72
XVII: THE WISDOM OF THEODERIC 76
XVIII: THEODERIC AND HIS FOREIGN NEIGHBOURS 86
XIX: THEODERIC'S EVIL DAYS 90
XX: A QUEEN'S TROUBLES 94
XXI: AN UNKINGLY KING 101
XXII: WITIGIS THE UNREADY 107

XXIII: THE YEAR-LONG SIEGE	113
XXIV: WITIGIS IN HIDING	124
XXV: THE GOTHS LOSE RAVENNA	129
XXVI: NEW GOTHIC VICTORIES	133
XXVII: THE FAILURE OF BELISARIUS	138
XXVIII: THE RUIN OF THE OSTROGOTHS	144
XXIX: THE VISIGOTHS AGAIN	152
XXX: LEOVIGILD AND HIS SONS	155
XXXI: THE GOTHS BECOME CATHOLIC	158
XXXII: A PRIEST-RIDDEN KINGDOM	161
XXXIII: THE STORY OF WAMBA	165
XXXIV: THIRTY YEARS OF DECAY	168
XXXV: THE FALL OF THE VISIGOTHS	172
XXXVI: CONCLUSION	174

Preface

This little volume is, so far as I have been able to discover, the first English book expressly treating of the history of the Goths. Adequately to supply the strange deficiency in our literature indicated by this fact is a task that will require powers far greater than mine. Some day, perhaps, the story of the Goths will be told in English by a writer possessing the rare combination of literary skill and profound scholarship that will be needed to do it justice. But in the meantime I would fain hope that this brief sketch may be found to have a sufficient reason for its existence. I have made no attempt to write a brilliant narrative, well knowing that success in such an attempt is beyond my reach. My aim has been to relate the facts of the history as correctly as I could, and with the simplicity of language required by the plan of the series in which the work appears—a series intended not for scholars, but for readers in whom little knowledge of general history is to be pre-supposed.

If this volume should fall into the hand of scholars, it will perhaps be obvious that I have not neglected to read most of the original sources of the history; but it may be still more obvious that I have not the thorough familiarity with them that might justly be demanded if I claimed for my work any independent historical value. Remembering the dangers of "a little learning," I have endeavoured to escape them by refraining from expressing any views which have not the sanction of at least one modern scholar of repute. The prescribed plan of the work has, of course, not permitted me either to adduce arguments or to cite authorities in justification of the particular conclusions adopted.

Among the English writers to whom I am indebted, the first place belongs to Gibbon, whose greatness appears to me in a new light since I have tried to compare a small portion of his wonderful work with the materials out of which it was constructed. I also owe much to Mr. Hodgkin's "Italy and her Invaders," and to various articles by Mr. E. A. Freeman. Among foreign writers my principal guide has been Dahn; I have also made extensive use of the works of Bessell, Waitz, Aschbach, Manso, and Lembke. To mention the titles of books that have been merely consulted on special points seems to me to be unnecessary, and, unless elaborate explanations could be added, likely to be also misleading.

Some surprise may perhaps be occasioned by the date chosen for the accompanying map. My reason for selecting the year 485 rather than 526 is that, if only one map is to be given, the map representing the state of Europe at the culminating period of the Visigoth dominion, is more useful for the illustration of Gothic history as a whole, than one relating to the later and intrinsically more interesting epoch.

I: WHO WERE THE GOTHS?

More than three hundred years before the birth of Christ, a traveller from the Greek colony of Marseilles, named Pytheas, made known to the civilized world the existence of a people called Guttones, who lived near the Frische Haff, in the country since known as East Prussia, and traded in the amber that was gathered on the Baltic shores. For four whole centuries these amber merchants of the Baltic are heard of no more. The elder Pliny, a Roman writer who died in the year 79 after Christ, tells us that in his time they were still dwelling in the same neighbourhood; and a generation later, Tacitus, the greatest of Roman historians, twice mentions their name, though he spells it rather differently as Gotones. In his little book on Germany, he says—in that brief pointed style of his which it is so difficult to translate into English —"Beyond the Lygians live the Gotones among whom the power of the kings has already become greater than among the other Germans, though it is not yet too great for them to be a free people." And in his Annals he mentions that they gave shelter to a prince belonging to another German nation, who had been driven from his own country by the oppression of a foreign conqueror. These two brief notices are all that Tacitus, who has told us so much that is interesting about the peoples of ancient Germany, has to say of the Gotones. But if he could only have guessed what was the destiny in store for this obscure and distant tribe, we may be sure that they would have received a far larger share of his attention. For these Gotones were the same people who afterwards became so famous under the name of Goths, who, a few centuries later, crowned their kings in Rome itself, and imposed their laws on the whole of Southern Europe from the Adriatic to the Western sea.

It is the story of these Goths that in the present volume we are going to relate, from the time when they were still living almost unnoticed in their northern home near the Baltic and the Vistula, down to the time when their separate history becomes blended in the history of the southern nations whom they conquered, and by whom they were at last absorbed. In many respects the career of this people is strikingly different from that of any other nation of equal historic renown. For three hundred years —beginning with the days of Tacitus—their history consists of little else than a dreary record of barbarian slaughter and pillage. A century later, the Goths have become the mightiest nation in Europe. One of their two kings sits on the throne of the Caesars, the wisest and most beneficent ruler that Italy has known for ages; the other reigns over Spain and the richest part of Gaul. We look forward two hundred and fifty years, and the Gothic kingdoms are no more; the nation itself has vanished from the stage of history, leaving scarcely a trace behind.

The story we have to tell lacks many of the elements to which the history of most nations owes a large part of its interest. Except a part of a translation of the Bible, the Goths have left us no literature; the legends which they told about the deeds of gods and heroes have nearly all perished; and even the history of their short period of greatness has to be learned from ignorant and careless writers, who have left untold a great deal that we would gladly know. And yet the story of the Goths is not without powerful attractions of its own. In all history there is nothing more romantically marvellous than the swift rise of this people to the height of greatness, or than the suddenness and the tragic completeness of their ruin. Amongst the actors in this story are some whose noble characters and deeds are worthy of eternal remembrance; and the events which it records have influenced the destinies of the whole civilized world. And while for an Italian, a Frenchman, or a Spaniard, Gothic history is important as a part of the history of his own country, for us who speak the English tongue it has a special interest of another kind, because the Goths were in a certain sense our own near kindred. It is true that we are a people of mingled origin; but we are to no small extent descendants of the Teutonic race, from which we have inherited our language, and to this race the Goths also belonged. The Gothic language, as it is known to us from Bishop Wulfila's translation of the Bible, is very much like the oldest English, though it is still more like the language that was spoken by the ancestors of the Swedes and Norwegians. There is little doubt that in the first century all the Teutonic peoples could understand one another's speech, though even then there must have been among them some differences of dialect, which grew wider as time went on. Now since the Gothic Bible is some hundreds of years older than any book in any of the sister dialects, it is the most important help we possess towards finding out what the old Teutonic speech was like before it was developed into the different languages which we call English, German, Dutch, Swedish, and Danish. And so it comes about that scholars, who inquire into the origin of English words and the reasons for the rules of English grammar, find that they can obtain a great deal of light from the study of the long-dead Gothic tongue.

Besides the Gothic Bible there have been preserved two or three other short pieces of writing in the Gothic language. One of these—a fragment of a calendar—contains the word Gutthiuda, "people of the Goths." The word thiuda is the same as the Old-English theod, meaning people; and from the compound Gut-thiuda, and from other evidence, it may be inferred that the name which, following the Romans, we spell as "Goths" was properly Gutans— in the singular Guta. Like all other names of nations, this word must originally have had a meaning, but it is very difficult to discover what that meaning was. It has often been asserted that the name of the Goths has something to do with the word God (in Gothic guth). We might easily believe that an ancient people might have chosen to call themselves 'the worshippers of the Gods' but although this interesting suggestion was proposed by Jacob Grimm, one of the greatest scholars who ever lived, it is now quite certain that it was a mistake. It seems now to be generally thought that the meaning of Gutans is "the (nobly) born."

About the year 200, when they were living on the north shore of the Black Sea, the Gutans or Goths divided themselves into two great branches, the Thervings and the Greutungs. These two peoples had also other names, which are much better known in history. The Thervings were called Visigoths (i.e., West Goths), and the

Greutungs Ostrogoths (East Goths). These latter names referred at first to the situation which the two divisions then occupied, one east, the other west of the river Dniester; but by a curious coincidence they continued to be appropriate down to the latest days of Gothic history, for when the Goths conquered the South of Europe, the Visigoths went westwards to Gaul and Spain, while the Ostrogoths settled in Italy. Probably the Thervings and Greutungs were the only people to whom the name of Goths in strictness belonged. There was, however, a third tribe, the Gepids, whom the other two recognized as being, if not exactly Goths, at any rate, their nearest kinsfolk, and as having originally formed one nation with them. About the origin of these Gepids, the Gothic historian, Jordanes (who lived in the sixth century, and was, perhaps, bishop of Crotona in Italy) tells a curious story, founded, it seems, on ancient popular songs. He relates that the original home of the Goths was in "the island of Scanzia"—that is to say, in the Scandinavian peninsula; and that they came to the mainland of Europe in three ships, under the command of a king named Berig. One of the ships was a heavy sailer, and arrived long after the others; and for this reason the people who came over in her were called Gepids, from a Gothic word gepanta, meaning slow. Of course this is not the real explanation of the name of the Gepids, but the story must be regarded as an ancient Gothic joke at their expense. Jordanes says that the Gepids were a dull-witted and heavy-bodied nation; and as a matter of fact we generally find them lagging a little behind the Goths in their southward march.

Whether the Goths did originally come from Scandinavia is a question that has been much disputed. The traditions of a people contained in its songs are not to be lightly put aside, and there is no reason to doubt that the Goths once inhabited the northern as well as the southern shores of the Baltic. But it cannot be said that apart from tradition there is any real evidence of the fact. It is true that the southern province of Sweden is still called Gothland; but the Gautar (called Geatas by the Anglo-Saxons), from whom this province took its name, were not identical with the Goths, though doubtless nearly related to them. On the other hand, the island called Gothland, in the Baltic, was anciently called Gutaland, which seems to show that its early inhabitants were really in the strict sense Goths. And according to the Norse sagas and the Anglo-Saxon poets, the peninsula of Jutland was anciently occupied by a branch of the Gothic people, who were known as Hrethgotan, or Reidhgotar.

There were also a number of smaller tribes, such as the Herules, Scirians, Rugians, and Turcilings, who accompanied the Goths as subjects or as allies in their southward march, and who seem to have been more closely akin to them than any other of the great divisions of the Teutonic race. The great nation of the Vandals, moreover, originally the neighbours of the Goths on the west, who about the same time as they did, though by a different path, wandered from the Baltic to the Danube, and afterwards played an important part in history, are said by Roman writers to have been identical with the Goths in language, laws, and manners. The Romans naturally often confounded the two peoples together, and not unfrequently they applied the name of Goths in a loose sense to all those Teutonic nations who invaded the southern lands. In this volume, however, we are concerned only with the fortunes of the Visigoths and Ostrogoths, and shall only mention these other peoples when they come in our way.

The Goths are always described as tall and athletic men, with fair complexions, blue eyes, and yellow hair—such people, in fact, as may be seen more frequently in Sweden than in any other modern land. A very good idea of their national costume and their general appearance may be gained from the sculptures on "The Storied Column," as it is called, erected at Constantinople by the Emperor Arcadius in honour of his father Theodosius, which represent a triumphal procession, including many Gothic captives. The dress of the men consists usually of a short tunic with girdle, wide turned-down collars, and short sleeves; an inner garment coming down to the knees; and trousers, sometimes reaching to the ankle, and sometimes ending just below the knees. The last mentioned article of dress is often referred to as distinguishing the Goths from the bare-legged Romans. A king or chief, who sits with two attendants on a car drawn by oxen, is similar in his attire to the rest of the captives, but his superior rank is denoted by the collar and skirt of his tunic being cut into an ornamental pattern. All the men wear long curly hair and long beards. Some of them are bareheaded, while others wear caps of somewhat fantastic shapes. Some of the Gothic figures in the procession seem not to be prisoners of war, but auxiliaries in the Roman service, as they appear without any marks of humiliation, and several of them carry Roman armour. Their leaders are on horseback, and are dressed in a style similar to that of their captive countrymen, with the addition of long fur cloaks—a garment which was proverbially characteristic of their people. The female captives appear clad in long robes down to the feet; some have their heads covered with kerchiefs, while others are bareheaded, with long streaming hair. We may safely rely on the general accuracy of this interesting portraiture, for at the end of the fourth century the appearance of the Goths had become familiar to all the inhabitants of Constantinople.

That the Gothic people had many noble qualities was frequently acknowledged even by their enemies, and is abundantly proved by many incidents in their history. They were brave, generous, patient under hardship and privation, and chaste and affectionate in their family relations. The one great reproach which the Roman writers bring against them is that of faithlessness to their treaties, a charge frequently made by civilized peoples against barbarians, and one which the barbarians have too often had good .reason to retort. In the first flush of victory they were sometimes terribly cruel; but on the whole there is nothing in their history more remarkable than the humanity and justice which they exercised towards the nations whom they had conquered; and there are many instances on record in which Romans were glad to seek under the milder sway of the Goths a refuge from the oppressions of their own rulers. It is true, however, that their history gives but little evidence of their possession of the gentler virtues until after their conversion to Christianity—an event which had unquestionably a very profound effect on their national character. The Roman clergy, by whom the Goths were disliked both as alien conquerors and as heretics, were often constrained to own that these barbarians obeyed the precepts of the gospel far better than did their own countrymen.

We have no contemporary description of the state of society which existed amongst the Goths when they were living in their ancient abodes near the Baltic; but it was probably in its main features similar to that of the other Teutonic peoples as described by Tacitus. By combining the information supplied by Tacitus with what we know of the manners and institutions of the Goths in later days, it is possible to arrive at some general conclusions respecting their mode of life before their southward wanderings began. We must imagine them as dwelling, not in cities or compact villages, but in habitations scattered over the woods and plains, each with its own enclosure of farm land, which they cultivated with the help of slaves, the descendants of captives taken in war. Their chief subsistence, however, was not derived from their crops, but from their vast herds of cattle, which they pastured on their wide common lands. Their drink was mead and beer, in which, no doubt, like the other Teutonic peoples, they often indulged to excess. At their feasts they entertained themselves with songs relating the deeds of famous heroes of the past. At the season of new moon the men of each district assembled in the open air to administer justice and to make laws for themselves; and from time to time the whole nation was gathered together to discuss great questions such as those of war or peace. The kings were chosen by the voice of the assembled people from certain great families, two of which, the Amalings and the Balthings, are known to us by name. The Amalings were said to be descended from a hero whose deeds had earned for him the title of Amala, 'the mighty,' the name of the Balthings is derived from the same root as our English word bold. Of these two noble houses we shall hereafter have much to say, for the Amalings became the royal line of the Ostrogoths, while the Visigoths chose their kings from the Balthings.

Of the religion of the Goths in their heathen days we know but little. Their native historian tells us that they worshipped certain beings called Anses, and this word is plainly the same as sir (plural of Ass or Ans), the name which the Scandinavians applied to the greater gods of their mythology. No ancient writer has mentioned the name of a single Gothic deity, but there is reason to believe that amongst their chief gods were the Great Twin Brethren, corresponding to Castor and Pollux, and we may feel sure that, like all their Teutonic kindred, they worshipped Wodan, the spirit of wind and storm, the inspirer of poetry and wisdom. Another of their gods, no doubt, was Tiw, whose name shows that he was once the same with Dyaus, Zeus, Jupiter, the ancient sky-god of the Indians, Greeks, and Romans, and whom the Teutonic warriors invoked as their god of battles. Probably, also, they worshipped—under what names we know not—the Sun-god and the Thunder-god, whom the Scandinavians called Baldr and Thorr. And there is proof that Halya, which in the Gothic Bible is the word for "hell," must originally have been the name of the goddess of the lower world. But which of these divinities were regarded as higher than the rest, and what other gods and goddesses were reverenced besides them, are questions that cannot be answered. Images of the gods (not complete statues, but pillars surmounted with the likeness of a human head), raised aloft on chariots, were carried from place to place to receive the adoration of the people. The sodden flesh of animals was offered in sacrifice, and sometimes we read that human victims were laid upon the altars, but whether this is fact or fable we cannot tell. The Gothic temples were served both by male and female priests, and during the warlike journeyings of the nation the place of a temple was supplied by a sacred tent. These few particulars are all that we really know about Gothic heathendom, for when the people became Christians their clergy strove to blot out the recollections of their old beliefs, and in this endeavour they succeeded only too well.

One more fact, and that a very interesting one, is known respecting the early condition of the Goths. They possessed an alphabet of their own, the letters of which were called "runes." We cannot suppose, however, that they had any extensive written literature, for they seem in their heathen days to have used no more convenient writing material than boards and wooden staves, on which their inscriptions were carved. It is not likely that the great bulk of the people knew how to read and write. The word rune literally means a secret or mystery, and that shows that the art of writing; was looked upon with superstitious awe as a sort of half-miraculous endowment. Very likely the knowledge of it was kept carefully in the hands of the priesthood, or some learned caste. The Goths used their runes for inscribing the names of their dead heroes on their tombstones, and for marking their swords and jewels with the owner's name. Their wise men wrote witchcraft spells to hang up in the people's houses to drive away bad spirits or to bring good luck. Sometimes, perhaps, a new law might be carved in wood or stone to be handed down to later ages; letters (very short and pithy we may be sure they would be) might be sent from one chief to another about matters too weighty to be trusted to word of mouth; or a poet might now and then call in the aid of the rune-man to preserve the memory of one of his songs. Perhaps too there were some rude attempts at history writing, such as we have in the early part of the Saxon Chronicle—just brief memoranda of events put down at the time, saying that "such a king died; So-and-so was made king; Goths fought with Gepids; Gepids were beaten, with great slaughter: this or that chief was killed." But all this is only guessing, for only one or two Gothic inscriptions, and those very short ones, have been preserved. From the Goths, however, the Runic alphabet passed to the kindred nations dwelling near the Baltic, and it is found on hundreds of tombstones and memorial pillars in Scandinavia, Iceland, and the British Isles. Two of the characters, p and p, were adopted in Old English to express the sounds of th and w, for which the Roman alphabet supplied no proper sign. When people write y instead of the, or y instead of that (as is still sometimes done in England), they are really using one of the "runes" inherited from the heathen Goths who lived two thousand years ago. A specimen of the Gothic runes may be seen in the accompanying engraving of a gold necklet found in 1838 amid the ruins of a heathen temple near Bucharest, in the country where the Goths were dwelling early in the fourth century. The inscription has been read by some scholars as Gutannom hailag, "sacred to the treasure of the Goths."

The Goths certainly did not invent these letters for themselves, and there has been a great deal of discussion on the question how they got them. If we compare the oldest runes with the Latin letters, or, what is very much the same thing, with an early form of the Greek letters, we see at once that several of them are just the Latin or old Greek characters, altered so as to render them more convenient for cutting on wood. It is usually believed amongst scholars that the runes are of Latin origin; but as the evidence seems to show that they were first used in the far north-east, where Roman influences could hardly have reached, we prefer to accept the view of Dr. Isaac Taylor, that they are a corruption of an old Greek alphabet used in certain colonies on the north-west coast of the Black Sea. But how the knowledge of this alphabet was carried to the Goths dwelling six hundred miles away, and what caused the changes in the sounds expressed by some of the letters, are questions we have no means of answering.

Before we leave the subject of this chapter, there is one more point that must be touched on, because it affects our understanding of some parts of the succeeding history. In ancient times the countries north of the Danube mouths were inhabited by a people called Getes (in Latin Getae). You may remember that the poet Ovid was sent to live among this people when Augustus banished him from Rome. Now in the third century after Christ the Goths came and dwelt in the land of the Getes, and to some extent mingled with the native inhabitants; and so the Romans came to think that Goths and Getes were only two names for the same people, or rather two different ways of pronouncing the same word. Even the historian Jordanes, himself a Goth, actually calls his book a Getic history, and mixes up the traditions of his own people with the tales which he had read in books about the Getes. In modern times some great scholars have tried to prove that the Getes really were Goths, and that the early territory of the Gothic nation reached all the way from the Baltic to the Black Sea. But the ablest authorities are now mostly agreed that this is a mistake, and that when the Goths migrated to the region of the Danube it was to settle amongst a people of a different race, speaking a foreign tongue.

As late as the middle of the second century (unless, as is not unlikely, the geographer Ptolemy copied his information from much earlier writers) the "Gythones" or Goths were still dwelling along the eastern bank of the Vistula. A few years later they began their great southward journey, and left their ancient homes to be occupied by new possessors, the kinsmen of the Slavonians and Lithuanians.

II: FROM THE BALTIC TO THE DANUBE

The emigration of a settled people from the country which it has occupied for hundreds of years, is a very different sort of thing from the movements of mere wandering hordes like the Huns or the Tartars. It is true the Goths were only barbarians, and the ties which bound them to their native soil were far less complex and powerful than those which affect a civilized community; and no doubt they had often made long expeditions for plunder or conquest into the adjoining lands. But still we may be sure that the resolution to forsake their ancient homes, and to seek a settlement in unknown and distant regions, must have cost them a great deal of anxious deliberation, and that they must have been impelled to it by very powerful motives. What these motives were we can only faintly guess. It can scarcely be supposed that the Goths were driven southward by the invasion of stronger neighbours, for the peoples who afterwards occupied the Baltic shores seem to have been certainly their inferiors in warlike prowess. Most likely it was simply the natural increase of their population, aided perhaps by the failure of their harvests or the outbreak of a pestilence, that made them sensible of the poverty of their country, and led them to cast longing eyes towards the richer and more genial lands further to the south, of which they had heard, and which some of them may have visited.

Our only information about the path along which they travelled is derived from their own traditions, as recorded by Jordanes in the sixth century. A great deal of the story told by that historian, however, seems to be either his own guesswork, or to be taken from the history of the Getes and Scythians. Putting all this aside, we find that the Goths, Gepids, Herules, and some other kindred peoples, united into one great body, first wandered southward through what is now Western Russia, till they came to the shores of the Black Sea and the Sea of Azov, and then spread themselves westward to the north bank of the Danube. As they went their numbers were increased by the accession of people of Slavonic race, whom they conquered, or who joined them of their own accord. One of the nations whom they overcame, the Spali, is mentioned by name. About these early wanderings Jordanes tells two legendary stories, evidently derived from Gothic popular ballads. One of these relates that the Goths, led by their king, Filimer, the son of Guntharic, had to cross a great river into a beautiful and fertile country, called Ovim or Ocum. When the king and most of the people had passed over in safety, the bridge broke down and part of the host was left behind in a sort of enchanted land, surrounded by a belt of marshes through which no traveller had since been able to find his way; but those who passed near its borders ages afterward could often hear the lowing of cattle and the distant sound of Gothic speech. The other story embodies the hatred felt by the Goths for their enemies the Huns. King Filimer, it was said, expelled from the camp the women who practised magic arts—the Halirunos, as they were called, that is to say, the possessors of the "rune" or secret of Halya, the goddess of the lower world. Banished into the deserts, these women met with the evil spirits of the waste, and from the unholy marriage of witches and demons sprang the loathsome savages whom the Goths had afterwards so much reason to dread.

The real history of the Goths begins about the year 245, when they were living near the mouths of the Danube under the rule of Ostrogotha [Austraguta], the first king of the Amaling stock. Ostrogotha was celebrated in tradition for his "patience" but in what way he displayed that virtue we are not informed, for history tells only of his victories. Whether on account of his patience or his deeds in war, his fame was widely spread, for one of the oldest of Ango-Saxon poems mentions him as Eastgota, the father of Unwen." The name of this son is given by Jordanes as Hunuil, but probably the Anglo-Saxon form is the right one.

There is evidence that about twenty years before this time the Goths had become allies of the Romans, who paid them a yearly sum of money to defend the border of the empire against the Sarmatian barbarians who lay behind them. But in the reign of the Roman emperor Philip the Arab, this payment was stopped, and King Ostrogotha crossed the Danube and plundered the Roman provinces of Moesia and Thrace. The Roman general Decius, who afterwards became emperor brought an army against them; but the Goths retreated safely across the Danube, and it is said that large numbers of the Roman soldiers deserted to the barbarians, and offered to help them to make another attack. The Gothic king collected an army of thirty thousand men, partly belonging to his own people and partly to other barbarian nations, and sent them over the river under the command of two generals, named Argait and Guntharic, who ravaged the province called Lower Moesia, and laid siege to its capital, a city which the great emperor Trajan had built, and named Marcianopolis in honour of his sister Marcia. The inhabitants were glad to bargain with the Goths to raise the siege on receiving a heavy payment in money, and then the barbarians went back into their own land.

After this the kingdom of Ostrogotha was attacked by the Gepids, who had separated themselves from the Goths, and under their king, Fastida, had conquered the Burgunds, another Teutonic people. They now demanded that Ostrogotha should give them a portion of his territory. The "patient" king tried hard to persuade them not to make war on their own brethren; but he was not patient enough to grant what they required, and the two nations met in conflict near a town called Galtis. The fight was long and terrible; "but at last," says Jordanes, sneering at the "sluggish" Gepids, "the more vigorous nature of the Goths prevailed," and Fastida had to retire within his own dominions.

Ostrogotha died about the year 250, and was succeeded, not by his son Unwen or Hunuil (who, however, became the ancestor of later Gothic kings), but by a King Cniva, who was not an Amaling at all. The new chief at once engaged in an expedition across the Danube into Moesia and Thrace. He sent out several bodies of his army to plunder different parts of the country, while he himself besieged the town of Nicopolis (now Nikopi on the Yantra), whose name, "City of Victory," preserved the memory of a battle in which Trajan had been successful against the barbarians. The emperor Decius, who had been elected by the army a year before, was a man of great energy and of noble character, and he at once hurried off to relieve the town. When the Goths heard that the Roman army was approaching, they abandoned the siege, and made their way through the passes of the Balkan mountains to attack the great city of Philippopolis. Decius followed them in haste, but the Goths unexpectedly turned on their pursuers, put them to flight, and plundered their camp. The barbarians were now able to carry on the siege of Philippopolis undisturbed. The inhabitants made a brave defence, and slew many thousands of their assailants. But at last they were obliged to yield; the town was taken, and it is said that a hundred thousand persons were massacred. A vast quantity of plunder fell into the hands of the Goths, besides many prisoners of noble rank. Amongst these was Priscus, a brother of the late emperor Philip, whom the Goths persuaded to assume the title of emperor, and to conclude a treaty of peace with them.

Meanwhile the emperor had not been idle. He rallied his scattered forces, and placed garrisons along the Danube and at the passes of the Balkans. The Goths felt how much they had been weakened by their losses in the long siege, and sent messages to the Romans, entreating that they might be allowed to return home in safety on giving up their plunder and their prisoners. But Decius thought he had the victory in his own hands, and demanded that they should submit without conditions. The Goths determined to fight for their freedom. The two armies encountered each other near a little town of Moesia, which the barbarians called Abritta, and the Romans, Forum Trebonii. Scarcely had the battle begun when Decius's eldest son, Herennius, whom he had made joint emperor, fell wounded by an arrow. A crowd of barbarians rushed upon him, and plunged their spears into his body. When the soldiers saw their young commander slain, their courage at first gave way. The bereaved father urged them on with the words: "The loss of one soldier makes little difference to the commonwealth." Then, overwhelmed with grief, he rushed into the thick of the conflict, resolved either to avenge his son or to share his fate. The fight was fierce and bloody. Two divisions of the Goths were routed; the third line, protected by a morass, awaited the attack of the Romans, who, unacquainted with the ground and burdened with their heavy armour, were utterly defeated. The emperor was killed, and his body was never found. Never before had the Roman Empire known so sad a day as this, which saw the ruin of a great army, and the death by barbarian hands of one of the worthiest emperors who ever ruled.

Broken and disorganized, the Roman army offered no further resistance to the Goths, who carried devastation over the provinces of Moesia, Thrace, and Illyria. The new emperor, Trebonianus Gallus, found that it was hopeless to try to drive them out by force of arms, and he agreed to leave them in possession of their prisoners and their booty, and to pay them a large sum of money yearly on condition that they should leave the Roman territories unmolested.

III: FIRE AND SWORD IN ASIA AND GREECE

There was a terrible outcry amongst the Romans when it became known that the emperor Gallus had agreed to bribe the Goths to keep the peace. Everybody said that Gallus was a traitor, and some people even accused him of having intentionally caused the ruin of Decius by his bad advice. To make matters worse, a great plague broke out all over the empire, caused, the Romans fancied, by the anger of the gods at the treachery of their emperor. And before long it turned out that the disgraceful bargain that Gallus had made had not even answered its purpose, for a portion of the Goths, faithless to their engagements, continued to ravage the provinces of Illyria. They were defeated by a general named Aemilianus, who assumed the title of emperor. Gallus was murdered by his own soldiers, who joined the army of the usurper; but soon afterwards he, too, was assassinated, and the empire came into the hands of Valerian and his son Gallienus.

The reigns of these two emperors, which extended from the year 253 to the year 268, were full of misfortunes for the empire. The Germans threatened it on the west; on the east there were troubles with Persia ; and all the while news kept coming from the provinces that one portion or another of the army had rebelled, and set up an emperor of their own. To grapple with these difficulties needed a great ruler at the head of affairs. Valerian was a brave and good man, but he foolishly went on an expedition against Persia, and in the year 260 was taken prisoner, and never came back. When Gallienus heard that his father was a captive, he took the matter very coolly, and his courtiers, instead of being disgusted with his heartlessness, only complimented him on his "resignation." He was not a coward, nor was he either cruel or vicious; but he cared for nothing but amusing himself When he heard of any great misfortune that had happened in some distant province, he used to make some foolish joke about it, and then went on writing pretty verses, or completing his collections of pictures and statues. Such was the sovereign who ruled the Roman world at a time when, more than ever in its past history, the manifold perils that threatened it demanded the energies of a hero and a statesman.

During these dreary fifteen years the history of the Goths is a frightful story of cruel massacres, and of the destruction and plunder of wealthy and beautiful cities. One branch of the people obtained possession of the Crimea, sailed across the Black Sea, and took the great city of Trebizond, from which they carried away an abundance of spoil and a vast multitude of captives. A second expedition resulted in the capture of the splendid cities of Chalcedon and Nicomedia, and many other rich towns of Bithynia. The cities were strongly fortified, and possessed ample garrisons, but such was the wild terror inspired by the Goths that resistance was hardly ever attempted. It is, however, the third of these plundering raids that is most worthy of attention, not only because it was conducted on a larger scale than the two previous ones, but because of the interest which we feel in the classic lands over which it extended. A fleet of five hundred vessels, conveying a great army of Goths and Herules, sailed through the Bosphorus arid the Hellespont. On their way they destroyed the island city of Cyzicus, and made landings at many points on the west coast of Asia Minor. Amongst other deeds of wanton devastation, they burnt the magnificent temple of "Diana of the Ephesians," one of the seven wonders of the ancient world, with its hundred lofty marble columns and its many beautiful statues, the work of the greatest sculptors of Greece. Then, crossing the Aegean Sea, they anchored in the port of Athens; and now that city, which had given birth to the finest poetry, philosophy, and art that the world had ever known, became the plunder of barbarian pirates.

Whatever havoc the Goths may have made at Athens, at least they did not burn the city, and we know that they left many noble buildings and works of art to be destroyed long after by the Turks. About their doings here we have only one anecdote. The Goths, it is said, had collected into a great heap all the Athenian libraries, and were going to set fire to the pile, dreading, perhaps, lest the magical powers dwelling in the foreign "runes" should work some mischief on the invading host. But there was among them one aged chief, famed for his wisdom, who persuaded them to change their purpose. "Let the Greeks have their books," he said, "for so long as they spend their days with these idle toys we need never fear that they will give us trouble in war." Although this story rests on no very good authority, there is no reason why it may not have been true. Perhaps the Goth was not altogether wrong. A people that has a vigorous national life gains fresh strength from the labours of its scholars and thinkers; but when a nation cares for nothing but books, its absorption in literature only hastens its decay, and the literature itself becomes pedantic and trifling, and gives birth to little "that the world would not willingly let die." So it was amongst the Greeks of the third century. But even while they were in Athens the Goths were taught that learning did not always make men cowards. For an Athenian named Dexippus, a man of letters whose studies had made him mindful of the ancient greatness of his country, collected a band of brave men and burned many of the Gothic ships in the harbour of Piraeus.

But there were not many Greeks like Dexippus, and the Goths and Herules met with little resistance as they ranged over the land, enriching themselves with the spoils of many a wealthy city, once great in arts and in war. When they had exhausted the plunder of Greece they marched to the Adriatic, and it seems they were thinking of invading Italy. But the emperor Gallienus, at last roused from his inaction, came to meet them at the head of his army. The barbarian chiefs began to quarrel amongst themselves, and one of them, Naulobatus, with a large body of Herules, deserted his countrymen, and entered the Roman service. Naulobatus was gladly received by the emperor, who bestowed on him the rank of consul, the highest honour that could be gained by a Roman subject. The main body of the Goths separated into two bands. One of them went back to the east coast of Greece, and there took shipping, and after landing at Anchialus in Thrace, got back in safety to the settlements of their people at the north of the Black Sea. The other band made their way into Mcesia, and continued to ravage that country for a year with impunity, because the quarrels between the Roman generals rendered any effectual resistance impossible.

One of these generals, however, was a brave and able man named Claudius, and when, in March, 268, Gallienus died by an assassin's hand, Claudius was declared emperor in his stead. He at once set to work to reorganize the Roman armies, and to clear the empire of the northern barbarians. His task seemed, indeed, a desperate one, for he had to grapple with a new invasion, more terrible than any that the empire had hitherto suffered. The Goths dwelling near the mouths of the Dniester, excited by the tales which their countrymen had brought them about the wealth and fruitfulness of the southern lands, had resolved to conquer the Roman Empire, and make it their settled home. They were joined by a multitude of Slavonic tribes, whom they had either subdued or had persuaded to enter into alliance with them. Through the Black Sea and the Hellespont sailed a vast fleet, conveying an army numbering three hundred thousand warriors, accompanied by their wives and children. The invaders landed at Thessalonica, and hearing of the approach of Claudius, hastened to meet him, glorying in the hope of an easy victory. The battle that took place at Naissus (now Nissa, in the middle of Turkey) was, perhaps, not a victory for Claudius; some writers say he was beaten. But the Goths lost fifty thousand men; and what was more, they lost their confidence in their own strength. Battle after battle succeeded, and soon the mighty host of the invaders was utterly broken. Thousands of Gothic prisoners were sold into slavery; many of the young men were taken to serve in the imperial armies; and the shattered remnant of the people fled into the recesses of the Balkan mountains, where their numbers were lessened by the cold of winter and the outbreak of a dreadful plague. In this plague, however, Claudius himself died, in the spring of the year 270. In memory of his victories the Roman people gave him the surname of Gothicus; and his name ought ever to be held in honour as that of one of the few great conquerors whose exploits have been of lasting benefit to the human race. It is terrible to think what would have been the consequences to the world if the Gothic enterprise had then been successful. The South of Europe would have been depopulated by fierce and lawless massacre; the masterpieces of ancient art and literature would have perished, and the traditions of many ages of civilization would in a great measure have been blotted out. It is true that by the victories of Claudius the triumph of the Goths was only deferred. But it was deferred until a time when they had become Christian, and in some degree civilized, and when they had learned to use their victories with gentleness and wisdom. When they came to subdue the empire, it was no longer as savage devastators, but as the saviours of the Roman world from the degradation into which it had sunk through the vices of a corrupt civilization, and through the misgovernment of its feeble and depraved rulers. Although a foreign conquest always must be productive of some evil, yet, on the whole, the Gothic rule in Italy, while it lasted, was such a blessing to the subject people that we may well feel sorry that it came to an untimely end.

The dying emperor recommended as his successor Aurelian, one of his generals, whom the soldiers who served under him knew by the nickname of "Your hands to your swords!" The army accepted the choice, and Aurelian ruled the empire well and wisely for five years. As soon as the new emperor had been proclaimed the Goths again tried their fortune in war, under a chief named Cannabaudes. The battle was indecisive, and the Roman losses were heavy, but the Goths had suffered so much that they were glad to accept an offer of peace. Aurelian, hearing that he was wanted to repel a German invasion of Italy, thought it wise to allow them favourable terms. It was agreed that they were to be granted a free retreat into Dacia, and that province, including what is now the kingdom of Roumania and the eastern part of Hungary, was abandoned to their sovereignty, the native inhabitants being invited to cross the Danube into Moesia. In return for these concessions the Goths were to furnish a body of two thousand horsemen to the Roman armies, and as security for their faithfulness a number of the sons and daughters of Gothic nobles were entrusted to the care of the emperor, who caused them to receive the education of persons of rank, and afterwards employed the youths in honourable offices in his own service, and gave the maidens in marriage to some of his principal officers. The result of these measures was that the Goths lived in unbroken alliance with the Roman Empire for fifty years, learning the arts of peace from the natives of Dacia, and gaining new strength for the time when they were again to distinguish themselves by deeds of arms.

IV: HOW THE GOTHS FOUGHT WITH CONSTANTINE

During the fifty years' peace the history of the Goths is a blank. No chronicler has preserved even the name of any of their kings, or a single anecdote, true or fabulous, about their doings in that tranquil time. Probably we have lost little by this silence of the historians; for the story of an uncivilized people does not contain much that is worth telling, when there are no battles or migrations to record. We should like to know, however, on what sort of terms the Goths lived with the native Dacians, for there is good evidence that the whole of that people did not avail themselves of Aurelian's invitation to emigrate into Moesia, but continued in their ancient homes under Gothic rule. There is some reason for thinking that they were not reduced to slavery, but that the Goths learned to respect the superior civilization of their neighbours, and that the native inhabitants and the new settlers gradually became united into one people. If this were so, we can understand how it came to pass that, as we have already seen, the Gothic historian of the sixth century could reckon the heroes and sages of ancient Dacia among the ancestral glories of his own nation.

But we must not suppose that Dacia was the only country occupied at this time by the Goths. Vast as were the numbers of the host that sailed from the northern shores of the Black Sea in the year 269, a large Gothic population still remained behind. Whether or not. the Goths of Southern Russia were included in the treaty which Aurelian made, they seem at any rate to have abstained from any invasion of the Roman Empire throughout the fifty years of which we are speaking. The Goths of Dacia and their eastern kinsmen were distinguished by the old names of Visigoths and Ostrogoths. How far they were respectively the descendants of those who had borne these names in earlier times we cannot tell. The Ostrogoths seem to have formed a united nation, while the Visigoths were independent of them, and were divided into separate tribes under different chieftains, without any common head.

Quiet and uneventful as were these fifty years in the history of the Gothic people, they were full of stirring incidents in the history of the Roman Empire. In the course of this period the Roman world was ruled by several emperors of uncommon ability, amongst whom was one man of surpassing genius, named Diocletian, who introduced important changes into the government. But of these it is not necessary here to speak, nor of the civil wars and the struggles with the Franks and other nations, which the empire had to sustain.

When the Goths first broke their long peace with Rome, it was in the reign of the emperor Constantine the Great. Two of the actions of this emperor had a profound effect on all succeeding history. He established Christianity as the state religion of the empire; and he removed the seat of government from Rome to his new city of Constantinople. Henceforward we have to remember that although the empire is still called Roman, the ancient capital of the world from which that empire took its name is now only its second city.

The first conflict between the Goths and Constantine took place in the year 322, one year before the defeat of his colleague and rival Licinius made him undivided sovereign of the empire. The Visigoths and Ostrogoths, in one united army, joined by Slavonic tribes from the far east, had made an attack, under the command of a king named Aliquaca [Alhwakars] on the Roman provinces south of the Danube. The emperor defeated them in three successive battles, and compelled them to submit. But he thought it well to offer them honourable terms of surrender, and the result showed that he was wise in so doing; for when in the following year he fought his decisive battle against Licinius at Hadrianople, he was assisted by the army of Aliquaca, consisting, we are told, of forty thousand men.

Eight years after this, however, Constantine had again to meet the Goths as enemies. It seems that the Vandals, or a part of them, were then living in what is now Western Hungary, divided from the Gothic territory by the river Theiss. Quarrels broke out between the two neighbouring peoples, and the Goths invaded the Vandal territory in overwhelming numbers. The Vandals appealed for help to the emperor, who listened to the prayer, and marched in person to chastise the aggressors. When the Goths heard of his approach, they crossed the Danube led by their two kings Araric and Aoric, and hastened to meet the Roman army. In the first battle Constantine underwent a serious defeat—for the first time in his life. But in the succeeding battles of the campaign the victory was all on the side of the Romans. The emperor was helped by the descendants of the Greek colonists in the Crimea, who were no doubt glad of the opportunity to revenge themselves on their old oppressors. The Goths were thoroughly humbled, and were glad to beg for peace. It was always Constantine's policy—in dealing with barbarians at least— to try by kindness to make friends of his vanquished enemies; and the Gothic kings and nobles received handsome presents and special marks of honour. Once more a treaty of alliance was made between the Goths and the Romans, and by way of security for his faithfulness, King Araric had to leave his eldest son as a hostage in the emperor's hands.

After this war was ended the Goths seem not to have troubled the Roman Empire for more than thirty years; but in other directions they made important conquests. When Araric died, the people chose a new king, who was of another family. His name was Geberic, and he was descended from a line of famous heroes. We know nothing about his father Hilderic or about Ovida and Nidada, his grandfather and great-grandfather, but from the way in which Jordanes mentions them it is plain that their names and deeds must in his time have been very familiarly known from the old Gothic ballads. King Geberic determined to accomplish the task, in which his predecessor had failed, of dislodging the Vandals. Constantine did not say him nay, for the Vandals, ungrateful for the help which the Romans had given them, had themselves been making plundering raids into the Roman provinces. On the banks of the river Marosh a battle was fought, in which Wisumar, the Vandal king, was killed, and his army was routed with great slaughter. The conquered Vandals once more appealed to Constantine, and he gave them permission to settle in Pannonia and other parts of the empire. The Goths took possession of the deserted territory; and being thus freed from enemies on the west, they soon began to engage in schemes of aggression against their eastern neighbours. But of these we shall have to speak in the next chapter.

V: THE GOTHIC ALEXANDER

We come now to a reign which marks a great epoch in the history of the Gothic people. Ermanaric, who seems to have been chosen king about the year 350, was a great warrior, like many of his predecessors; but his policy, and the objects for which he fought, were markedly different from theirs. The former kings of the Goths had been content to conduct expeditions for the sake of plunder into the territories of neighbouring nations, or to lead their subjects in search of new homes in other lands. But the Gothic people had now once more acquired a settled territory; and bitter experience had compelled them to renounce the hope of conquests in the more genial and wealthy countries of the south. These new conditions gave a new direction to their warlike ambition. Ermanaric made no attempt to invade the provinces of the Roman Empire; but he resolved to make his Ostrogothic kingdom the centre of a great empire of his own. The seat of his kingdom was, as tradition tells us, on the banks of the Dnieper. We have a long list of the peoples whom he subjected to his sway; but the names have been so blundered by the copyists that it is useless to repeat them here.

We can however form some notion of the vast extent of his empire from the fact that amongst the nations he subdued were the Esthonians, living far away on the shores of the Gulf of Bothnia. Another of the peoples whom he conquered was the Herules, who, as we have already seen, had once formed one nation with the Goths, but had before this time made themselves independent, and were living under the rule of a king called Alaric—a name which a generation later became famous as that of the great hero of the Visigoths. A Roman historian compares Ermanaric to Alexander the Great; and many ages afterwards his fame survived in the poetic traditions of Germans, Norsemen, and Anglo-Saxons. These traditions are more fabulous than historical; they bring together as contemporaries persons whom we know to have lived at periods a hundred years apart; but we can gather from them that while Ermanaric was feared and admired as a great conqueror and an able ruler, he was bitterly hated as a cruel and selfish tyrant.

Ermanaric was the first king since Ostrogotha who belonged to the Amaling family. Down to this time, the Gothic kings seem to have been chosen by free election from any of the noble families, and we have no proof that a son ever succeeded his father. But henceforward the kingship of the Ostrogoths became hereditary among the descendants of Ermanaric.

During this time the Visigoths appear to have been practically independent, divided into separate tribes ruled by their own "judges" or chieftains; but, while these chieftains seem to have been free to make war and peace on their own account, it is probable that in theory they acknowledged the supremacy of the Ostrogothic king.

But the great empire of Ermanaric, which, like that of Napoleon, had been created by conquest in one lifetime, was doomed, like Napoleon's, to an inglorious end.

For in the king's old age there appeared upon the scene a new enemy, with whom he was unable to contend. The Tartar people of the Huns had forsaken their ancient camping grounds in Asia, and in overwhelming numbers poured westward over the plains of Russia. Nation after nation was subdued as they advanced, and compelled to join the devastating horde. Their approach inspired amongst the subjects of Ermanaric a wild panic, which was caused, not merely by their vast multitude, and by the fame of their unresisted career of conquest, but by the superstitious horror which their strange and terrible appearance excited. Dwarfish, and, as it seemed, deformed in figure, but of enormous strength, their swarthy and beardless faces of frightful ugliness ("with dots instead of eyes," says Jordanes), and rendered still more hideous by tattooing, it is no wonder that they were regarded by the Goths rather as demons than as men. A Roman writer compares their aspect to that of the roughly hewn caricatures of human faces which were carved on the parapets of bridges. The aged king of the Goths tried to urge his people to resistance, but they were paralysed by terror, and the subject tribes gladly hailed the invasion as an opportunity to throw off the yoke of the detested tyrant. When Ermanaric saw that his empire was falling to pieces, he is said to have taken his own life in his despair. This seems to be the true story of his end ; but the account given by Jordanes does not mention the suicide, and mixes up the history with a romantic legend, which appears in many differing forms in German and Scandinavian traditions. According to one of the later versions of this legend, the tyrant had sent his son to woo for him the beautiful Swanhilda, the daughter of a queen named Gudrun. But the son, prompted by an evil counsellor, won the maiden for his own bride. Ermanaric, "the furious traitor," as an Anglo-Saxon poet calls him, cunningly disguising his anger, enticed Swanhilda by fair words into his own power, and then in his fierce revenge ordered her to be torn in pieces by wild horses. Her brothers (named Sorli and Hamdhir in Norse story, Sarus and Ammius according to Jordanes) attacked Ermanaric, and cut off his hands and feet, leaving him to linger in misery and helplessness until his hundred and tenth year.

Ermanaric died in the year 375, and the Ostrogoths were subdued by the Hunnish king Balamber. For a whole century they remained subject to the Huns, even fighting on the side of their masters against their own kinsmen the Visigoths. Of the history of the Ostrogoths during this time of humiliation there is not much to tell. They did not submit to the savage invaders quite without a struggle. One large body of them, led by two generals, Alatheus [Alhthius] and Safrax, taking with them a boy of Amaling descent named Wideric, whom they chose as their king, emigrated westward soon after Ermanaric's death, and joined the army of the Visigoths, where we shall hear of them again. A few years later, one portion of the Ostrogoths who were left behind, chose a king named Winithari [Winithaharyis], a grandson of Ermanaric's brother, and tried to throw off the Hunnish yoke. While the Huns were busy with new conquests, Winithari overran the country of the Antae, a Slavonic people whom the Huns had made tributary; and the Gothic historian confesses without shame that his countrymen crucified the king of the Antae and seventy of his nobles. But the rest of the Ostrogoths, under Hunimund, the son of Ermanaric, continued to be subject to the Huns, and joined the army of Balamber to crush the revolt of their countrymen. In two battles Winithari was victorious, but in the third he was defeated and killed. Balamber married an Amaling princess named Waladamarca, and the Ostrogoths submitted quietly to his sway. They were allowed, however, to choose their own kings, who assisted the Huns in their conquests. Hunimund famed for his beauty, won victories over the German nation of the Sueves. His son Thorismund conquered the Gepids, and was killed "in the flower of his youth," by a fall from his horse.

We are told that the Ostrogoths were so stricken with grief for the death of their young hero that they chose no other king for forty years. Of course we cannot believe this ridiculous tale, which seems to have been taken from the Gothic ballads. The plain prose account of the matter would probably be, that the Ostrogoths were unable to choose a king who was approved of by their Hunnish masters, so that the latter kept the government in their own hands. The young prince Berismund, whose right it was to succeed his father Thorismund, was naturally discontented at being excluded from the throne, and went away to join the Visigoths, who were then settled in Gaul. It seems he thought that the Visigoths would make him their king; but he found that the throne was already occupied, and he kept his Amaling descent a secret. The king of the Visigoths received him kindly, and promoted him to high rank on account of his bravery; but during his lifetime it was never known who he was.

When the forty years were ended—about the year 440—the Huns once more allowed the Ostrogoths to have a king of their own. His name was Walamer, and he was the son of Wandalhari, and the grandson of King Winithari. He had two brothers, Theudemer and Widumer, to whom he entrusted the care of portions of his kingdom, and who succeeded him when he died. The unity and the mutual affection of these three brothers are described by Jordanes, in almost poetical words, as having been something singularly beautiful. During the greater part of Walamer's life, the three brothers were faithful servants of the Huns, and their subjects fought, against their own kin, in the armies of Attila. But, when Attila died in 453, his sons quarrelled for supremacy, and the Ostrogoths regained their freedom. The Huns made an effort to reconquer them, but were defeated by Walamer in a decisive battle. On the day when the news was brought to Theudemer of his brother's triumph, a son was born to him. This "child of victory" was the great Theoderic [Thiudareiks], who was destined to fulfil the omen of his birth, and to raise the Ostrogothic nation to the highest position among the people of the Teutonic stock. The name of Theoderic is the most glorious in Gothic history; but before we begin his story we must turn back a hundred years, and inquire what the Visigoths had been doing while their eastern brethren were the humble vassals of a horde of Asiatic savages.

VI: THE JUDGES OF THE VISIGOTHS

We told you in the last chapter that during the third quarter of the fourth century the Visigoths formed part of the great empire of the Ostrogoth Ermanaric. In the earlier part of the famous conqueror's reign, while his power was still at its height, it is very probable that they were his subjects in reality as well as in name. But when the Ostrogothic kingdom began to be invaded by the Huns, and the conquered nations were claiming their freedom, the Visigoths seem to have been allowed to manage their own affairs as they liked, and to wage war or make treaties on their own account, without waiting for the approval of the Amaling king.

The Visigoths were divided into three tribes or petty kingdoms, which were ruled by "judges" named Athanaric, Frithigern, and Alawiw. Of these three chieftains Athanaric was the most powerful, and the other two seem to have recognized his claim to leadership. He had inherited his power from his father Rothestes, who had been a faithful ally of the Romans, and had received the honour of a statue or a memorial column at Constantinople. Athanaric is said to have been a brave warrior, but his history perhaps gives more evidence of his cunning than it does of his bravery.

In order to understand the story of the Visigoths under their "judges," we must take a glance at the events that had been happening at Constantinople.

When Constantine the Great died in 337, he was succeeded first by his three sons, and afterwards by his nephew Julian, who is called the Apostate, because he forsook Christianity, and during his two years' reign set up heathenism as the religion of the empire. After Julian's death, the Romans thought they had had enough of the house of Constantine, and chose as their emperor Jovian, an officer of the imperial household. But he only lived a year after he was raised to the throne, and then the diadem was bestowed on Valentinian, the most successful general of his time.

Valentinian, though uneducated, was a man of strong mind and resolute will; but he perceived that the government of the Roman world was a task too heavy for one man to manage. He therefore determined to share the supreme power with his brother Valens, whom he sent to Constantinople as emperor of the East, while he kept for himself the rule over the western provinces. Unfortunately Valens, though a brave soldier and a well-meaning man, had little decision of character or knowledge of men; and just at this time the Eastern empire needed a strong and skilful ruler even more than did the empire of the West. To make the matter worse, Valens did not even know Greek, which was the language spoken by the greater part of his subjects. It was not long before the emperor found himself entangled in fearful difficulties; and his weak and vacillating policy— doing a thing one day and undoing it the next, losing precious time in long deliberation, and then acting rashly after all— brought on a succession of calamities that came very near destroying the Eastern empire altogether.

Since the time of Constantine, the Visigoths had faithfully observed the treaty which they had made with that emperor, and had continued to supply their promised number of men to the Roman armies. Athanaric, so far as we can discover, honestly intended to continue the policy of friendship with Constantinople, but he made a great mistake which cost him and his people dearly. A cousin of the emperor Julian, named Procopius, rebelled against Valens, expelled him from Constantinople, and got himself proclaimed emperor. He called on the Visigoths to fulfil their treaty engagements; and Athanaric, regarding Procopius as the real emperor, at once sent over thirty thousand men into Thrace. Apparently Athanaric did not go himself, for his father (so at least he said afterwards) had made him swear never to set foot on Roman soil. We can imagine how the thirty thousand would enjoy the opportunity of returning, actually under imperial sanction, to their old sport of plundering the Thracian provincials. But while they were ravaging the country, never dreaming of resistance, they suddenly learned that Procopius was dead, and that Valens was again master at Constantinople. Instead of having earned the gratitude of the Roman Empire, they had made it their enemy.

By cutting off their supplies and provisions, and preventing them from retreating across the Danube, the generals of Valens managed, without very much fighting, to compel the Goths to surrender at discretion. The Romans spared their lives, but sold the common soldiers into slavery, and sent the chiefs to live as prisoners of war in distant parts of the empire.

When Athanaric heard of this disaster, he sent ambassadors to Constantinople; but it was not by any means to beg humbly for mercy from the conqueror. Instead of that he assumed an air of injured innocence. His envoys bitterly reproached the astonished Romans with an unprovoked breach of the treaty between the two nations. All that the Visigoths had done, they said, was to render their promised assistance to the Roman Empire. To be sure they had in their simplicity supported the wrong emperor; but instead of being angry with them for their mistake Valens ought to have been thankful to them for their good intentions! They therefore demanded that their prisoners of war should at once be set at liberty.

One would suppose that this audacious demand would have been at once rejected with laughter; but Valens seems at first to have been half inclined to agree to it. However, he wrote for advice to his brother Valentinian, who, as might have been expected, told him to go and attack Athanaric in his own country. Valens did so, and the war lasted three years. The Romans won most of the battles, but they did not make much progress towards subduing the country, and they were glad at last to agree to a peace. The cunning Athanaric consented that the Gothic chieftains should be deprived of the pensions they had been accustomed to receive from the Romans; but he managed to procure an exception in his own favour, and to get himself recognized by the Romans as king of all the Visigoths. When the conditions of peace were agreed upon, Valens wished that the treaty should be ratified at a personal interview between himself and Athanaric, for whom he seems to have "conceived a good deal of respect. Athanaric, however, pleaded that the oath he had taken to his father prevented him from crossing the Danube into Roman territory, and he threatened that he should consider the peace broken if the emperor set foot in Dacia. He proposed that the meeting between Valens and himself should take place in boats in the middle of the Danube. There is something amusing in the clever way in which Athanaric continued to avoid everything that looked like a confession of defeat. Valens must have felt that the barbarian was laughing at him, but he did not venture to refuse the offered arrangement. The treaty was confirmed, and the emperor, as well as Athanaric, had to give hostages as security for its faithful observance. The result of these negotiations was anything but a brilliant success for the ruler of Constantinople, but of course he celebrated a triumph when he got home, and the Court scribes and orators talked as if Valens had been another Claudius Gothicus.

For the next two or three years (the peace was concluded in the year 369), Athanaric was busy persecuting the Christians (who, as we shall find in the next chapter, were becoming numerous among the Visigoths), and in a petty war with Frithigern, who was defeated and driven out of the country, though he was soon reinstated by the Romans. However, in the year 376 the judges of the Visigoths had made up their quarrels, and Athanaric was acting as commander-in-chief of the armies of the whole nation, which were massed on the west bank of the Dniester, with the Huns facing them on the other side. As the enemy had no boats, Athanaric thought himself safe from immediate attack. But one moonlight night a body of the Huns made their horses swim over the river, and surprised the Gothic camp. Athanaric had to retreat hastily to the west of the river Pruth, where there were some deserted Roman earthworks which he meant to repair, and by means of them to offer defiance to the foe. But the Visigoths were stricken with panic, and would think of nothing but flight. Frithigern and Alawiw sent ambassadors to the emperor, begging him to let them cross the Danube. When Athanaric saw that he could not persuade the people to offer any resistance, he went away with a few hundred men towards the northwest, into a country which the Roman writers call Caucalanda, a name which is evidently meant for hauhaland, the Gothic form of our English word Highland, and probably denotes the mountain region of Transylvania.

And so Athanaric disappears from our story for four or five years, during which time his rival Frithigern was practically king of all the Visigoths.

VII: THE APOSTLE OF THE GOTHS

We must now turn aside for a little while from the direct course of our history to tell the story of a Goth who, in the midst of all the confusion of this age of turbulence and bloodshed, spent his life in quietly doing good, and whose influence on the future history of his nation was quite as powerful as that of any of the soldiers and statesmen of his time. Milton expressed a sad truth when he said that the victories of peace are "less renowned" than those of war; but although the name of Wulfila the Bishop is not so famous as those of many men far less worthy to be remembered, it will no doubt be familiar to many readers to whom the names mentioned in the preceding chapters were altogether unknown.

It seems that Wulfila was born about the year 310 or 311, but where his birthplace was in the wide tract of country then inhabited by the Goths, we do not know. It is said that he was not of pure Gothic descent, for his grandfather was a native of Cappadocia—one of those unfortunate prisoners whom the Goths carried away from their homes when they ravaged Asia Minor about the year 267. However this may be, his parents gave him a Gothic name, and his whole life proves that he was a thorough Gothic patriot at heart.

You may remember that after their king Araric had been defeated in battle, the Goths made a treaty of alliance with the emperor Constantine; and in the year 332 they sent ambassadors to the imperial city to settle the conditions of peace. How it came to pass that the young Wulfila accompanied this embassy we can only guess. Perhaps the grandson of the Cappadocian captive had learned to speak Greek as well as Gothic in his own home, and so was useful as an interpreter; or perhaps he may have been one of those young Goths who, along with King Araric's son, were to be left in the emperor's hands as security for the treaty being faithfully kept. Whether by his own choice or not, we know that he remained at Constantinople, and received a good education, learning to speak and write Latin as well as Greek.

But Wulfila was like Moses, who, though "learned in all the wisdom of the Egyptians," and living in comfort and honour in Pharaoh's court, could not be content while his own people were in misery. Whether Wulfila was a Christian before he went to Constantinople we do not know; certainly there had been some few Christian Goths before his time. But if he was not already a Christian, he very soon became one, and his mind was filled with a burning desire to go as a missionary to convert his countrymen from their cruel heathen ways. With this end in view he became a priest, and when he was thirty years old the bishops assembled at the Council of Antioch ordained him bishop of the Goths dwelling north of the Danube.

For seven years after this Wulfila was preaching the gospel to his countrymen in Dacia, and gained vast numbers of followers in spite of bitter opposition from Athanaric. The persecution at last became so fierce that Wulfila wrote to the emperor Constantius asking him to let the Christian Goths have a home in the Roman lands, where they could be safe from the fury of their oppressors. The permission was granted, and Wulfila, with many thousands of his converts, crossed the Danube, and settled near Nicopolis in Moesia, at the foot of the Balkan mountains. Constantius had a great admiration for Wulfila, and often used to speak of him as "our sec-second Moses." The people whom Wulfila led into Moesia (the Lesser Goths, as they were called), continued to dwell there for some centuries, peacefully cultivating their lands, and taking no part in the fierce wars that raged all around them.

But all the Christian Goths did not leave Dacia along with Wulfila, and their numbers grew so fast that about the year 369 Athanaric thought it necessary to resort to cruel measures in order to suppress them. His rival, Frithigern, however, was either a Christian himself, or at any rate favourable to the Christians, and when Athanaric, as we described in our last chapter, went away into the Transylvanian "highlands" there was no longer any resistance to the spread of the gospel. In a very few years nearly the whole people, Visigoths and Ostrogoths alike, learned to call themselves Christians.

It may be well to explain here that those Christians from whom Wulfila had received his religious teaching at Constantinople belonged to what was called the Arian sect: that is, they differed from the general body of the Church in believing that the Son of God was a created being. The Goths, who were converted to Christianity through the preaching of Wulfila and his disciples, naturally became Arians too. It is important to remember this, because many of the troubles of the Goths in later years arose from the fierce mutual hatred that existed between Arians and Catholics. The two parties often thought each other worse than heathens, and persecuted each other cruelly. As for Wulfila himself, however, he cared a great deal less about the harder questions of theology than he did about the plain and simple truths which help men to act kindly and justly towards one another, and to look up with love and reverence to the Giver of all good.

For three and thirty years Wulfila lived among his people in Moesia, teaching the newly converted heathens the lessons of Christian faith and life, and training clergymen to carry on his work after his death. But in addition to these labours he had imposed on himself an important and difficult task, which must have occupied a large portion of his life. He perceived clearly that if Christianity was to take deep root amongst the Goths, and to continue to be held by them in its purity, it was necessary that they should be able to read the Scriptures in their own tongue. And therefore he set himself to work to produce a translation of the Bible into Gothic.

Before, however, Wulfila could give his countrymen the Bible, he had to teach them to read, and, in fact, to reduce their language to a written form. It is true that, as we have already said, the Goths had already an alphabet of their own. But Wulfila probably thought that the Runic alphabet was better forgotten, because of the heathenish things that were written in it; at all events he chose to write his Gothic Bible in Greek letters—large capitals, such as were commonly used in books at that time. There were, however, some Gothic sounds which could not be correctly expressed by means of the Greek alphabet, and for these Wulfila adopted the Runic characters, altering their shapes, however, so as to give them as far as possible the general appearance of Greek letters. Our earliest manuscripts of the Gothic Bible were written about 150 years after Wulfila's time, and probably the forms of the letters had before then undergone a little change, but it is still quite easy to see that the Gothic alphabet is merely the Greek alphabet with half a dozen new signs.

Wulfila's translation was a wonderful piece of work for the age in which it was written. It cannot have been very easy, in the fourth century, for a Goth to acquire such a thorough knowledge of Greek as to enable him accurately to understand the text of the Scriptures; and to make a faithful translation out of one language into another requires a mind trained in habits of exact thinking. But there are very few passages in which Wulfila appears to have misrepresented the sense of his original. Many of the words which occur in the Bible had nothing properly corresponding to them in Gothic, because they denoted objects or actions peculiar to civilized life, or ideas belonging to Christian ways of thinking, which were quite strange to the minds of people who had been brought up in heathenism. The way in which Wulfila got over these difficulties is often very curious. The word he uses for "writing," for instance, meant properly "painting" or "marking," and to express the meaning of "reading" he used the word "singing"— no doubt because in reading the Bible it was customary to adopt a chanting tone. Our Anglo-Saxon ancestors expressed these ideas in a different way: they retained the old words that had been used in the days when people carved the runes on pieces of wood. Our word "write" properly means to scratch or engrave, and our word "read" meant originally to guess or give the answer to a riddle, just as "rune" itself meant a secret or mystery which it required a clever man to unravel. Wulfila seems to have avoided these expressions on purpose, because he regarded Christian writing as altogether a different kind of thing from heathenish rune-carving.

Here is the Gothic Lord's Prayer as it is in Wulfila's Bible, with a word-for-word translation, which will show how much, even yet, our language resembles that of the Goths. The English words that are in italics are of the same origin as the Gothic words which they translate.

We do not know how much of the Bible Wulfila translated into Gothic. One ancient writer says that he translated all but the books of Kings, which he left out because he thought that the stories of Israel's wars would be dangerous reading for a people that was too fond of fighting already. It is quite in accordance with what we know of Wulfila's character that he should have felt some uneasiness about the effect that such reading might have on the minds of his warlike countrymen ; but one would have thought that the books of Joshua and Judges would have been even more likely to stimulate the Gothic passion for fighting than the books of Kings. Probably the truth is that Wulfila did not live to finish his translation, and no doubt he would leave to the last the books which he thought least important for his great purpose of making good Christians.

The part of Wulfila's Bible that has come down to us consists of a considerable portion of each of the Gospels, and of each of St. Paul's Epistles, together with small fragments of the books of Ezra and Nehemiah. Six different manuscripts have been found. The most important of these was discovered in the sixteenth century in a monastery at Werden in Germany. After having been in the possession of many different owners, it was bought in 1662 by the Swedish Count de la Gardie, who gave it the binding of solid silver from which it is commonly called the Codex Argenteus, or Silver Book; it is now in the University of Upsala,,and is regarded as one of the choicest treasures possessed by any library in Europe. It is beautifully written in letters of gold and silver on purple parchment, and contains the fragments of the Gospels. Of the other five manuscripts one was discovered in the seventeenth century in Germany, and the rest in Italy about seventy years ago.

Wulfila visited Constantinople in the year 360, and was present at a church council held there. In 381, when he was seventy years old, he was sent for by the emperor Theodosius to dispute with the teachers of a new sect that was gaining many converts among the Goths. But almost as soon as he had arrived at Constantinople he was seized with the illness of which he died. His last act was to write out, as his "testament," a profession of his Christian faith, which his disciple Auxentius has affectionately preserved.

VIII: FRITHIGERN AND VALENS—THE BATTLE OF HADRIANOPLE

At the end of our sixth chapter, we left Frithigern and his Visigoths on the north bank of the Danube, in continual dread of an attack from the Huns, and eagerly awaiting the reply of the emperor Valens to their request for permission to cross the river and become subjects of the Roman Empire. Valens was in Asia (probably at Antioch) where the ambassadors of Frithigern presented themselves before him. They told him of the terrible danger to which their countrymen were exposed, and promised that if they were granted a home in Thrace the Visigoths would become his faithful and obedient subjects. The answer, yes or no, had to be given at once: there was no time for hesitation. To do the advisers of Valens justice, it was not altogether "with a light heart" that they came to the decision which well-nigh involved the empire in irretrievable ruin. Some of them, at any rate, clearly perceived the danger that there was in admitting such a vast and unruly multitude into the Roman territories. Others, however, urged that the empire was in need of men; its population had for a long time past been growing smaller; and here was a golden opportunity of adding at one stroke a million of subjects to the dominions of their sovereign. After much anxious discussion, the prayer of the Visigoths was granted. Possibly the experiment might not have turned out so badly if the Goths, when they had been admitted into the empire, had been treated with generosity and confidence. But first to accept them as subjects, and then to let them be goaded into rebellion by every sort of oppression and insult, was a course that could only end in the most frightful calamity.

Orders were sent to the Roman governors on the banks of the Danube to make preparations for bringing the Visigoths across the river, and when a sufficient number of boats had been collected, the great immigration began. Day after day, from early morning till far into the night, the broad river was covered with passing vessels, into which the Goths had crowded so eagerly that many of them sank on the passage, and all on board were lost. At first the Romans tried to count the people as they landed, but the numbers were so vast that the attempt had to be given up in despair.

If the Goths at first felt any thankfulness to the Romans for giving them a safe refuge from their savage enemies, their gratitude was soon turned into fierce anger when they got to know that their children were to be taken from them, and sent away into distant parts of the empire. The reason for this cruel action was that the Romans thought the Goths would keep quiet when they knew that their children might be killed if a rebellion took place; but it only filled the minds of the barbarians with a wild longing for revenge. Valens thought he could make himself safe against his new subjects by ordering the fighting men to be deprived of their weapons; but the Goths, who were rich with the plunder they had taken in many wars, found that it was easy to bribe the Roman officers to let them keep their arms.

When Valens heard that the Visigoths, instead of being a defenceless multitude, were a powerful army, and that they showed signs of fierce discontent, he felt that he had made a great mistake. He tried to remedy the mischief by ordering that the Goths should be divided into several bodies, and removed to different parts of the empire. Just at this time those Ostrogoths who had not submitted to the Huns asked the emperor that they too might be allowed to cross the Danube and become Roman subjects. Of course the request was refused; but the Ostrogoths took no notice of the refusal, and finding an unguarded place, they passed the river, and joined themselves to the subjects of Frithigern.

When this vast multitude of strangers had been brought into the Roman provinces, it was needful to consider how they should be supplied with the necessaries of life. Valens had given orders that arrangements should be made to furnish the Goths, at reasonable prices, with the provisions they required, until they should be able to maintain themselves by agriculture and the rearing of cattle. But unfortunately the Roman governors of Thrace, Lupicinus and Maximus, were avaricious men, who saw in the distresses of the Goths a chance of making themselves rich by ill-gotten gains. These men kept the food supply in their own hands, and doled it out to the Goths at famine prices, forbidding every one else to sell to them more cheaply. Pressed by hunger, the miserable people had to give a slave as the price of one loaf, or ten pounds of silver for an animal, and they were often compelled to feed on the flesh of dogs or of animals that had died of disease. Some of them even sold their own children, saying it was better to let them go into slavery to save their lives than to keep them where they would die of hunger.

During all these terrible hardships, Frithigern succeeded in keeping his followers from breaking out into revolt, and even from relieving their wants by plunder of their neighbours. He seems to have been really anxious to maintain friendship with the Romans if he could; and no doubt, also, he thought of the Gothic boys and girls who were kept as hostages in distant lands. But all the time he took care that the Goths should be ready to rise as one man, if the burden of oppression should become too heavy to be borne.

The occasion was not long in presenting itself Lupicinus had invited Frithigern and the other chiefs to a banquet at Marcianopolis, and they were accompanied by a few attendants into the palace, the Gothic people being encamped outside the walls of the city. While the feast was going on, an uproar arose at the city gates between the Roman soldiers and the hungry Goths, who saw before them a market well supplied with food, which they were prevented from buying. Some of the soldiers were killed, and news of what had happened was brought secretly to Lupicinus, who, awakened out of a drunken sleep, gave orders for the slaughter of Frithigern's followers. Frithigern heard the outcry, and soon guessed what had happened. With rare presence of mind, he quietly said that it was needful for him to show himself to his countrymen in order to put a stop to the tumult; and beckoning to his companions, he boldly led the way through the streets and out at the city gates, while the Romans looked on, too much astonished to offer any opposition. When the chiefs reached the camp, they told their story to their countrymen, and announced that the peace with the Romans was at an end. The Goths broke into wild shouts of applause as they heard this longed for declaration. "Better," they said, "to perish in battle than to suffer a lingering death by famine." Very soon the sound of the Gothic trumpets warned the garrison of Marcianopolis that they must prepare for war.

Lupicinus hastily collected such an army as he could, and went out to meet the foe; but the Romans were beaten, and their cowardly general fled for his life before the battle was decided, and took refuge in the city. And now the Goths made amends for their past privations by plundering the innocent country people of the Thracian provinces. They were joined by some Gothic regiments in the imperial service, who had been driven into rebellion by the foolish insolence of the Romans; and the slaves who worked in the Thracian gold-mines, set free by the flight of their cruel masters, were glad to serve the Goths as guides, and to show them where the stores of food and of treasure had been hidden.

We need not say very much about the events which immediately followed. There was one great battle at a place called "The Willows," which was a victory for neither side, but resulting in terrible slaughter to both, so that long afterwards the field was white with the bones of the unburied dead; another great battle on the Hebrus, won by the Roman General Sebastian, who carried off a vast quantity of spoil, greater than could be stored in the city of Hadrianople or in the surrounding plains; and several less important conflicts, in which sometimes one side was victorious and sometimes the other. But in spite of all this fighting the Gothic army kept growing stronger and stronger, being joined continually by new bands—Taifals, Scythians, Ostrogoth deserters from the Huns, and even by some of the Hunnish hordes themselves.

In the summer of 378 Valens came back to Constantinople, and found himself the object of universal indignation. Whenever he appeared in public he was assailed by shouts of abuse for his folly in letting the Goths into the empire, and for his cowardice in not having marched in person to subdue them. Valens felt keenly that there was some truth in these reproaches. He knew that he had made a terrible mistake; and though he also knew that he had meant well, and that he was no coward, he had not the strength of mind to be indifferent to popular clamour. What added to the bitterness of his feeling was the knowledge that the people were making comparisons between himself and his nephew Gratian, the brave and accomplished young emperor of the West, who had been winning brilliant victories over the Germans on the Rhine and the Upper Danube. Valens resolved to risk everything in a desperate attempt to repair the consequences of his own error. He remained only a few days in the capital, and set out to take the command of the army, which was encamped under the walls of Hadrianople.

While the emperor and his generals were discussing their plans for the management of the war, there arrived at the camp one of Gratian's generals, named Richomer, who brought a letter saying that his master would soon be on the spot at the head of his army, and begging Valens on no account to risk a battle until Gratian had joined him. Well would it have been for Valens if he had listened to this advice; but his flatterers urged him not to let his nephew share in the glory of a victory which, they represented, he was sure to win; and he decided to hurry on his preparations so that the battle might be over before Gratian arrived.

The Romans had everything in readiness for the attack, when a Gothic Christian priest (some think it must have been the bishop Wulfila, but this is not very likely) accompanied by some other Goths of humble rank, presented themselves before Valens, bearing a letter from Frithigern, in which he offered to enter into a treaty of peace, on condition that the Goths should be recognized as masters of Thrace. In addition to this official despatch, which had no doubt been sent with the consent of the Gothic assembly, the priest had brought a private note from Frithigern, in which he informed Valens that he feared the Goths would not remain faithful to such a treaty if they got what they wanted too easily, and advised the emperor to make a display of force so that it might not appear that his concessions were the result of weakness. What the Gothic chief meant by these tactics it is not easy to see: the historian who tells this curious story intimates that the Romans could make nothing of these contradictory messages, and sent the ambassadors home without any reply.

It was on the morning of the 9th of August, 378, that Valens, leaving his treasure within the walls of the city, marched from Hadrianople to attack the enemy. After the army had proceeded for eight miles, under a blazing sun, they came unexpectedly in sight of the waggons of the Goths. The troops were hastily drawn up in battle array, while the barbarians broke out into the fierce chant with which they were accustomed to animate their courage before an engagement. The sudden advance of the Romans took Frithigern by surprise. The Ostrogoths under Alatheus and Safrax were many miles away in search of plunder, and had to be hurriedly sent for. In order to delay the fighting until his allies arrived, Frithigern sent to the Romans what we should call a flag of truce, pretending that he wished to make terms for surrender. The Romans fell into the trap, and answered that they were willing to agree to a parley if the Gothic chief would send some of his highest nobles as the bearers of his proposals. The messenger returned saying that Frithigern was willing to come and negotiate in person, provided that some officer of distinguished rank was previously sent to the Gothic camp as a hostage. This unexpected offer was hailed by the Romans with delight, and they at once began to discuss whom they should send. The unanimous choice fell on the tribune Equitius, commandant of the palace, and a relative of Valens ; but he stoutly refused the dangerous office, saying that he had escaped from barbarian captivity once in his life, and there was no knowing what desperate thing the Goths might do if they got him in their power. The dispute was settled by Richomer, who nobly volunteered to accept the unwelcome task himself. During all these long discussions, the Roman soldiers were kept under the burning sun, tormented by thirst and hunger, while the Goths remained comfortably in their encampment.

Richomer had already started on his way to the Gothic camp, when he was called back by the news that the battle had already begun. Some Iberian troops in the Roman service, tired of the delay, had made an attack on the enemy without waiting for orders. They were immediately routed; and just at that moment the long-waited for Ostrogoth cavalry burst ("like a thunderbolt," says a contemporary writer) upon the Roman army. Frithigern caused the trumpets to be sounded for the attack; the Roman cavalry was soon dispersed, and the infantry, surrounded and forced into a dense mass so that they could not use their weapons, and worn out by hunger and fatigue, were slaughtered by thousands. The Roman general Victor, perceiving that the emperor was in a position of danger, and forsaken by his guards, went to his relief; but when he reached the place Valens was not to be found. Victor and the other generals then left the field; but the massacre of the Romans went on until it was interrupted by the darkness of night.

For many days after the battle parties of the Goths were constantly on the field, plundering the dead, so that none of the Romans ventured to make a search for the body of the emperor. What his fate had been was not known until many years afterwards, when a young Roman, who had escaped from captivity among the Goths, related how he had been one of a party of youths who had conveyed Valens, wounded by an arrow, to a cottage on the battlefield, where they tried to attend to his wound. The enemy attempted to burst open the door, but failed, and, not knowing who was inside, set fire to the cottage. All the occupants perished except the narrator of the story, who jumped out of the window. The Goths were bitterly disappointed when they heard from the survivor that they had thrown away the chances of capturing a Roman emperor alive, and securing for themselves his ransom. Whether this tale was true or not, it was at any rate very generally believed. Several Catholic writers of the fifth and sixth centuries, who imagined that Valens had been the cause of the Goths becoming Arians, have shown the ferocity of their religious hatred by the remark that it was a just doom that he who had caused the souls of so many Goths to suffer eternal fire should be burned alive by Gothic hands.

For the second time in history a Roman emperor had perished amid the total ruin of his army, in conflict with the Goths. But even the day of Abritta had been less terrible than was the day of Hadria-nople. Two-thirds of the Roman army lay dead on the field, and amongst the slain were two generals of great renown, Sebastian and Trajanus, two high officers of the palace, Equitius and Valerian, and thirty-five tribunes. A contemporary historian says that no such disaster had befallen the Roman arms since that of Cannae. We can hardly doubt that if the Goths had been united and disciplined, and had known how to use their victory, the Eastern empire would have come to a speedy end. But this was not to be; the Goths could win battles, but the art of conquest they had yet to learn.

IX: THE GOTHS AND THEODOSIUS

On the morning after the battle, the victorious Goths at once began to lay siege to the city of Hadrianople, where they had got to know that the imperial treasure had been deposited. But "fighting with stone walls" requires more patience than the barbarians had yet learned to exercise. When their first assaults on the place were repulsed with heavy loss, they gave up the attempt in disgust, and after two days marched away to besiege Constantinople. Their first attack was so violent that they had nearly succeeded in forcing the gates, and perhaps if their fury had continued unabated the imperial city would have soon become their prey. But a band of Arab horsemen in the Roman service issued from the city, and a sharp conflict took place. The skirmish was indecisive, but a panic was created among the Goths by the sight of an act of cannibalism on the part of one of the Arabs, who sucked the blood of his slain adversary. The thought of having to fight with enemies of such inhuman ferocity chilled their courage, and after continuing the siege half-heartedly for a short time, they abandoned it as hopeless. Carrying away a large quantity of plunder from the suburbs outside the city walls, they wandered away to the north, and spread themselves once more over the provinces from the Black Sea to the Adriatic, which had so often before been the scene of their ravages.

We do not know much about what the Goths may have done in Thrace and Illyria during the two years following their great victory. The Roman writers complain bitterly of the havoc and devastation which they wrought, but they tell us no details. But surely the worst deeds of the barbarians can scarcely have equalled in cruelty and treachery the infamous act by which the civilized and Christian Romans revenged themselves on innocent persons for the defeat at Hadrianople. It will be remembered that on several occasions when treaties were made between the Goths and the Romans, a number of the children of Gothic nobles were given up to the Romans, as security for the faithful observance by the Goths of their engagements. As these young "hostages" had usually been sent away to the East, it happened that at the time we now speak of most of the cities of Asia Minor contained a considerable population of Gothic youths. The war minister of the Eastern empire, Julius, had heard rumours that great excitement prevailed amongst these young Goths at the result of the battle of Hadrianople, and that many of them had openly expressed disloyal sentiments. No successor had yet been appointed in the room of Valens, and Julius obtained from the Senate of Constantinople a vote authorizing him to do whatever he thought necessary for the good of the State. He then sent to the governors of the Asiatic provinces secret instructions that the Gothic youths should be induced, by promises of gifts and honours, to assemble on a certain day in the marketplaces of their respective cities. When they were collected together, the place of meeting was to be surrounded by troops, and the defenceless Goths were to be unsparingly massacred. This dreadful plan was successfully carried out, and its author was praised to the skies for having delivered the Eastern provinces from a terrible danger. It is true that these young Goths had been given up by their people as hostages, and the forfeiture of their lives, when the treaty had been broken, was "in the bond" but such an excuse does little to lessen the guilt of Julius, or of the Roman public which applauded his treacherous deed. Happily the ruler who was chosen to succeed Valens was a man of a spirit very different from that of Julius. It was in January, 379, that the great Theodosius was appointed by Gratian emperor of the East In his reign of sixteen years he proved once more, what every really great emperor since Aurelian had proved before him, that a policy of justice and kindness could convert even the turbulent Goths into faithful allies and subjects of the empire.

But before Theodosius could venture to do anything to conciliate the Goths, it was necessary that he should make them feel that he was to be feared. He had to reorganize his shattered army, and to teach his soldiers to overcome the terror which had been inspired by the crushing defeat of Hadrianople. His policy was not to risk any great battle, but to fight only when he had such advantages of position and numbers as made victory certain, so that his own troops grew gradually bolder, and the Goths became disheartened, as they saw that the gains of the contest, if not singly very important, always fell to the Roman side. The quarrels among the barbarians did much to help the Roman cause, and from time to time Gothic chiefs who thought themselves slighted by Frithigern deserted to the emperor, who gave them abundance of honours and rewards. One of these deserters, named Modahari, was entrusted with a high command in the imperial army, and gained for the Romans the greatest victory they obtained in the war.

Frithigern seems to have died sometime in 379 or 380, and in the latter year Athanaric crossed the Danube. On what ground he considered himself released from the oath by which he had professed to be prevented from treading Roman soil, we do not know, but very likely this had only been an excuse-He was soon acknowledged by the greater portion of the Visigoths as their king, and his first act was to make a treaty of peace with the emperor. Theodosius invited him to Constantinople, and entertained him splendidly. The sights which he beheld there impressed him with profound astonishment. "Often," he said, "have I been told of the grandeur of this city, but I never believed that the stories were true. The emperor is a god on earth, and whoever resists him is guilty of his own blood." Athanaric did not long survive his arrival at Constantinople. He died in January, 381, and was honoured with a royal funeral and a costly monument.

During the next two years those Visigothic tribes which had not joined in the treaty made by Athanaric were induced one after the other to make their submission to the emperor. In the year 386, the band of Ostrogoths who had formerly followed Alatheus and Safrax, and were now led by a chief named Audathaeus, had returned to Dacia after having made a raid into the north and west of Germany, and had attempted to cross the Danube into Thrace. Their fleet of boats, however, was unexpectedly attacked by the Roman soldiers; great numbers of the invaders perished by the sword or by drowning, and those who succeeded in reaching the southern bank at once surrendered to the Romans.

The sovereignty of Theodosius was now acknowledged by the whole Gothic nation, excepting only the Ostrogoths north of the Danube mouths and the Black Sea, who still continued under the Hunnish yoke. The emperor understood the character of his new subjects well enough to perceive that gratitude and honour were the ties which could best secure their faithfulness, and his conduct towards them was marked by kindness and confidence. The Visigoths were provided with lands in Thrace, and the Ostrogoths in Asia Minor; and large gifts of corn and cattle were made to them. They were allowed to govern themselves by their ancient laws. Their warriors were embodied into a separate army, under the name of allies, receiving handsome pay and honoured with many special privileges, and many of the Gothic nobles were promoted to high office in the state and in the imperial household. These measures had their intended effect. Although, no doubt, there were movements of discontent here and there, yet as long as Theodosius lived the great body of the Goths seem to have regarded their benefactor with feelings of passionate loyalty. In his wars against the Western usurpers, Maximus and Eugenius, the Gothic warriors rendered invaluable service.

It is plain that Theodosius took the best course that was open to him under the circumstances. The Goths could neither be expelled nor subdued by force. The only chance of rendering them harmless lay in winning their attachment, in making them feel that their rulers were their friends. For this purpose no cautious half-measures would have been of any use. The emperor's policy of unreserved confidence might appear too bold, but its seeming rashness was the truest prudence.

But indeed the state of things was such that every policy which could be adopted was full of terrible danger. Just imagine what the situation was. A vast people of foreigners, divided from their fellow-subjects in language, national feeling, and religion, and remembering that they had lately been the conquerors of the Romans, were settled in the heart of the empire; and forty thousand of their warriors were incorporated into a separate army, supplied with Roman weapons, and to be trained in the art of war under skilled Roman generals. And it was soon easy to see that the indulgence bestowed on the Goths had developed in them a pride which would not tolerate the smallest slight, and might easily prompt them to wish to be masters instead of subjects. It is said that Theodosius himself, though he was always regarded by the Goths as their friend, was not ill-pleased when he heard that they had suffered heavy losses in battle; and we can scarcely wonder if it was so. Even had Theodosius been succeeded by a long line of emperors as wise as himself, it is unlikely that the loyalty of the Goths to the empire could have been maintained for many years. But what might in that case have happened we do not know; whether the outbreak of the Gothic revolt might have been prevented or not, at any rate it was hurried on through the folly of the successors of the great emperor, and the recklessness of their selfish and ambitious ministers.

X: ALARIC THE BALTHING

In January, 395, the great Theodosius died. Owing to the line of the Western emperors having previously come to an end, he was at his death the sovereign of the whole Roman world. His dominions were divided between his two sons; the eldest, Arcadius, becoming emperor of the East, and the younger, Honorius, emperor of the West. They were both mere puppets in the hands of their ministers and favourites, and though Arcadius lived till 408, and Honorius till 423, our story would not lose much if we were never to mention their names again.

The favour shown by Theodosius to the Goths had excited a great deal of jealousy and discontent, which began to be very loudly expressed as soon as he was dead. Some people were foolish enough to demand that the new emperor should dismiss all his Gothic soldiers, and drive the whole nation back again over the Danube. Of course the Government could not attempt to carry out such extravagant proposals as these, but the popular clamour had its effect, and one of the first things that was done in the name of Arcadius was to lower the pay of the Gothic allies.

This was enough. The Romans had broken their treaty, and in a few weeks nearly all the Visigoths rose in rebellion.

Amongst the many Gothic chiefs employed in the Roman service was a young man not much over twenty years of age, named Alaric [Alh-reiks], a member of the princely family of the Balthings. Young as he was, he had rendered good service as a military commander; but when he asked for the promotion to which his deeds entitled him, he was refused. He joined the rebels, who at once chose him as their king ; and this was the beginning of the renowned Balthing dynasty of the Visigoths.

Led by their brave young king, the Visigoths marched through Macedonia and Thessaly, and entered Greece through the famous pass of Thermopylae. There were no successors of Leonidas and his three hundred Spartans to oppose their progress; the guards who were stationed at the entrance of the pass fled without striking a blow, and Alaric and his host hastened through Phocis and Boeotia, burning villages and carrying away the population as slaves, and were soon encamped before the walls of Athens. The Athenians paid a heavy ransom in money, and invited Alaric to a splendid banquet; and so the Goths departed, leaving the city unhurt. But the other famous cities of Greece, Megara, Argos, Corinth, and Sparta, fell into the hands of the barbarians; the inhabitants were killed or taken captive, and their treasures divided amongst the conquerors.

The great general of Honorius, Stilicho the Vandal, had already set out to meet Alaric with an army; but the government of Constantinople foolishly refused his help. But in the following year (396) they were glad to beg for it of their own accord. Landing at Corinth, Stilicho encountered Alaric in Arcadia, and succeeded in driving him into the mountain region of Pholoe, near the frontiers of Elis. It now seemed as if Alaric's escape was impossible; Stilicho had hemmed him in with a strong line of earthworks, and by turning aside the course of a river had deprived the

Gothic camp of its supply of water. The Romans abstained from making any attack, thinking that hunger and thirst would soon compel the Goths either to surrender or to risk a battle in which they were sure to be beaten.

Stilicho felt so sure that he had got Alaric in a trap that he allowed his own soldiers to roam about the country in search of plunder as they liked. But he did not know what a clever adversary he had to deal with. To the amazement of the Romans, Alaric broke through their lines, marched thirty miles away to the north through a difficult country, and had crossed the gulf that divides the Peloponnesus from the mainland before Stilicho could put his forces in marching order. Travellers who are acquainted with the ground say that this march of Alaric's was one of the most wonderful feats of the kind on record. The Roman general was making preparations for pursuit when he received information that the ministers of Arcadius had made a treaty with Alaric, who was then in possession of the province of Epirus. Stilicho therefore returned to Italy without having effected anything by his expedition.

Alaric had driven a hard bargain with the court of Constantinople. He was made military governor of Eastern Illyricum—that is to say, of nearly all the European portion of the eastern empire. The chief use that he made of this command was to set the Government factories to work at making weapons and armour for his own soldiers; and the ministers of Arcadius could, of course, do nothing to prevent him. He remained quiet for three years, arming and drilling his followers, and waiting for the opportunity to make a bold stroke for a wider and more secure dominion. In the autumn of the year 400, knowing that Stilicho was absent on a campaign in Gaul, Alaric entered Italy. For about a year and a half the Goths ranged almost unresisted over the northern part of the peninsula. The emperor, whose court was then at Milan, made preparations for taking refuge in Gaul; and the walls of Rome were hurriedly repaired in expectation of an attack. On the Easter Sunday of the year 402 (March 19th), the camp of Alaric, near Pollentia, was surprised by Stilicho, who rightly guessed that the Goths would be engaged in worship, and would not imagine their Roman fellow Christians less observant of the sacred day than themselves. Though unprepared for battle, the barbarians made a desperate stand, but at last they were beaten. The poet Claudian—the only true poet who lived in that dark age—in the poem which he wrote on the deeds of his patron Stilicho, tells us that the wife of Alaric was one of the captives taken, and in words which remind us of a fine passage in the Song of Deborah, describes how, before the battle, she had exulted in the prospect of adorning herself with the jewels of Roman matrons and being served by Roman captive maidens.

But although Stilicho was victorious at Pollentia, and obtained a large quantity of plunder and recovered many thousands of Roman prisoners, the Gothic loss of men does not seem to have been very great Alaric was able to retreat in good order, and he soon after crossed the Po with the intention of marching against Rome. However, his troops began to desert in large numbers, and he had to change his purpose. In the first place he thought of invading Gaul, but Stilicho overtook him and defeated him heavily at Verona. Alaric himself narrowly escaped capture by the swiftness of his horse. Stilicho, however, was not very anxious for the destruction of

Alaric, as he thought he might some day find him a convenient tool in his quarrels with the ministers of Arcadius. So he offered Alaric a handsome bribe to go away from Italy. The king was unwilling to agree, but the chiefs who commanded under him would not allow him to refuse. Finally Alaric accepted the money, and withdrew to Aemona in Illyria.

The departure of the Visigoths was hailed with great joy throughout Italy, and Honorius and Stilicho celebrated (in the year 404) a triumph in honour of their "victory." An arch which was erected for the occasion bore an inscription proclaiming that " the Gothic nation had been subdued, never to rise again." Six years later Alaric and his Goths had an opportunity of reading these boastful words as they rode through the streets of the conquered capital. After a stay of a few months in Rome, Honorius took up his residence in Ravenna, a city which for centuries afterwards continued to be the favourite abode of the sovereigns of Italy.

Of Alaric we hear little more for four years, but during this interval an important event occurred which belongs to the story of the Goths, though it is not easy to understand the circumstances which gave rise to it. In the year 406, Italy was suddenly overrun by a vast multitude composed of Vandals, Sueves, Burgunds, Alans, and Goths, under the command of a king named Radagais. To what nation this king belonged is not certain, but it seems likely that he was an Ostrogoth from the region of the Black Sea, who had headed a tribe of his countrymen in a revolt against the Huns. The invading host is said to have consisted of two hundred thousand warriors, who were accompanied by their wives and families. These barbarians were heathens, and their manners were so fierce and cruel that the invasion excited far more terror than did that of Alaric. It was commonly affirmed that Radagais had made a vow to burn the imperial city, and to sacrifice the Roman senators to his gods.

Stilicho found it hard work to collect an army capable of opposing this savage horde, and Radagais had got as far as Florence before any resistance was offered to him. But while he was besieging that city, the Roman general came upon him, and by surrounding his army with earthworks, compelled him to surrender. The barbarian king was beheaded, and those of the captives whose lives were spared were sold into slavery.

After this interlude, the second act of the drama of Alaric's life begins in the year 408. Stilicho, who had always had an idea that the Visigoths might some time be useful for his cherished purpose of humbling the eastern empire, had succeeded in persuading Alaric to enter the service of Honorius, and to undertake a plan for uniting all the Illyrian provinces under the dominion of the emperor of the West. Before the scheme had been completely executed, Stilicho changed his mind, and thought that it had better be put off till a more convenient time. Alaric now made his claim for the promised reward of his services, and Stilicho presented his demands before the Roman senate in a long speech, in which he praised Alaric as a faithful and valuable ally, and showed how dangerous it would be to refuse what he asked for. He also told the senate that the Gothic king had offered his services against the usurper Constantine, a private soldier whom the army had made emperor in Gaul, and whom the forces at the command of Honorius were quite unable to subdue.

The senators were very angry when they were asked to agree to the payment of tribute, as they called it, to a barbarian king. Some of them talked very grandly about letting their houses be burned over their heads rather than consent to such a disgraceful surrender. But Stilicho was still powerful, and after a long and fierce discussion the opposition cooled down. The grant—four thousand pounds' weight of silver—was voted with only one dissentient, Lampadius, who walked out of the senate house, telling his colleagues that what they had made was not a treaty of peace, but a contract of slavery.

The contract, however, was never fulfilled. Stilicho's rivals and enemies managed to get the emperor on their side, and in August, 408, the great general, the only able servant Honorius ever had, was murdered by the order of his ungrateful master. After Stilicho was dead, the Romans did not trouble themselves any more about the treaty. Alaric's repeated demands for its fulfilment received no answer, and at last he led his armies into the north of Italy.

The ministers of Honorius now did the most unwise thing that they possibly could have done. They dismissed the Gothic and other barbarian officers from their commands, and passed a law that no Arians or heathens were in future to be allowed to enter the imperial service. The barbarian troops, who were most of them Arians, and had been devoted to Stilicho, were of course thrown into great excitement by the proofs of the ill-will of the government, but did not at first venture to rebel, fearing that the Romans might revenge themselves upon their families. However, the mob of the Italian cities, having got to know that heretics and foreigners were now out of favour, rose and murdered the innocent wives and children of the barbarian soldiers, and looted their property. The result was that thirty thousand men, inflamed with the bitterest hatred, at once deserted from the Roman army and joined that of Alaric.

The march of Alaric over the north of Italy was like a triumphal procession. Without meeting any opposition, he plundered city after city till he came to the neighbourhood of Ravenna. Perhaps his first intention was to besiege the emperor in his own city; but Ravenna was protected by marshes, and Alaric did not think it worth while to attempt to capture it. He had a greater prize in view. He marched across the peninsula, and in the beginning of the year 409 his army encamped round the walls of Rome. Alaric was far too sagacious to sacrifice the lives of his soldiers by trying to carry the city by assault. He knew that a population of a million people would soon be starved into surrender, and so he contented himself with intercepting all the supplies of provisions, and waited quietly for the result. As soon as the Romans began to feel the distress caused by the siege, they threw the blame of their misfortunes on Stilicho's widow, who, they said, had sent for Alaric to revenge her husband's death; and without any pretence of a trial the senate ordered her to be strangled. The scarcity of food grew greater from day to day. But though many thousands of the people died of hunger, so that at last there was no room within the walls to bury them, the senate long refused to think of submission. Their hopes were kept up by messengers from Ravenna, who succeeded in entering the city in spite of the Goths, and brought them word that the emperor would soon send an army to raise the siege.

At last it was felt that the famine could be borne no longer, and two envoys of noble rank were sent to Alaric's camp to offer conditions of surrender. They began by trying to show Alaric that it would be prudent in him to grant the Romans honourable terms, for if he refused them the whole population would rise as one man, prepared to die rather than yield. When they were boasting of the enormous numbers of their people, Alaric said, "The thicker the grass, the easier it is to mow!" and burst into a loud laugh at the idea of the townspeople of Rome attempting to fight. The ambassadors were a good deal abashed by this reception of their arguments, and asked what were the terms which he would offer. He replied that he would spare the city on condition of receiving all the gold and silver within the walls, and all the foreign slaves. "What should we have left, then?" said one of the envoys in amazement. "Your lives!" replied the conqueror. The ambassadors had not a word more to say, and returned to tell their fellow citizens that there was no hope of mercy from the cruel Visigoth.

But Alaric only wished to give the Romans a fright: he did not really mean to insist on stripping them of everything they possessed. He succeeded, however, in making them believe he was thoroughly in earnest, and they were very glad when, after some further negotiation, he consented to fix a definite price for their ransom. The contract was a very curious one. Alaric was to receive five thousand pounds weight of gold, thirty thousand pounds of silver, four thousand silken robes, four thousand robes dyed with the costly Tyrian purple, and four thousand pounds of pepper. It seems odd to read of pepper being mentioned as an article of costly luxury, but it had then to be brought from India at great expense, and was used very freely in Roman cookery, the delights of which the Goths had learned to appreciate.

The price was paid, and Alaric moved his vast army away into Tuscany. He was careful to restrain his followers from committing any acts of rapine, and those Goths who were guilty of insulting Roman citizens were severely punished. The Gothic host was increased in numbers by forty thousand slaves, who had run away from their Roman masters, and by a large body of Goths whom Atawulf, the brother-in-law of Alaric, brought from the banks of the Danube.

Alaric had still no thought of upsetting the western empire. What he and his Visigoths wanted was to found a kingdom of their own under Roman protection. So from his camp in Tuscany he opened negotiations with the court at Ravenna, asking that he should be appointed chief of the Roman armies and should be allowed to settle with his followers in what are now the dominions of Austria. One of the ministers of Honorius, named Jovius, had actually agreed to grant him his demands; but the emperor and his courtiers, who were themselves out of danger at Ravenna, refused to confirm the treaty. Alaric was terribly enraged, and he proceeded to capture the harbour city at the mouth of the Tiber, where the Roman stores of corn were kept, and by the threat of a second famine forced the people of Rome to surrender.

Obeying the orders of their conqueror, the Roman senate declared that Honorius was deposed, and appointed Attalus, the prefect of the city, emperor in his stead. Attalus of course agreed to give Alaric the military rank and the dominions that he asked for. Most of the Italian cities, tired of Honorius, gladly-acknowledged the rival emperor, and when, accompanied by the army of Alaric, Attalus approached the gates of Ravenna, the ministers of Honorius offered, in his name, to agree to a division of the empire. Attalus refused this proposal, and demanded that Honorius should at once abdicate and retire into exile.

Honorius was already making preparations for a secret escape to Constantinople, when a quarrel broke out between Alaric and Attalus, who was scheming to make himself independent of the Gothic king. Alaric very quickly put an end to the plans of his puppet emperor. A great assembly of Goths and Romans was called together in a plain near Rimini, at which Attalus was made to appear dressed in the purple robe, and wearing the diadem; these signs of sovereignty were then solemnly taken away from him, and it was proclaimed that he was henceforth reduced to the rank of a private citizen. He seems to have taken his degradation very contentedly, and remained attached to the household of Alaric and his successor, who valued him as a pleasant companion and a skilful musician. How he afterwards again meddled in State affairs, unfortunately for himself, we shall have to mention in a succeeding chapter.

Alaric now sent the diadem and the purple robe of the deposed emperor to Honorius, as a token of his wish for peace and friendship. He renewed his proposals for a treaty, on the same terms as he had previously offered, and marching to within three miles of the gates of Ravenna, encamped there to await an answer. But a body of four thousand veteran soldiers, sent from Constantinople, having entered the city, the ministers of Honorius had recovered from their panic. The Gothic camp was attacked unexpectedly by a small company of men under Sarus the commander of the Gothic troops in the Roman service; and a herald was sent to proclaim to the Goths that Alaric was the perpetual enemy of the empire.

Instead of making an attack on the strongly fortified Ravenna, Alaric crossed the peninsula and laid siege, for the third time, to Rome. By a midnight attack — on the 24th of August, 410 — the Salarian gate was forced (or opened by treachery it is not certain which); and the great city, for the first time since its capture by the Gauls, eight hundred years before, was given up to the plunder of a foreign foe.

We may be sure that many dreadful things were done during the six days that the Gothic army remained in Rome. And yet, terrible as the fate of the city undoubtedly was, it was far less terrible than the Romans had feared—far less terrible than the fate which Rome underwent more than once afterwards at the hands of conquerors who called themselves civilized. Alaric remembered that he was a Christian, and he tried to use his victory mercifully. He told his soldiers that the plunder of the city was theirs, but that no man was to be killed who was not in arms; even of the soldiers, all were to be spared who took refuge in the churches of the two great apostles, St. Peter and St. Paul; and all the churches and their property were to be held sacred. But, though Alaric's commands were to some extent obeyed, so that some of the Roman writers speak with wonder of the moderation of the Goths, it was impossible to restrain the furious passions of such a vast multitude of conquerors. The streets, we read, were heaped with dead; men, and women too, were cruelly tortured to make them disclose the places where their wealth was hidden; and many thousands of people were sold into slavery. We cannot wonder at the thrill of horror which this event caused throughout Europe, nor that the Christians everywhere, when they heard the tale, thought that the end of the world was at hand.

Alaric now felt that it was useless any more to think of peace with the empire. Nothing remained but to establish himself as absolute master of Italy. But to do this, it was necessary that he should secure command of the corn supplies which came from the African ports; and when he marched from Rome, it was with the design of conquering the African provinces.

The Goths had reached the southern extremity of Italy, and had made one attempt to cross over into Sicily, which was defeated by the destruction of their fleet in a storm, when their king was taken sick, and died, at the age of only thirty-five years.

With bitter lamentation the Goths bewailed the death of their young hero. They knew that he had left behind him no successor who could carry out his mighty plans, and that the dominion of Italy could never be theirs. But, while they looked forward forsaking the country, they resolved to make sure that the sepulchre of their beloved king should not be violated by the hands of their enemies. They carried his dead body to the banks of the little river Busento, which flows by the town of Cosenza. They compelled their multitude of prisoners to dig out a new channel for the river, and in its deserted bed they made a grave for their king, burying with him a vast treasure of gold and silver, costly garments, and weapons of war. Then the river was turned back into its former channel, and the captives who had done the work were put to death, so that no Roman should ever know the spot where rested the remains of Alaric, king of the Visigoths.

XI: KING ATAWULF AND HIS ROMAN QUEEN

We must here for a moment interrupt our narrative to glance at certain events that had been taking place in the eastern empire while Alaric was fighting in Greece and Italy. The colony of Ostrogoths, whom Theodosius had planted in Asia Minor had, in the year 399, rebelled under a leader named Tribigild; the imperial general Gaina, himself a Goth, who was sent to subdue the rebels, ended by joining them, and becoming their chief. He crossed with his followers into Thrace, and excited great alarm at Constantinople, but was finally defeated, in the beginning of 401, by the king of the Huns, who sent the head of Gaina to the emperor as a sign of his friendly intentions. But all this has little bearing on the general history of the Goths, and after this brief digression we may continue the story of Alaric's followers, whom we left lamenting the loss of their beloved king, beside the river which flowed over his grave.

The new king whom the people chose in Alaric's place was Atawulf, Alaric's wife's brother, who has been mentioned in a preceding chapter. He made no attempt to carry out Alaric's purpose of invading Africa, and he does not seem to have had any clearly-defined plans of his own, for he spent two years in moving his army from the south of Italy to the northwest. It is said that a few years later he confessed that he had once had the intention to overthrow the Roman Empire and establish a Gothic Empire in its place, but that he had become convinced that the Goths were too rude and lawless to be capable of ruling the world, and so since then it had been his aim to do all he could to strengthen the Roman power. But this change in his views must have taken place before Alaric's death, for it is quite plain that he did not try to conquer Italy. Instead of that, he endeavoured to persuade the emperor to receive him as an ally. He had in his hands one argument which he thought would be powerful in inducing Honorius to consent to his demands. The emperor's favourite sister, Galla Placidia, was a prisoner in his camp, having been captured when the Goths had possession of Rome; and Atawulf offered to send her home if Honorius would make such a treaty as he wanted. But probably the terms he asked were too hard, and the great general Constantius, who now ruled over the weak emperor, refused to consent to them. It is thought, however, that when Atawulf, in the beginning of the year 412, left Italy, he had got a commission from Honorius to go and fight with Jovinus, who had made himself emperor in Gaul.

But when the Visigoths had entered Gaul Atawulf allowed Attains to persuade him that he had better try to make a friendly arrangement with Jovinus to divide the country with him. But Jovinus would not listen to the proposal, and so Atawulf returned to his original plan. The Goth Sarus, who was Atawulfs bitter enemy, had rebelled against Honorius, and was on his way to Gaul to support the usurper. Atawulf attacked him, and gained a complete victory, in which Sarus was killed.

Honorius now agreed to a treaty, which provided that Atawulf should receive a supply of corn for his army, and in return should set Placidia free, and send the heads of Jovinus and his brother Sebastian to the emperor at Ravenna. The latter part of the bargain was fulfilled by Atawulf, but the corn did not come, and he said he would keep Placidia until it was received. He went on fighting for his own hand against both the imperial forces and the remnants of the rebel army, and before the end of 413 was master of most of Southern Gaul, including the cities of Valence, Toulouse, Bordeaux, and Narbonne.

In Narbonne it was that he took up his abode, and there, in January, 414, the princess Placidia became his wife. The wedding was celebrated in the house of one of the wealthiest citizens of Narbonne, and Atawulf took care that it should be conducted in every respect according to Roman customs. The bridegroom was attired in Roman dress, and at the banquet he took the second seat, giving the place of honour to the princess. The presents to the bride included a hundred bowls filled with precious stones and gold pieces, which were laid before her by fifty noble youths dressed in splendid silken robes. The wedding chorus—an essential part of the Roman marriage ceremony among people of rank—was led by Attalus, who was famous for his skill in music.

Some of the Romans who heard of this marriage thought it was the event that was referred to in the words of the prophet Daniel: "The king's daughter of the south shall come to the king of the north to make an agreement; but she shall not retain the power of her arm, neither shall he stand, nor his arm, but she shall be given up." The rest of the verse could not well have been made to suit the occasion, but the prophecy, as far as this quotation goes, was admirably fulfilled in the events which followed.

No doubt Atawulf thought that the Romans of Gaul, who he knew would never own a Gothic king as their emperor, might be persuaded to submit to the rule of a daughter of Theodosius; and perhaps he thought also that Honorius would now himself be willing to acknowledge him, if not as sovereign of Gaul, at any rate as his own substitute and commander-in-chief there.

But he found himself mistaken. The Romans only thought that Placidia had disgraced herself by marrying a barbarian; and as for Honorius, he was still ruled by Constantius, whom this marriage made all the more bitter against Atawulf, for he had wanted Placidia to become his own wife.

As a last resort Atawulf caused poor Attalus to be proclaimed emperor once more. But Constantius came with a powerful army, and as the Roman fleets had cut off the supply of corn from the Gaulish ports, the Goths were in danger of being starved out. When Constantius advanced they fled from Narbonne, and after plundering the cities and country of the south of Gaul, crossed the Pyrenees into Spain. The unfortunate Attains was left to shift for himself He tried to escape by sea, but was captured by the Roman fleet, and was sent to Ravenna. His life was spared, but two of his fingers were cut off, and he was banished to one of the Lipari islands, where he ended his days.

Soon after arriving in Spain Atawulf captured Barcelona from the Vandals, and made that city his royal residence. Here a son was born to him, who received the name of Theodosius, and who, his parents hoped, would some day wear the diadem of his illustrious grandfather. But the child soon died, and was buried with great pomp in a coffin of solid silver.

In August, 415, Atawulf was murdered in his palace by Eberwulf, a former follower of Sarus, whom he had taken into his own service. Eberwulf, perhaps, meant treachery from the beginning, but Atawulf had irritated him by ridiculing his small stature. With his last breath the king charged his brother to make peace with the empire, and to send Placidia home to Ravenna.

But the brother who received this counsel was not allowed to succeed to the throne. The people blamed Atawulf for favouring the Romans too much, and they chose as their king a brother of Sarus, named Sigeric. His first act was to murder the six children of Atawulf's former wife, and he treated Placidia with the most shameful cruelty, making her walk twelve miles by the side of his horse. But in seven days he too was assassinated, and Wallia [Walya], a Balthing, though not related to Atawulf, was chosen in his stead.

Wallia treated Placidia kindly, but began by acting as the enemy of the Romans. Fighting both against the imperial forces and the Vandals and Sueves, he soon conquered the whole of Spain. But he was reduced to straits by a great famine, and like Alaric in a similar position, he made an attempt to cross over into Africa, to make the corn supplies of that province his own. Just as in Alaric's case, the attempt failed through storms, and Wallia had no other resource than to make his peace with the Romans. Honorius, or rather Constantius, was glad to accept his offer to send Placidia home, on condition of receiving 600,000 bushels of wheat, and being allowed to conquer Spain under the authority of the empire.

What became of Atawulf's widowed queen is not exactly part of the story of the Goths, but you may like to know how her strange history ended. When she got back to Ravenna she was compelled to marry Constantius, whom she disliked. Her husband was afterwards made joint emperor with Honorius, but only lived to possess the throne for seven months. As Honorius died childless in 423, he was succeeded by the infant son of Constantius and Placidia, Valentinian III, in whose name the empire was governed by the empress-mother until her death in 450. Among the famous monuments of Ravenna is the mausoleum which covers the remains of Placidia, together with those of Honorius, Constantius, and Valentinian.

XII: THE KINGDOM OF TOULOUSE

King Wallia was now no longer a rebel, but the recognized champion of the Roman emperor in Spain. With a well-provisioned army, and the support, instead of the opposition, of all the barbarians who wished to be loyal subjects of the empire, he soon succeeded in conquering the whole of the peninsula except the mountain region of the north-west, and in the year 417 he sent to Honorius two captive Vandal kings who formed part of the procession in the triumph which the emperor celebrated at Rome.

For some reason or other it did not suit Constantius's purpose to allow the Visigoths to settle down in Spain, and he proposed that instead of that country they should have the province known as the second Aquitania. Wallia must surely have been overjoyed when he received this splendid offer. The province, which included Bordeaux, Agen, Angouleme, Poitiers, and many other cities, was one of the most beautiful and fertile in all the empire. "The Pearl of Gaul," "The Earthly Paradise," "The Queen of Provinces," are amongst the titles which it received from poets and orators of that time. To receive the undisputed possession of such a "land of corn and wine and oil," in exchange for a country exhausted as Spain was by many years of barbarian ravage, where he would have had to maintain his dominion by continual conflict with powerful enemies, was a piece of good fortune which Wallia could scarcely have dreamed of. And the concession included also some important cities beyond the Aquitanian frontier, chief amongst them being Toulouse, which became the residence of the kings of the Visigoths, and the capital of their dominions.

It was at the end of the year 418 that the Goths marched out of Spain to occupy their new kingdom; and in the following year Wallia died. He left no son to succeed him, though he had a daughter who became the mother of Rikimer, a man famous in the history of the Roman Empire.

The Visigoths chose as his successor, Theoderic, who seems to have been a Balthing, though not related either to Wallia or to Atawulf. You must be careful not to confound this Visigoth Theoderic, or his son of the same name, with the great Theoderic the Amaling, who began to reign over the Ostrogoths about the year 475. Theoderic the Visigoth was not such a great man as his namesake, but he must have been both a brave soldier and an able ruler, or he could not have kept the affection and obedience of his people for thirty-two years. His great object was to extend his kingdom, which was hemmed in on the north by the Franks (a German people who had just been allowed to settle in the country now called France, after their name); and on the west by another people of German invaders, the Burgunds; while the Roman Empire still kept possession of some rich cities, such as Aries and Narbonne, which were temptingly close to the Gothic boundary on the south.

When the emperor Honorius died, in 423, Theoderic led out his armies, professedly to fight for Placidia and her infant son (Valentinian III) against a usurper named John; but his real object was to add some of the rich Roman cities to his own dominions; as very soon appeared, for when John died and the rebel army had submitted, he did not lay down his arms, but captured several towns, and began to besiege the great city of Aries. The famous Roman general Aetius, who had at first supported the usurper, but had made his peace with Placidia, attacked the besieging party, and defeated them, taking their commander Aunwulf prisoner.

For many years the relations between the Goths and the Romans were very unsettled, treaties being made and quickly broken whenever it suited the convenience of either side. In 437 the Goths had been trying to take Narbonne, and the Roman generals, Aetius and Litorius, resolved to put them down thoroughly. Aetius did gain a great victory, but he was called away to Italy, and Litorius had not the skill to finish the work. He besieged Theoderic in his capital city, Toulouse, with such an overwhelming force that the Goths thought their case was hopeless, and sent Orientius the bishop of Auch, with many other bishops and clergy, to try to persuade the Roman general to grant honourable terms of peace. Litorius, who was more than half a heathen, treated the messengers with contempt; and so Theoderic gave the order to prepare for battle. Until the conflict began, the king was clothed in the dress of a penitent, and spent many hours in prayer. His soldiers, inspired by their king's piety, and by the thought that they were fighting for Christianity against heathenism (for Litorius's army was mostly composed of Huns), made a furious attack upon the camp of the besiegers, who were totally defeated. Litorius was taken prisoner, and had to walk through the streets of Toulouse in the triumph which Theoderic celebrated after the Roman fashion. The Christian writers tell how Litorius's soothsayers had promised him that he should go in triumph through the city—a promise which, like many of those given by heathen oracles in older days, was fulfilled in another sense than that in which it was understood.

After this sudden change in the position of affairs, the Romans themselves were fain to sue for peace. Theoderic, puffed up by his success, at first refused to come to any terms unless the Romans would leave him in undisturbed possession of the whole of Southern Gaul, west of the Rhone. But his friend Avitus, a distinguished Roman senator, of whom we shall hear again, persuaded him to renew the alliance, though what the conditions were we do not know.

Theoderic, however, did not think the Roman treaty was likely to last, and determined to have a second string to his bow. In order to secure the friendship of the Vandals, he gave his daughter in marriage to the son of their king, the fierce and cruel Gaiseric, who had lately conquered the Roman provinces of Africa, and had made Carthage the capital of his kingdom. The marriage had a frightful sequel. Gaiseric suspected that his daughter-in-law was plotting to poison her husband, and he cut off her nose and ears, and sent her back to her father.

Of course it was now impossible to think any more of alliance with the Vandals; and in the year 450 the Visigoths and the Romans were drawn more closely together by the approach of a great common danger.

The Huns, who for three-quarters of a century had been occupying the old seats of the Goths north of the Lower Danube and the Euxine, had under their famous king, Attila, moved westward, and were threatening to over-run both Gaul and Italy. The Hunnish army consisted, it is said, of half a million men, belonging to all the nations whom the Huns had subdued on their march. The Ostrogoths and Gepids, and many other Teutonic tribes, formed part of this immense host, and were marching to fight against their brethren in language and race, under the command of an Asiatic savage. In the face of such an enemy, Roman and Frank and Visigoth felt that they must forget their differences, and unite for mutual defence. Attila cunningly tried to persuade first one and then another of these three nations to take his part against the rest. But they saw very well that unless they joined to oppose his progress, Attila would conquer them one by one. Theoderic was, indeed, at first disposed to adopt a policy that was both selfish and foolish, namely, that of remaining quietly in his own kingdom, and only defending himself when he was attacked. Aetius had arrived at Aries from Italy, at the head of a small army, but he had no force sufficient to meet Attila without the aid of the Visigoths. After long persuasion from Aetius and Avitus, Theoderic was made to see the necessity of joining in the defence of Christendom against the heathen horde. But precious time had been wasted in these discussions, and before any resistance could be offered, Attila had marched, plundering and burning towns and desolating the country, through the regions since known by the famous names of Lorraine and Champagne, and had begun to besiege the important city of Orleans.

The city was strongly fortified and bravely defended; but after a struggle of some days the gates were forced, and the vanguard of the Huns had passed through, when (as the church legend tells us in language borrowed from the story of Elijah), the messenger whom the holy bishop Anianius had sent to the walls to search the horizon beheld at last "a little cloud like a man's hand," which told that the saint's prayers were answered, and that the army of deliverance was approaching.

As soon as the coming of Aetius and Theoderic was known to Attila, he abandoned the neighbourhood of Orleans, and hastened across the Seine, to await the enemy in the plains of Champagne. The great battle—one of those which have decided the fate of Europe—was fought near the village of Moirey, a few miles from Troyes. It began with an attack by the Franks upon the Gepids, who were defeated with great slaughter. The Alans, who occupied the centre of the allied army, were routed by the Huns, and the Roman troops of Aetius were thrown into confusion; Theoderic was killed by a dart from the hand of an Ostrogoth named Andagis; but the bravery of the Visigoths carried the day, and Attila was compelled to retire to his camp, having lost a hundred and sixty thousand men.

Theoderic was buried on the spot where he fell, in sight of the vanquished enemy, with all the marks of honour which the Goths bestowed on their royal dead. His son Thorismund, to whose valour and skill the victory was chiefly due, was chosen by the army to be king in his father's stead.

In grim despair ("like a wounded lion," says Jordanes) Attila waited for the attack which he expected would result in the total ruin of his army. He ordered a funeral pile to be constructed, on which, in the event of defeat, he resolved to perish by fire, so that he might not fall, either alive or dead, into the power of his enemies.

The anticipated assault, however, was not made. Although the young king of the Visigoths was eager to complete his triumph and to revenge his father's death, he listened to the advice of Aetius, who— fearing, it is said, lest the Gothic power should become dangerously great—recommended him to return to Toulouse in order to prevent his brothers from seizing on the kingdom in his absence. And so Attila was allowed to retire from Gaul undisturbed. His army was still strong enough to enable him to ravage the north of Italy for two years, and to compel the Romans to make a humiliating treaty of peace. But the battle of Moirey had not been fought in vain. The question whether barbarism or civilization should prevail in Western Europe was decided; and when Attila died in 453, the vast confederation of nations over whom he ruled had fell to pieces. The Ostrogoths established a kingdom in Pannonia, which included nearly all the present Austrian dominions south and west of the Danube; the Gepids settled east of them in Dacia; and the broken remnant of the Huns, after a fruitless invasion of the eastern empire, wandered away into Southern Russia, where they were overwhelmed by the successive swarms of kindred savages who continued to stream westward from Asia.

Thorismund did not long enjoy his kingdom. He quarrelled with Aetius about the division of the Hunn's spoils, and began to levy war upon the Romans; against the wish of the more powerful party among his subjects, who desired to remain in friendship with the empire. A rebellion broke out, and in the year 453 Thorismund was murdered by two of his brothers, one of whom, Theoderic II., succeeded him in his kingdom, and reigned thirteen years.

The second Theoderic was no mere barbarian, but a man of cultivated mind, refined taste, and pleasing and graceful manners, though, like many other men of whom all this can be said, he was capable of the basest treachery and cruelty.

During Theoderic's lifetime events succeeded each other very fast at Rome. Valentinian III, Placidia's worthless son, was murdered by a senator, Petronius Maximus, who assumed the imperial diadem. He had reigned only four months when the Vandals under Gaiseric landed at the port of Rome. Maximus was about to take flight, but the people, disgusted with his cowardice, attacked him in the street, stoned him to death, and threw his body into the Tiber. Gaiseric entered Rome unresisted, and the work of destruction and plunder went on for fourteen days. The city suffered far more terribly than it had suffered at the hands of Alaric. All the gold and silver, and valuable possessions of every kind, whether public or private property, which could be removed, were carried away to the ships of Gaiseric. Amongst the spoil taken by the Vandals was the seven-branched candlestick, and the sacred vessels of the temple of Jerusalem, which had fallen into the hands of Titus when he captured the city. Many thousands of prisoners were taken to be sold into slavery at Carthage, and the empress Eudoxia, the widow of Valentinian, who had been compelled to marry her husband's murderer, was now obliged to follow in the train of the barbarian conqueror.

When the news of Maximus's death was received in Gaul, the Roman subjects in that province elected the prefect Avitus (whom we have already mentioned as the friend of the first Theoderic) to be emperor in his stead. The Visigoth king strongly supported his claim, and the senate at Rome did not dare to reject a candidate who was put forward by the most powerful king in Western Europe. The eastern emperor, Marcian, gave his consent, and Avitus took up his residence in the palace of the Caesars.

As the vassal of Avitus, Theoderic made an expedition against the Sueves, who had been attacking the little that remained of Roman territory in Spain. The Sueves were beaten, and their king, Rekihari, was captured and cruelly put to death. Theoderic would soon have conquered the whole peninsula, but in October, 456, his career was stopped by the news that the emperor had been deposed and killed. Avitus had incurred the displeasure of the "Warwick the king-maker" of those days—Rikinjer, the general of the barbarian troops in the Roman service. This remarkable man was the son of a Suevic father, and of the daughter of Wallia, king of the Visigoths. At this time he was practically sovereign of the western empire; and although he never took the imperial title himself, he continued, until his death in 472, to appoint and depose emperors just as he pleased. The history of Rome under the nominal rule of Majorian, Severus, Anthemius, and Olybrius, does not belong to our story; but the growing weakness of the empire, caused by the political confusion, and the occasional struggles between these emperors and their master, allowed the Visigoth kings to pursue their schemes of conquest without any serious check.

In 466, Theoderic, who had gained his throne by the murder of his brother, was himself murdered by his younger brother Euric. A skilful general and a cunning statesman, utterly destitute of conscience, shrinking from no act of cruelty or treachery necessary for the accomplishment of his plans, Euric raised the Visigoth kingdom to its highest point of power. He conquered the whole of the Spanish peninsula, with the exception of the north-western corner, which he allowed the Suevic kings to hold as his vassals, and he destroyed the small remnant of Roman dominion in Gaul.

If you glance at the map accompanying this volume, you will see how Gaul was divided at the time of Euric's death in 485. The Visigoths held nearly all the country south of the Loire and west of the Rhone, besides the region since known as Provence, which includes the great cities of Aries and Marseilles. Their eastern neighbour was the kingdom of the Burgunds, ruled over by Gundobad, the nephew of Rikimer. North of the Loire was the so-called "Roman Kingdom," which had been founded by Syagrius, the son of the Roman general Aegidius, and which had its capital at Paris. And behind the kingdom of Syagrius, in the tract including Northeastern France, Belgium, and Holland, dwelt the nation of the Franks, who were destined in a few years to conquer the whole of Gaul, and eventually to bestow upon it the new name which it bears to this day.

If the successors of Euric had been endowed with genius and energy equal to his, it is possible that the Visigoths might have made themselves masters of the whole Western world. But there was in the kingdom one fatal element of weakness, which perhaps not even a succession of rulers like Euric could have long prevented from working the destruction of the State. The Visigoth kings were Arians; the great mass of their subjects in Gaul were Catholics, and the hatred between religious parties was so great that it was almost impossible for a sovereign to win the attachment of subjects who regarded him as a heretic. The Arian Goths, to do them justice, scarcely ever were guilty of religious persecution. But when the Catholic bishops were found preaching rebellion, and conspiring against the throne, Euric put some of them to death, banished others, and refused to allow successors to be consecrated in their dioceses. Where there were no bishops, of course priests could not be ordained; the parishes were left without clergy, and the whole church organization fell into a state of ruin which excited the bitterest indignation both in the kingdom itself and among Catholic Christians in all the neighbouring lands.

Euric's son and successor, Alaric II, inherited neither his father's ability nor his strength of will. Before he had been two years on the throne, he had shown his own weakness by an act which disgusted many of his faithful subjects, and only earned for him the contempt of those whom it was intended to please.

The king of the Franks, Clovis, who, though only a boy, had already shown the talents of a great general, had conquered the kingdom of Paris. King Syagrius fled to Toulouse, and was at first received with welcome. But when Clovis demanded that he should be given up, Alaric did not dare to refuse, and Syagrius, loaded with chains, was delivered into the hands of the Frankish ambassadors. "Faithless" as the Goths were often called by their enemies, they were always proud of their observance of the duties of hospitality, and they were bitterly ashamed of this cowardly and treacherous deed of their king. And Alaric's Gaulish subjects, who looked eagerly forward to an opportunity of rebellion, were greatly encouraged by this proof of the feebleness of the hands into which the sceptre of the terrible Euric had fallen.

The only hope of deliverance from the Visigoth yoke, however, lay in a conquest of the kingdom by the Franks; and as Clovis was a heathen, there was reason to fear that the Catholics might find themselves worse off under his rule than even under that of Alaric. Some of the bishops, indeed, went so far as to say that it was better to serve a heathen than a heretic, and sent messages to Clovis assuring him of their sympathy in case of an invasion. But they did not succeed in persuading their people to join them: however discontented they might be under Alaric, the Southern Gauls felt that to place themselves in the hands of Clovis, might be a remedy worse than the disease.

This state of things continued until the year 496, when the news came that Clovis had professed himself a Christian, and had been baptized by a Catholic bishop. The thought of inviting a Prankish invasion now rapidly gained ground among the southern Catholics, whose discontent with their own condition was increased by the reports which they received of the growing wealth and prosperity of the Church in Clovis's dominions. Many of the clergy began openly to preach rebellion, and to offer public prayers for the coming of the deliverer from the north.

Alaric felt his danger. At first he tried his father's plan of banishing the rebellious bishops, and when that did not seem to answer, he tried to win over the Catholics by kindness, granting them increased privileges, and authorizing them to hold a council and to fill up the vacant bishoprics. But it was all to no purpose. The Catholics did not want to be tolerated or patronized, they wanted to rule. Alaric's concessions therefore satisfied nobody, while they were looked upon as a proof of weakness, which encouraged the hope that the Visigoth rule might be brought to an end without much difficulty.

Meanwhile the Prankish clergy were pressing on their king the duty of declaring a holy war against the heretic oppressor of their brethren. Clovis, we may be sure, was not unwilling, but first of all he had a quarrel to settle with his brother-in-law Gundobad, king of the Burgunds, who like Alaric was an Arian, though, unlike him, he had been able to gain the affection of his Catholic subjects. Gundobad was defeated, and the Burgunds entered into a treaty of alliance with the Franks. Although Alaric saw the danger to his own kingdom from the growth of the Prankish power, he did not dare to offer Gundobad any armed support, but he was imprudent enough to express his sympathy with the Burgunds. His utterances were reported to Clovis, who was very angry. Alaric was in a great fright, and wished to explain away what he had said. He wrote a letter to "his brother" Clovis, begging him to grant him an interview.

The two kings met on an island in the Loire, near Amboise, where they feasted together, and conversed with every appearance of friendliness. But every one knew that the peace would not last long. The situation was like that in the fable of The Wolf and the Lamb. However much Alaric might cringe and flatter, Clovis would devour him all the same, as soon as he found it convenient to do so.

It was in the year 507 that Clovis declared war against the Visigoths. The real motive was the king's ambition and desire of conquest. Of course he tried to find an excuse for his aggression; but he did not consider it worth while even to pretend that Alaric had injured him. All he had to say was "that it was a shame that the Arians should possess the finest country in Gaul, and that it was his duty as a Catholic king to drive them out, and to add their lands to his own dominions." Neither Clovis, nor his clergy, or people, thought that any other justification was needed; and the Franks went to war against the Visigoths, like the Hebrews against the people of Canaan, convinced that they were doing God service, and that He was on their side.

Perhaps this was the first time that a Christian nation ever made war with no other professed reasons than those of religious differences; unhappily it was very far from being the last.

Alaric was in despair. He had to meet not only the Franks, but the Burgunds as well; his army had been for many years neglected, and his treasury had become empty. He compelled, or tried to compel, all the able-bodied men in his kingdom to become soldiers, and tried all sorts of means to get money to pay them. First he had recourse, like James II of England and many other kings in their time of need, to the plan of debasing the coinage, and then he compelled the rich people to lend him money, which there was little hope of their ever getting back. But with all his efforts Alaric could neither raise the men nor the money that he needed. His only hope lay in foreign help. His father-in-law, the great Theoderic the Amaling, who, as you will learn in another chapter, was at this time King of Italy, had promised to send him a body of troops. Alaric was therefore anxious to put off fighting until these Ostrogoth allies had arrived, and so he abandoned the defence of the northern and eastern parts of his kingdom, and took up his position in the south-west, near Poitiers. Just at this time one of the Catholic bishops in Alaric's dominions—Galactorius of Beam—raised an army in his own diocese, and marched at its head intending to join the Franks. Before he had got very far, however, this warlike prelate was attacked by the Goths, and fell, as his fellow religionists thought, "gloriously fighting."

As the ancient heathen had their "oracles," so the Christians of the sixth century had theirs. It was to the tombs of famous saints that people used to resort when they wished to know whether any undertaking which they had engaged in would be successful or not. The priest in charge of the tomb would receive their questions, and on the following morning communicate the answers which he professed the saint had revealed to him in a dream. When Clovis with his army had entered Tours, he sent messengers to inquire at the sepulchre of St. Martin what would be the result of his war against the Visigoths. The messengers were told that the answer would be contained in the words of the psalm which they should hear as soon as they entered the church. The verses proved to be the following: "Thou hast girded me with strength unto the battle: Thou hast subdued under me those that rose up against me. Thou hast also given me the necks of mine enemies, that I might destroy them that hate me."

Encouraged by this response, the Franks marched through the territories of Alaric, eager for the conflict with the enemy whom God had given into their hands. The church historians tell of the "signs and wonders" which were granted them on their way to assure them of the continuance of the Divine favour. It is said that when they had come to the banks of the river Vienne, their progress was stopped by finding the stream swollen by the heavy rains, so that it seemed impossible for them to cross. But while they were considering what to do, a beautiful white hart was seen to wade across the river, thus showing them the place of a ford, over which the army was able to pass. The place was long afterwards called "the hart's ford." Very likely this story was suggested by the name itself, which may be compared with those of Hertford and Hartford in England. As the Franks approached the city of Poitiers, they saw in the sky above the cathedral a blaze of light which reminded them of the "pillar of fire" that went before the chosen people in the desert.

The rapidity of Clevis's advance was something quite unexpected by the Visigoths. Alaric still clung to the hope of being able to avoid a battle until the arrival of Theoderic's Ostrogoths, and wished to retreat. But the Franks were of course anxious to fight as soon as possible, and they were so close behind, and their movements were so rapid, that a retreat on the part of the Goths would have been nothing but a flight. Alaric's officers were of opinion that it was better to offer a bold front to the enemy where they were than to be pursued and overtaken, and the king, sorely against his will, was obliged to yield to their advice. He drew up his army on "the field of Voclad" (the name still survives as Vouille or Vougle) on the banks of the Clain, a few miles south of Poitiers, and prepared to receive the attack of the Franks.

The battle which followed decided the fate of Gaul. The Visigoths were totally defeated, and their king was killed. Alaric's son, Amalaric, a child five years of age, was carried across the Pyrenees into Spain. During the next two years Clovis conquered, with very little resistance, almost all the Gaulish dominions of the Visigoths, and added them to his own. The "Kingdom of Toulouse" was no more.

So, as Jordanes says, the greatness of the Visigoths, which had been built up by the first Alaric, fell to ruin under the second. But Clovis was not allowed to fulfil his intention of thoroughly destroying their power, for the great Theoderic of Italy took up the cause of his grandson Amalaric. The final result of many struggles between Theoderic and the Franks was that the Visigoths were allowed to remain masters of Spain, and of a strip of sea-coast bordering on the Gulf of Lyons.

Of the fortunes of this diminished kingdom, which lasted just 200 years, we shall afterwards have to tell. But for the present we must leave the Visigoths, whose history is no longer the main thread of the story of the Goths. We have to relate how the Ostrogoths won the kingdom of Italy, how they ruled there, and how at length they fell.

XIII: HOW THE WESTERN EMPIRE CAME TO AN END

We must now go back to the year 472, when Rikimer the emperor-maker died. The last emperor whom he had made, Olybrius, survived him only two months; and, after some time, Gundobad, Rikimer's nephew—the same whom we have before spoken of as King of the Burgunds—appointed a certain Glycerius to the vacant throne. The choice did not please the eastern emperor, Leo, and Julius Nepos, Prince of Dalmatia, and a nephew (by marriage) of Leo's wife, was proclaimed at Constantinople, Emperor of the West. Nepos sailed to Italy to take possession of his empire in the spring of 474. There was not much trouble with Glycerius, who was soon persuaded to resign his diadem, and accept consecration as Bishop of Salona in Dalmatia. But in the August of the following year, Nepos himself had to take refuge in his inherited dominions. The army had revolted, and the commander-in-chief, an Illyrian named Orestes, had seized the reins of government.

This Orestes had had a strange history. About thirty years before the date of the events just mentioned, his native country—the northern part of what is now called Croatia—had been given up by the Romans to the Huns. Orestes, who was then quite a young man, finding himself one of Attila's subjects, offered his services to the Hunnish king, and seems to have acted as his secretary. In this capacity he was in the year 448 sent on a mission from Attila to the eastern emperor, Theodosius II, and we read of his being terribly indignant because he was not regarded as a person of equal consequence with his fellow-envoy, Edica the Scirian. By what curious chances it came about that the former secretary of Attila now found himself at the head of the Roman army, and master of the Roman state, history does not tell.

Orestes did not choose to call himself emperor, thinking, perhaps, that it was safer for the wearer of the diadem and the real holder of power to be different persons. He contented himself with the title of Patrician, the same which had been borne by Rikimer and by Aetius; and bestowed the imperial crown on his son, a boy of fourteen, who was named Romulus after his maternal grandfather. Very likely Orestes may have thought what a lucky omen it was that the new emperor should bear the name of Rome's first sovereign, and may have flattered himself that his son's reign would be the beginning of a new age of glory and prosperity for the empire that had fallen so low. But the people looked on the election of the boy-emperor as a good joke, and turned his grand title of Augustus into the playful diminutive Augustulus. And so "Romulus Augustulus" is the name by which the son of Orestes is always known in history.

It was not long before signs of serious trouble showed themselves. The barbarian troops in the Roman service demanded of the Patrician that he should make them a gift of one-third of every landed estate in Italy. Orestes refused, and the whole mixed multitude of Goths, Scirians, Rugians, Turcilings, Herules, and Alans, which now formed the great bulk of the military force of the western empire, rose at once in rebellion. They chose as their king Odovacar or Odoacer [Audawakrs], the son of that Edica the Scirian, whom we have mentioned as having been associated with Orestes in Attila's embassy to Constantinople. The Scirians were one of those smaller peoples who spoke the same language of the Goths, and hence Odovacar is often spoken of as "King of the Goths." But he was really not the king of any nation, but only of the mingled host, belonging to many barbarian races, who served under the Roman standards.

There is a story which tells how, when Odovacar was a young man, poor and unknown, he was wandering in Southern Germany, and paid a visit with some of his companions to a saintly hermit named Severinus to ask for his blessing. His coarse dress showed his poverty, but the attention of the saint was at once attracted by his stature, which was so tall that he had to stoop in order to come under the lowly roof of the cell. Severinus soon saw that the young Scirian was as remarkable for his powers of mind as for his noble form and bearing, and prophesied that there was a glorious career before him. Odovacar informed him that he was intending to go to Italy to seek employment in the Roman army. "By all means go," said Severinus, "although you are now-poorly clad in skins, I foresee that it will not be long before you make many men rich with your princely gifts."

Orestes was killed in the tumult; some say that Odovacar slew him with his own hand. But the king of the barbarians took pity on "Romulus Augustulus," and gave him a pension of six thousand gold pieces yearly, and a splendid palace at Misenum, on the bay of Naples, which had belonged to the great Roman general, Lucullus.

It was in the year 476 that Orestes was put to death. For four years longer Odovacar seems to have kept up the pretence of being the servant and protector of the boy emperor. But in the year 480 Augustulus was made formally to resign his throne, and to add his signature to a memorial which the senate addressed to the eastern emperor Zeno, saying that they had determined to abolish the useless dignity of emperor of the west, and asking him to proclaim himself the sovereign of the whole Roman world. Of course they added the request that Zeno would entrust the government of the western provinces to that excellent statesman and soldier Odovacar, and confer on him the rank ot Patrician.

The memorial was carried to Constantinople by delegates from the senate, who were accompanied by ambassadors sent by Odovacar himself. No doubt Odovacar thought that Zeno, who had just been restored to the throne from which he had been driven by rebellion, would be highly flattered by the prospect of becoming, if only in name, the emperor both of east and west.

But on the same day on which the envoys presented themselves at the palace, there arrived ambassadors from Nepos to congratulate Zeno on his restoration, and to beg for his assistance in regaining his lost empire. Nepos was related by marriage to the empress, and had too many friends at the court at Constantinople for Zeno to venture to betray his cause. He angrily upbraided the senate for their treason against their rightful sovereign. To Odovacar himself he sent a polite letter, recommending him to acknowledge his allegiance to Nepos, and to seek to obtain from him the office which he desired. In the letter, however, he addressed Odovacar by the title of

"Patrician," which, he said, he felt sure Nepos would willingly grant when he was asked.

But although Zeno might refuse to acknowledge the action of the senate, it was none the less the fact that the abdication of Romulus was the end of the western empire. The year 480 is a memorable date in history, and the name of "Romulus Augustulus" a memorable name, though the poor boy-emperor himself never did anything to make it so. From this time forward the proud title of Augustus remained the exclusive possession of the rulers of Constantinople, until three centuries later it was assumed by the Prankish king who was crowned at Rome as the successor of the emperors of the West.

Before this fateful year had closed, Nepos was assassinated by a certain Count Ovida. Zeno made no attempt to appoint a successor, and no longer refused to be regarded as sovereign over the western provinces.

Of course this sovereignty was only an empty name, for Odovacar was practically king of Italy, and all the rest of what had been the western empire was in the hands of other barbarian kings. The rule of Odovacar, so far as it depended on himself, was wise and merciful. Although an Arian, he gave the Catholics full liberty of worship; the Roman state officials were allowed to keep their places, and the system of government was little changed. But the barbarian soldiers received their promised third part of the Italian lands, and they subjected the Roman country people to a great deal of insult and oppression, which the king was unable to prevent. Property and life became insecure; agriculture and trade fell into neglect, and altogether the state of Italy under Odovacar was one of great wretchedness.

Although Odovacar would tolerate no interference with his government, he tried to gain Zeno's goodwill in various ways. He sent over to Constantinople the insignia of the imperial palace, and caused statues of the emperor to be erected in Rome and elsewhere. He also undertook an expedition to Dalmatia against the murderer of Nepos, who was taken prisoner and put to death.

But Zeno was anxious to be master of Italy in reality as well as in name, and if he had had a powerful army at his command he would very promptly have made an attempt to drive out the Usurper by force of arms. For several years his weakness compelled him to put off his design, but about the year 489 he granted permission to the king of the Ostrogoths, the famous Theoderic the Amaling, to invade the country, and to take possession of it in the name of the empire.

Before we tell of the struggle that took place between Odovacar and the Amaling, we must relate the story of Theoderic's early life.

XIV: THE BOYHOOD OF THEODERIC

Theoderic, the son of Theudemer, as we have already mentioned at the end of our fifth chapter, was born on the day when his uncle Walamer, king of the Ostrogoths, won the great victory that set his nation free from the dominions of the Huns. The home of the Ostrogothic nation was then (about A.D. 454) in the region which we call South-western Austria, and Theoderic's birthplace was somewhere not very far from Vienna. After the Ostrogoths had established their independence, they entered into an alliance with the eastern emperor Marcian, who agreed to pay them a large sum of money every year, to enable them to defend their kingdom and furnish men when required for the service of the empire.

While Marcian lived the treaty seems to have been observed on both sides. The next emperor, Leo of Thrace, owed his position to the favour of the "Patrician" Aspar, a barbarian who had at Constantinople the same rank and the same influence that Rikimer had at Rome; and Aspar caused the yearly subsidy to be taken away from Walamer and given to another Gothic chieftain, a relative of his own, Theoderic Strabo, the son of Triarius. Who this man was we do not certainly know, but possibly the body of Goths whom he commanded may have been descendants of those who sixty years before had been defeated with Gaina in Thrace. We shall have frequently to speak of him in the following chapters, and in order to distinguish him from the other Theoderic, we shall always give him his Latin name.

King Walamer tried all peaceable means to induce the emperor Leo to restore him his yearly pay, but when he found that his representations were of no avail he led his army into Illyria, and soon made the Romans feel that it was much better to have him for a friend than for an enemy. In the year 462 the treaty was renewed. The emperor agreed to make Walamer a regular payment of three hundred pounds weight of gold every year, besides paying the arrears that had already been incurred. In return the Ostrogoths undertook to guard the borders of the empire, and the little Theoderic, then eight years old, was sent to Constantinople as a hostage to ensure fulfilment of their part of the bargain. His father was not very willing to let him go, but king Walamer persuaded him to consent—urging the great advantage which it would be for the boy, who would one day be king of the Ostrogoths, to have received an education in the imperial palace.

The young Gothic prince soon became a great favourite with the emperor. He remained ten years at Constantinople, and seems to have been brought up just like the son of a Roman of high rank. The most celebrated teachers in the capital were secured for his education, and although no doubt he was more distinguished for success in athletic exercises than in book-learning, we need not believe the common story that when he became king of Italy he was unable to write, and had to make his official signature with the help of a gold stencil-plate. His residence in Constantinople certainly taught him to appreciate the advantages of civilized ways of life, and inspired him with a desire to impart those advantages to his own people.

When Theoderic was eighteen years old, he was allowed to return home, receiving on his departure many splendid presents from the emperor and his court. During his period of exile, king Walamer had been killed in a battle against the Scirians, and Theudemer had become king in his stead. It was hard work for the Ostrogoth kingdom to maintain itself against the attacks of the surrounding peoples. On one side it was assailed by the Gepids and Sarmatians, on another side by the Alamans, Sueves, and Rugians; and the remnant of the Huns had not given up trying to recover their lost dominion. When Theoderic returned home, he found that his father was away fighting the Alamans in the northwest, while the opposite extremity of the kingdom was threatened by a Sarmatian king named Babai, who had captured the Roman fortress of Singidunum (now Belgrade).

The young prince soon showed that his education at Constantinople had included some lessons in the art of war. Without waiting for his father's permission, he collected a band of six thousand men, and attacked Babai on his own ground. Singidunum was taken; the Sarmatian king was killed, and his family and his treasure carried off in triumph to the Ostrogoth capital. In spite of his friendly relations with the emperor Leo, Theoderic did not give back Singidunum to the Romans. Perhaps indeed they never asked for it, for the rulers at Constantinople were kept too busy with their home troubles to think much about the outlying parts of the empire, and Theoderic had at any rate relieved them of one dangerous enemy.

But the limits of Theudemer's kingdom were too narrow for the numbers of the people, and the continual conflicts with the border tribes left them little opportunity for tilling their fields; besides, after nearly a century of wandering about under the dominion of the Huns, they could not be very well fitted to settle down peacefully as farmers. When the Ostrogoths found themselves in danger of famine, they begged their king to lead them forth to war — no matter against what enemy, if only they might have the chance of supporting themselves by plunder.

The king could not refuse his people's demand. The army was divided into two bodies, one led by Theudemer himself, the other by his brother Widumer, and it was decided that they should attack severally, the eastern and the western Roman Empire. In the presence of the assembled people the two chiefs solemnly cast lots to determine the direction in which each of them should march.

The lot so fell out that Widumer led his division of the people to Italy. It was in the short reign of Glycerins, and that emperor—it was almost the only official act of his that we know of, except his abdication—induced the invaders, by the gift of a large sum of money, to go away into Gaul, where they united themselves with the Visigoth subjects of Euric.

The great mass of the Ostrogoth nation, however, followed their king into the region between the Danube and the Balkan mountains, which had so often, in years gone by, had the misfortune to be ravaged by Gothic invaders. The city of Naissus and several others fell into their hands, and the Romans of Constantinople were so alarmed by their successes that they were glad to purchase peace. The Ostrogoths were invited to settle in Macedonia, and received large gifts of land and money. Amongst the cities which were abandoned to them was Pella, famous as the birthplace of Alexander the Great.

Just after the conclusion of this treaty (in the year 474) Theudemer died, and his son Theoderic, at the age of twenty years, began his long and glorious reign as king of the Ostrogoths.

XV: THE RIVAL NAMESAKES

The emperor Leo died in the same year as Theudemer, and was succeeded by his son-in-law, "Trasacodissa the son of Rusumbladeotus," a native of Isauria in Asia Minor, who had exchanged his barbarous-sounding native name for the more pronounceable Greek name of Zeno. You will remember that it was to this emperor that the senate of Rome, under the dictation of Odovacar, offered in 480 the sovereignty of Italy and the West.

Zeno was, as the historians of that time tell us, "a coward who trembled even at the picture of a battle." There was no act of meanness and no humiliation from which he would have shrunk if it were necessary in order to avoid war. But the two principal "foreign powers," if we may call them so, with whom he had to do, Theoderic, king of the Ostrogoths, and Theoderic Strabo, were bitter enemies to each other, and if Zeno tried to please one of them he Was sure to bring down on himself the wrath of the other. So he was constantly seeking by flattery and rich presents, to attach to his own side whichever of the two Gothic chiefs happened to be strongest, and at the same time so to arrange matters that both of them should suffer as much damage as possible from their mutual conflicts.

Before Zeno had been a year on the throne, he was driven out of Constantinople by a rebellion in which Basiliscus, the brother of Leo's widow, was made emperor. Strabo supported the usurper, and while he reigned held the rank of Patrician and commander-in-chief But the Ostrogoths were on Zeno's side, and after two years Basiliscus was dethroned, and Zeno came back to Constantinople. The emperor made a great display of his gratitude to Theoderic the Amaling for his share in defeating the rebels; he gave him the title of Patrician, adopted him as his son, conferred on him a high command of the imperial armies, and made him a grant of large sums of money. Theoderic, however, knew very well that "his father" Zeno would not at all scruple to betray him whenever it suited his convenience, and so, to make his own position more secure, he removed his people from their Macedonian abodes, and settled them along the southern bank of the Danube, from Singidunum down to the river mouth.

Meanwhile Theoderic Strabo and his Goths ranged undisturbed over Thrace, and maintained themselves by the plunder of the country people of that province. He is said to have been guilty of many acts of cruelty, such as cutting off the right hands of the prisoners whom he took, so that they might never be able to fight against him. But the plunder of Thrace was soon exhausted, and when Strabo found it difficult to obtain food for his army he sent ambassadors to Zeno to say that he was willing to make peace—on condition of being put into the position then occupied by his rival. He argued that Theoderic the Amaling had acted like a rebel, in occupying the Danube region without permission, and that it would be to the emperor's interest to break with the Ostrogoths, and entrust Strabo himself with the duty of punishing their breach of faith.

Zeno thought that Strabo's wish for peace was a sign of weakness, and therefore rejected the proposals with the utmost scorn, and gave orders to his generals to prosecute the war with all possible vigour. But Strabo's Goths showed unexpected powers of resistance; the Roman troops were beaten, and there actually seemed reason to fear that the enemy might soon threaten Constantinople itself. It was now the emperor's turn to try to make peace, and he sent to offer Strabo the undisturbed possession of the territory he had conquered, on condition that he should abstain from further hostilities against the empire, and should send his son as a hostage to Constantinople.

But Strabo by this time had got to know his own strength. He had learned, too, that he had many friends in the capital itself, and believed that it might not be difficult for him to obtain an entrance into the city and to make himself master of the empire. He accordingly rejected the proposed conditions, and Zeno in his despair was reduced to implore the help of the Ostrogoths.

Theoderic the Amaling, however, shrewdly suspected that Zeno meant to lead him into a trap, and it was a long time before he could be persuaded to move. He made the emperor swear a solemn oath never to make peace with Strabo, and promise that before he arrived in presence of the enemy he should be joined by a Roman army of eight thousand horse and thirty thousand foot. Having received these assurances, Theoderic led his soldiers into Thrace. After a long and toilsome march through a desolate country, he suddenly came in sight of Strabo's army, posted in a strong position on a mountain called Sondis. There was no sign of the coming of the promised Roman troops, and it soon became clear that Zeno had never meant to send them.

Theoderic's situation was a desperate one. It was impossible to attack Strabo in his encampment on the mountain, and just as impossible to retreat to a safer position. He remained for several days undecided, perhaps hoping against hope that his Roman allies might after all arrive. Strabo made no attempt to assume the offensive, but rode every day to a place which was out of the reach of bowshot, and where his powerful voice could be heard in the Ostrogoth camp. "Goths!" he said, "will you let yourselves be led by that foolish boy to fight against your own brothers? Will you be made to play the game of the Romans, who desire nothing better than to see us cut each other's throats? What has Theoderic ever done for you? Some of you were rich once: he has made you poor. Nobles and freemen as you call yourselves, he has led you out like slaves to perish in this desert that he may earn honours and wealth from the enemies of our people." Such words as these excited fierce discontent amongst the Ostrogoths, and their king was compelled to enter into an alliance with his rival. And so, while Zeno was expecting the welcome news of a bloody battle between his enemy and his too dangerous ally, he learned instead that the two chiefs had united against him, and were prepared to march together upon Constantinople unless the demands of both were fully satisfied.

The treacherous emperor could think of no other plan than that of bribing one of the new allies to betray the other. First he tried what he could do with the Amaling. He offered him immense sums of money paid down, and a larger yearly income than he had before received from the empire. He also promised him the hand of the daughter of Olybrius, the late emperor of the West. But Theoderic was not to be induced to become a traitor, and Zeno then endeavoured to buy over the other of the confederates. In this attempt he was successful. Whatever Strabo might have said about the wickedness and folly of a war between "brethren," he had no objection to fight against the Ostrogoths if the price offered was high enough, and he accepted the emperor's proposal to invest him with the honours and commands which had been held by the Amaling, and to allow him to maintain thirteen thousand Gothic soldiers at the emperor's cost.

It is no wonder that Theoderic was very angry at this shameful breach of faith. The first thing he did was to invade Macedonia, where it is said that he put the garrisons of several cities to the sword without quarter; then, crossing over the mountains into Epirus, he came to the Adriatic coast, and took possession of Dyrrhachium (Durazzo), the great seaport from which ships used to sail for the south of Italy.

But Zeno soon became dissatisfied with the conduct of Strabo, and so he sent ambassadors after the Amaling to try to make peace with him. He offered to grant the Ostrogoths a tract of country in Epirus, and to provide them with money to buy corn until they could raise their first harvest. Theoderic insisted on better terms; but while the negotiations were going on, his brother Theudamund was treacherously attacked by a Roman general, who took five thousand prisoners. After this the parley was broken off, and the war began afresh.

In the year 481 a rebellion broke out in the neighbourhood of Constantinople, led by two generals named Illus and Romulus. Strabo undertook, in consideration of a heavy increase of pay, to put down the rising; but he played the traitor after all, and joined the rebels in an unsuccessful attempt to take Constantinople. Soon afterwards he was accidentally killed, his horse having run away with him and thrown him against the point of a spear, which had been fixed before a tent.

So now Theoderic the Amaling was freed from the rivalry of his troublesome namesake. His army was soon joined by the greater part of Strabo's followers, and he became so formidable and did so much damage to the empire that Zeno was glad to purchase his friendship at any price. In 483 the Ostrogoths received an ample grant of land near the Danube. Two years later, Theoderic marched against the rebel forces under Illus, and gained a complete victory, for which he was rewarded with a triumph and an equestrian statue at Constantinople. But very soon the emperor and the king were quarrelling again, and the Ostrogoths took up arms and began to ravage the neighbourhood of Constantinople.

At last, however, a settlement was arrived at which satisfied both parties. Zeno gave permission to Theoderic to go and wrest Italy from the hands of Odovacar, to establish his own people there, and to rule the country as the emperor's representative.

This plan enabled Zeno to get rid of the Ostrogoths, whose expensive help was no longer necessary to him. At the same time, it was just what Theoderic himself desired. Although circumstances had compelled him to become something like a bandit chief, it had always been his great ambition to be the king of a settled and civilized people. And now, with the express sanction of the sovereign whom he regarded as the rightful lord of the world, he was to place his subjects in that very land in which, more than in any other he might reasonably hope to mould them into a great nation, which should be as glorious in the arts and the virtues of peace as in those of war.

XVI: HOW THE OSTROGOTHS WON ITALY

It was in the year 488 that Theoderic received the emperor's permission to go to Italy and fight against Odovacar. He betook himself at once to his headquarters at Novae, on the south bank of the Danube (near Sistova), and called on his people to make ready for emigrating into their "promised land." The preparations were quickly made, for the Ostrogoths had only been in Moesia five years, and it was easy for them to resume the wandering life to which they had so long been accustomed. Theoderic was so eager to get to Italy that he began his march at the end of the autumn, thus exposing his people to suffer the hardships of winter in addition to those of a long journey over rugged mountains and through the territories of unfriendly tribes.

It is thought that the people whom Theoderic led out of Moesia numbered not less than a quarter of a million. For about three hundred miles this vast multitude, with all their cattle and their baggage, proceeded along the bank of the Danube without meeting opposition. But when they came to Singidunum, the place where Theoderic, when a boy, had gained his famous victory, their progress was stopped by the Gepids, who had now taken possession of the country which the Ostrogoths had occupied in King Walamer's and King Theudemer's days.

Theoderic sent messengers to Thrafstila, king of the Gepids, asking permission for the Ostrogoths to pass through his country. Thrafstila refused, and there was a great battle near a river called Ulca. The ground was marshy, and at first the Gepids were beginning to win, because they knew the place better than the new-comers; but Theoderic's own bravery inspired his soldiers with such enthusiasm that the defeat was changed into a complete victory. The Gepids had to forsake the field in confusion, and left behind them many waggons full of provisions, which the Ostrogoths were very glad to get hold of

After the victory by the Ulca, Theoderic led his people along the river Save, and then over the steep passes of the Julian Alps. But however impatient the king might be to enter on his future kingdom, it was only possible to move very slowly forward, for amongst the throng were many thousands of women and young children, and more than once sickness broke out amongst them, and compelled them to interrupt their march. And so it was not until nearly a year after the beginning of their journey that the Ostro-gothic host stood ready to cross the Isonzo, the boundary river of Italy. On the opposite bank of the stream they saw the powerful army of Odovacar encamped to prevent their passage.

Theoderic's soldiers were weakened by their long journey and the hardships they had gone through on their way, but they still proved more than a match to Odovacar's followers—a disorderly crowd made up of a number of petty tribes, whose chiefs scorned to obey the orders of a commander whom they accounted no nobler than themselves. On August 28, 489, the Goths forced the passage of the river, and Odovacar retreated to Verona.

After giving his army a little breathing-time, Theoderic broke up his camp near the ruins of Aqui-leia, and set out to make a second attack upon the enemy. It was on the 30th of September that the great battle of Verona was fought, which decided the fate of Odovacar's kingdom. On the morning of the battle Theoderic care-carefully dressed himself in his most splendid clothing, ornamented by the hands of his mother and his sister, saying with a smile that he hoped his bravery in the fight would show who he was, but at any rate his apparel should show it. Odovacar's men fought desperately, and the losses of the Ostrogoths were enormous. But once more the king's skilful leadership, and the animating example of his own dauntless courage, carried the day, and Odovacar fled in confusion. With the remnant of his army he endeavoured to find shelter within the walls of Rome; but the senate had no mind to side with a beaten rebel against the victorious representative of the emperor, and ordered the gates to be closed. Odovacar then marched across the country, burning villages and destroying the crops, and took refuge in the impregnable fortress of Ravenna. Meanwhile Theoderic's victory had placed him in possession of the strong cities of Verona and Milan, and he soon received the submission of a large portion of Odovacar's army.

Amongst the chiefs who deserted to Theoderic was a certain Tufa, who had held a high command in Odovacar's army. This man succeeded in thoroughly gaining Theoderic's confidence, and undertook, if he were entrusted with a large body of men, to besiege Odovacar in Ravenna. The king agreed to his proposal, and at Tufa's own request a number of Theoderic's principal officers were attached to the expedition. But before he reached the neighbourhood of Ravenna Tufa deserted back again to his former sovereign, and Theoderic's officers were loaded with chains and sent to Odovacar, by whom they were kept for some time in prison, and then shamefully murdered. The soldiers who had submitted to Theoderic when Odovacar's cause seemed hopeless now forsook him by thousands, and joined the army of Tufa. For a time it seemed as if the tide of fortune had turned, and Odovacar was, after all, going to recover his lost dominions. The Ostrogoths were compelled to abandon Milan and Verona, and to retire to the neighbourhood of Pavia.

But Odovacar was unable to follow up his advantage. His followers, unlike those of his adversary, were a mere band of mercenaries, held together by no tie of national sentiment, and feeling little attachment to the person of their leader. They soon began to desert in large numbers; and the quarrels between the generals rendered it impossible to take any effectual action. In August, 490, the arrival of a body of Visigoths sent by Alaric of Toulouse enabled Theoderic to inflict a crushing defeat upon his enemy, and before very long Odovacar was closely besieged in Ravenna. Just about this time it is said that an event took place which resembles that which is so gloomily celebrated in English history under the name of St. Brice's day. The partisans of the emperor, according to a concerted plan, massacred the supporters of Odovacar all over Italy. Before the year 490 had closed, the only important place in Italy, except Ravenna itself, which had not submitted to Theoderic was the seaport of Rimini (Ariminum) on the Adriatic. The senate at Rome despatched its most distinguished member, the consul Faustus, to Constantinople, to ask that Theoderic might be invested with the royal robes, and be authorized to bear the title of king of Italy. But when the envoy arrived at Constantinople the emperor Zeno was breathing his last, and the petition seems to have remained unanswered.

It was not till the blockade of Ravenna had lasted for two years and a half that the pressure of famine compelled Odovacar to offer terms of surrender. The bishop of Ravenna acted as mediator, and Theoderic was so tired of the long siege that he was glad to agree to conditions which were extravagantly favourable to his rival. It was stipulated that Odovacar should be allowed to live in Ravenna with the title of king, and should be treated, so far as pomp and ceremony were concerned, as the equal of his conqueror. His son Thelane, whom he had shortly before, in imitation of the example of Orestes, proclaimed emperor of the West, were delivered up to the Ostrogoths as a hostage, and on March 5, 493, Theoderic entered the city, and took possession of the imperial palace in "the Laurel-grove."

The two kings met one another with a great show of friendliness, but before many days had passed Theoderic heard that Odovacar was plotting his assassination. At any rate that was what he said afterwards to justify his own cruel and treacherous action. On the 15th of March he invited his rival to a banquet at the "Laurel-grove" palace. In two side chambers to the right and the left of the seat which the royal guest was to occupy he placed armed men, who were instructed on hearing a certain signal to rush out and cut down Odovacar and his followers. As soon as Odovacar had taken his seat, two soldiers of Theoderic approached him, pretending that they wished to ask some favour from him, and seizing his hands as if in the eagerness of their entreaty. The signal was given, and the armed men came into the hall, but when they saw that their business was to be the murder of a defenceless man, and not, as they had expected, the frustration of an attack upon their own king, they stood as if stupefied. Theoderic then drew his sword, and raised it to strike Odovacar. "Where is God?" exclaimed the unhappy victim. "This is how you treated my friends!" shouted Theoderic, and dealt him such a violent blow on the collar-bone that the body was almost cut in two. Theoderic looked with astonishment at the effect of his stroke, and said with an inhuman sneer, "The poor wretch must have had no bones." Thus died Odovacar, at the age of sixty years. He was buried outside the city, in a piece of ground which was close to the Jews synagogue, and was deemed to be polluted by the neighbourhood of infidel worship. His wife, Sunigilda, was starved to death in prison, and his son was sent as a prisoner to King Alaric at Toulouse, but afterwards escaped to Italy and was there killed.

We have told this sad story of Odovacar's end as it is related by a historian of the seventh century. It contains some things that sound rather improbable, and we would fain hope that some of the circumstances of treachery and brutality have been exaggerated. When we think how gloriously Theoderic reigned over Italy for thirty-three years, how he laboured to secure the happiness of his subjects, and how Goths and Romans alike acknowledged the even-handed justice of his rule, we cannot help believing that the act by which he gained his kingdom was not altogether the cold-blooded treason which his account represents it to have been. Nothing that we know of Odovacar, on the other hand, forbids us to think him capable of plotting the murder of the rival with whom he had sworn peace and friendship. If Theoderic had indeed discovered evidence of such a plot we can scarcely wonder that he should be moved to take violent means to render its execution impossible. But whatever may be said in palliation of the murder of Odovacar, we cannot help feeling sorry that the reign of the great Theoderic should have begun with this fierce and lawless deed.

XVII: THE WISDOM OF THEODERIC

Once more we have to lament the truth of Milton's saying, that the victories of peace are "less renowned" than those of war. Far more interesting, if it could only be told, than the records of all the battles which Theoderic ever won, would be the story of the peaceful achievements which followed. By what means the Gothic usurper succeeded in giving order and prosperity to the land so long the prey of lawlessness and oppression, by what arts he so won the hearts of his subjects, both Romans and Goths, that when he died he was mourned as no ruler had been for centuries past, are questions which history gives us very imperfect answers.

The earliest act of Theoderic's which we read of after the death of Odovacar did not seem to promise well for the wisdom and gentleness of his rule. He published an edict by which all those Romans who had in any way exhibited any sympathy with Odovacar against himself should be deprived of their privileges as citizens, including the right of disposing of their own property by will. This measure was felt to be a great injustice, because many of those whom it affected had supported the cause of Odovacar under compulsion, and were quite ready, if treated with kindness and consideration, to become faithful subjects of the new king.

Fortunately the sufferers by this edict found a powerful intercessor. When, during the war with Odovacar, Theoderic had taken up his quarters in the city of Pavia, he had had a great deal of intercourse with the bishop Epiphanius, and, though the bishop was a Catholic, the holiness of his character had inspired in the king's mind the profoundest veneration. "There is not such a man in all the east," Theoderic said; "it is a privilege even to have seen him." It was this venerable man whom the Romans begged to plead their cause. Accompanied by Laurentius, bishop of Milan, he journeyed to Ravenna, and sought an audience of the king, who received him with every mark of honour, and listened with great attention to his speech. Epiphanius reminded Theoderic (not without some dexterous flattery mingled with his admonitions) of the many signs of Divine favour which had attended his career in Italy, and exhorted him to testify his gratitude by imitating the Divine example of mercy. He urged that Odovacar had fallen because of the harshness and injustice of his rule, and counselled Theoderic to be warned by the fate of his predecessor, concluding with an appeal which might almost be translated in the familiar words:

"Consider this, That in the course of justice none of us Should see salvation: we do pray for mercy, And that same prayer doth teach us all to render the deeds of mercy."

There was a pause of some moments after the bishop had spoken, and every one present awaited the king's reply with deep anxiety. Theoderic began by saying that it was not always that the necessities of government permitted of the exercise of mercy, and by appealing to the Scriptural example of Saul, who incurred the Divine wrath by his ill-timed compassion for a vanquished enemy. But he added that as heaven itself yielded to the bishop's prayers, no mere earthly power could resist them: and he ordered his secretary to prepare a decree of general amnesty.

Theoderic certainly could have taken no better means of winning the goodwill of his new subjects. And the fact that this act of mercy had been granted to the entreaties of a Catholic bishop made a great impression on the minds of the Catholics, and did much to soften the prejudice which was naturally felt against the heretic king.

After this question was decided, Theoderic had a private conversation with Epiphanius, in which he spoke of the deep grief he felt on account of the wretched condition into which Italy had been brought by continual war. He referred especially to the misfortunes which had befallen the bishop's own northern diocese through the invasion of the Burgunds, who, in 490, had carried away large numbers of the peasantry as prisoners into Gaul. "I know," said Theoderic to the bishop, "that Gundobad, king of the Burgunds) has a great desire to see you; if you go to plead the cause of the Italian captives he will be persuaded to set them free, and I will supply you with money sufficient for their ransom."

Epiphanius was moved to tears by this proof of the king's interest in the people whose welfare lay so near to his own heart. He eagerly accepted the commission that was offered to him, and at once set out, braving the bitter cold of March, across the Alps to visit King Gundobad at Lyons. The king received him graciously, and granted the free release of all those captives who were under his own control. Those who were slaves belonging to private persons had to be ransomed with Theoderic's gold. From Lyons the bishop went to Geneva, where he had the same success with the other Burgund king Godegisel; and he was accompanied to Italy by many thousands of the rescued captives, who returned to bring back to fertility their long-deserted fields, and, we may be sure, to invoke blessings on the name of their deliverer Theoderic. Not to leave his work incomplete, the king bestowed large gifts of seed-corn and of cattle upon the returned peasants.

The first great problem that the king had to encounter was how to satisfy the claims of his Gothic soldiers for lands in reward of their services, without exciting rebellion amongst the Roman proprietors at whose expense these grants were made. It was, however, fortunate for Theoderic that his predecessor had already despoiled the Roman landowners of a third of their estates, so that for the most part the Goths had only to step into possession of the share which Odovacar's men had held, and the Roman lord was no poorer than he had been for thirteen years previously. The king, moreover, wisely placed the carrying out of this measure for the Gothic settlement in the hands of a distinguished Roman named Liberius, who had been one of Odovacar's ministers, and who knew how to manage the matter so as to spare his countrymen's feelings as much as possible. Theoderic had a great respect for Liberius, and, in a letter to the senate some time after his death, he praises him especially for his honesty in never concealing his grief for Odovacar in order to curry favour with Odovacar's enemy and successor. Only a man of real nobleness of mind would have singled out such a characteristic for praise in a public document, and this is one of the many things which lead us to believe that the deed by which Theoderic gained the crown was not the shameful treachery that it is recorded to have been. Theoderic goes on to say that the goodwill and harmony which existed between Goths and Romans was very largely due to the tact and skill with which Liberius conducted the division of the estates and the apportionment of the burdens of taxation.

Although Theoderic did not care to run the risk of offending both his Goths and the Court of Constantinople by calling himself Caesar or Emperor, yet those titles would have exactly expressed the character of his rule—so far at least as his Roman subjects were concerned. When the Emperor Anastasius in 497 acknowledged him as ruler of Italy, he sent him the purple cloak and the diadem of the Western emperors; and the act showed that Anastasius quite understood the difference between Theoderic's government and that of Odovacar. In fact, though not in name, the Western empire had been restored with much the same institutions as it had had under the best of the Caesars. Although the army was Gothic, the great offices of state were filled by Romans, and the senate, if it had less real power than it had sometimes managed to obtain under weaker sovereigns, was treated with a show of respect and deference which was some consolation for its political insignificance. Its members were appointed to act as judges in the courts, and in all cases in which Romans were concerned the Roman law still retained its authority.

One great evil from which the Roman Empire had suffered for many reigns past was the illegal exactions on the part of the officers entrusted with the collection of revenue. So long as the emperors could raise the money they wanted, they had cared little how their officials might enrich themselves by extortion. Theoderic kept a strict watch on the conduct of his officials. All persons who had grievances against them were encouraged to bring forward their complaints; rigorous inquiries were made, and the accused, if found guilty, were severely punished. It was the king's special study so to apportion the taxes that the burden fell as equally as possible, and—unlike the Eastern emperors of the same period, who were notorious for always exacting "the uttermost farthing"—he was always ready to grant exemptions or reductions of taxation to districts that were suffering from bad harvests or similar causes of distress. The official letters of Theoderic's secretary Cassiodorus make us acquainted with many of these timely acts of generosity, which contributed more than anything else to make the Roman subjects submit gladly to the rule of the barbarian king. One interesting instance of the same kind is known to us from another source, the biography of Epiphanius, the Catholic bishop of Pavia, whom we have already spoken of as being greatly respected by Theoderic. In the year 496 the people of Epiphanius's diocese had had their crops destroyed by floods, and the good bishop once more journeyed to Ravenna to plead the cause of his beloved flock. Theoderic listened with sympathy to the story of the sufferings of the people, and though he talked a good deal about the difficulties that lay in the way of making a sacrifice of revenue, he gladdened the bishop's heart by consenting to reduce the taxes for that year to one-third of their amount. Epiphanius returned to Pavia with the good news, but the rejoicings of his people were soon mixed with sorrow, for a few days after his arrival he died from the effects of a cold taken during his journey.

The one great obstacle to Theoderic's popularity was that he was an Arian, while the great mass of his Roman subjects were Catholics. But in his government he never allowed himself to make any difference between the two parties. One of his most honoured Gothic generals, Ibba, was a Catholic; and the Catholic clergy, if they were by their character worthy of their office, were regarded by him with as much respect as those of his own creed. This tolerant conduct was not merely adopted because Theoderic feared to offend the Catholics. He had really a profound conviction of the truth, known to so few in his age, that kings have no right to meddle with the religious faith of their subjects, and that persecution, though it may make men hypocrites, will never make them sincere believers. The best proof that Theoderic's toleration was a matter of principle is seen in his conduct towards the Jews. Ever since the Roman Empire had become Christian, this unhappy people had been subjected to cruel persecution, and even the Visigoths in Gaul had shamefully oppressed them. If Theoderic had followed this bad example he would no doubt have been applauded both by the Romans and by many of his own countrymen. But he had courage and firmness enough not only to announce publicly that " the benefits of justice are not to be denied even to those who err from the faith," but to act up to this maxim in the most uncompromising manner. In one instance a Jew at Rome had been murdered by his Christian slaves. The perpetrators of the crime were condemned to death. The people of the city could hardly believe that such a monstrous sentence would be carried out, and, when the execution actually took place, the mob made a furious attack on the Jews, and burnt their synagogue. The offenders were brought before the senate for trial, and pleaded the many acts of extortion of which they said the Jews had been guilty. They were told that these complaints were nothing to the purpose; if the Jews had acted illegally the courts were open, but acts of violence would meet with due punishment, whether committed upon Jew or Gentile. Another case of synagogue burning occurred at Ravenna, and in that instance the building had to be restored at the expense of those who had destroyed it, while those of the offenders who had not means to pay were whipped through the streets. In some places the Jews had been robbed of their synagogues by Christian priests, who had converted the buildings Into churches, and now argued that twenty or thirty years' possession gave a title to the ownership. But Theoderic would listen to no such reasoning; the churches had to be restored to their original use, notwithstanding all the fierce indignation of the Christians, few of whom had any sympathy with the spirit of the text, "I hate robbery for burnt offering." It is true that Theoderic, or his secretary, when writing to the Jews to announce some concession or act of justice In their favour, generally takes the opportunity to lecture them on the sin of unbelief, and to express compassion for their gloomy prospects in the next world. But he is always careful to add that their perversity in this respect Is no reason for treating them with injustice. One of his letters written on an occasion of this kind ends with the significant words, "Religion is not a thing which we can command, because no man can be compelled to believe against his will." It is to Theoderic's eternal honour that he was willing to brave the fierce Indignation of the vast majority of his subjects for the sake of doing justice to a weak and oppressed people.

We have already said that Theoderic, though bearing the title only of king, aspired to fulfil the perfect Ideal of a Roman Caesar. He did not neglect to display the bounty and magnificence which were appropriate to the character. You remember how "Bread and Circus games" was the demand which the Roman populace used to make of their rulers in the palmy days of the empire. It was long since these demands had been satisfied by imperial generosity, but now once more the poor of Rome and the other Italian cities received their periodical gifts of food, and the public spectacles were exhibited with something like their ancient splendour, though happily without the cruel fights of gladiators, in which the heathen world delighted. The king himself took great pleasure in the theatre and in exhibitions of gymnastic skill.

To those who are accustomed to regard "the Goths" as tasteless destroyers of the vestiges of ancient civilization, it will seem strange to be told of the extraordinary zeal which Theoderic displayed in the preservation of the buildings and statues of antiquity. But perhaps there had never been a Roman emperor who was so anxiously concerned about this matter as this barbarian king. In the official letters of his secretary Cassiodorus we find continual proofs of Theoderic's endeavours to arrest the destruction of the works of ancient art. Judging him by his conduct in this respect, we might fairly say that he was the first civilized ruler that Italy had had for centuries. The Christian emperors had allowed their subjects to use the temples and other public edifices of heathen days as quarries for their own buildings, and not seldom had they been themselves guilty of pulling down venerable historical monuments to erect new buildings in their place. Theoderic indignantly forbade this work of waste and ruin. He was himself a great builder, and bestowed honours and rewards freely on those who adorned the cities with splendid works of architecture; but it was a saying of his that "reverently to preserve the old was even better than to build afresh."

Except an act of extortion or oppression on the part of one of his own officials, nothing excited his anger so fiercely as any wanton destruction of works of art. On one occasion he was informed that a bronze statue had been stolen from a public place at Como during the night. In hot haste he writes to Thankila the senator (from his name evidently a Gothic officer, and apparently governor of the city), ordering him to offer a reward of a hundred gold pieces for the discovery of the perpetrator, and to have a strict inquiry made of all the metal smiths of the town, as it was probable that such a theft could not have been carried out without skilled assistance. This letter was promptly followed by another, in which a free pardon was offered to the guilty person if he confessed and made restitution, otherwise, in the event of a discovery, the penalty was to be death. In the year 500 Theoderic spent six months at Rome, and in his letters he often refers to the profound admiration which had been inspired in him by the contemplation of the treasures of ancient art. The grandeur of the forum of Trajan, especially, is often mentioned by him. While at Rome, he decreed that a sum of 200 pounds weight of gold (£8,000 sterling, or 40,000 dollars) should be set apart every year for the repair of the walls and the public buildings. It used to be the fashion to blame "the Goths" for the destruction of the monuments of ancient Rome; but the truth is that we are indebted to a Gothic king for the preservation of many a noble building which, but for his pious care, would have totally disappeared.

Theoderic was earnestly desirous that his reign should be distinguished, not only as a period in which the ancient masterpieces were protected and valued, but also as a period of original artistic productiveness. In this it was impossible for him to succeed, for in the many years of misery and disorder from which Italy, and the Roman world generally, had suffered, the nobler arts had fallen into hopeless decline. But at any rate he spared no labour or cost in seeking out and rewarding the best architects, sculptors, and painters that could be found; and one branch of art, namely, mosaic-work, may be said to have attained perhaps its highest level in his reign. When we read of the enormous number of works which Theoderic carried out—building of churches, theatres, palaces, public baths, not only in Rome, Ravenna, and Verona, the three capitals of his kingdom but in many of the smaller cities of Italy—we are at first tempted to accuse him of recklessly lavish expenditure; but we are informed that although he found the treasury deeply in debt, his wise management not only enabled him to find money for all these costly undertakings, but to leave the finances of the kingdom in a thoroughly prosperous condition.

Although Theoderic was not so ignorant of books as he is commonly said to have been, it is not likely that he had any great appreciation of literature. But to protect and encourage literature was part of the duty of a pattern Roman emperor, and Theoderic was not wanting in this respect. The age was one of miserable degeneracy, in letters even more than in art; but the principal writers and scholars of the time, such as they were, were all rewarded by Theoderic with honours and official rank. There was Cassiodorus, whom he made his "quaestor" and secretary of state—an orator, historian, theologian, and grammarian, many of whose writings still exist. Poor enough in literary merit they certainly are, but they show a good knowledge of classical literature, and give us besides a very favourable impression of the author's upright and kindly character. His twelve books of official letters, written in the names of Theoderic and his successors, are of great value to the historian, though they are perhaps the most bombastic State papers ever known in Europe, not excepting the Latin charters of some of the Anglo-Saxon kings. One work of his which has unfortunately perished in his History of the Goths, of which the history by Jordanes, so often quoted in the early part of this book, is a very clumsy abridgement. Jordanes says that he had managed to get a loan of Cassiodorus's history for three days, and that his own book was written chiefly from the hasty notes he had been able to make in that time.

There was also Symmachus, famed in his own day for learning and eloquence, the author of a Roman history in seven books, which has not been preserved. Theoderic gave him the office of Prefect of the city of Rome and of patrican. We shall in a future chapter have to tell how Symmachus was put to death on suspicion of treason, sharing the fate of his more renowned son-in-law, the philosopher Boethius.

Of Boethius himself there is much more to be said, for he is by far the greatest literary name of Theoderic's reign, or indeed of the whole sixth century. Of noble rank, and born to great wealth, he devoted his leisure to the study of science, and to the task of rendering the treasures of Greek learning accessible to his countrymen. It was from his translations and commentaries that the Western world became acquainted with the writings of Aristotle on logic, which had so powerful an influence that they set all the great minds of Europe, for eight or nine centuries, studying nothing else than the theory of reasoning and subtle questions of metaphysics, which were profitless because unanswerable, even if they had any rational meaning at all. He also translated Greek treatises on music, astronomy, and mathematics; he wrote poetry and books on theological controversy, and his skill in mechanics was greater than that of any man of his time. When quite a young man he was made, by Theoderic, consul and patrician, and afterwards Master of the Offices; and for many years there was no man whom the king more deeply honoured and esteemed. How this career of prosperity and dignity came to a sudden end—how Boethius was accused of treason, judged guilty, and condemned to death—we shall relate further on.

Theoderic's great anxiety, however, was to restore to Italy its long-lost material prosperity and plenty. Of course when the country was firmly and justly ruled, and the people had protection against violence and fraud, there was very soon a revival of agriculture and trade. Theoderic was eager to help on this revival by active means. He encouraged the opening of iron mines in Dalmatia, and gold mines in the south of Italy. He assisted the development of the shipbuilding and fishing industries. He promoted the draining of the marshes at Terracina and Spoleto, and granted the reclaimed land, free from taxes, to those who had borne the cost of the undertaking. He spent large sums yearly in the repair of the highways, and in the restoration of the old aqueducts and the building of new ones. The extortions of the custom-house officers, which in the days of the empire (as Cassiodorus says) "foreign merchants had dreaded more than shipwreck," were now firmly put down, and the import duties were assessed by a committee, among whose members were the bishop and several influential citizens of the seaport town. A uniform standard of weights and measures was introduced; the coinage, which had been debased, was restored to its proper value, and the uttering of false money was severely punished.

Some other things which Theoderic did with the same object do not seem to have been equally well advised. He appointed in every town a committee, consisting of the bishop and some of the citizens, to fix the price of articles of food, and inflicted severe punishment on all tradesmen who ventured to charge higher rates. The exporting of corn from Italy was forbidden under heavy penalties; and if a corn merchant was found "speculating for a rise," as it is called, that is to say, buying up a large quantity of grain when it was cheap, in order to sell it at a great profit when it became dearer, the king compelled him to sell out his stock immediately at cost price.

No doubt these measures did more harm than good; but they were well meant, and show how zealously Theoderic strove to promote the welfare of his subjects, especially of the poorer part of them. And on the whole his philanthropic policy was wonderfully successful. In after times people looked back to the reign of Theoderic as to a period of almost fabulous plenty and prosperity.

So much for Theoderic's relations with his Roman subjects. With the Goths his relations were to some extent different. Though they lived amongst the Romans, the Goths did not become blended with them; they were still a separate nation, with their separate laws and a separate system of government. Just as in their earlier days, the army and the nation were really the same thing; the officers who led the people in war judged and ruled them in peace. It must be remembered that Theoderic had no soldiers except his Goths; the native Italians were not allowed to enter the army. The Goths of each province were governed by a military chief, called the "Count of the Goths," who in time of peace was accountable only to the king himself. When a lawsuit arose between Goth and Goth, it was judged by the count, according to Gothic law; while cases between Goth and Roman were tried before the count and a Roman judge sitting together.

But still the political constitution of the Ostro-gothic kingdom had undergone a great change. The Gothic warriors had gained a settled home, lands, and money; but they had paid for these advantages by the loss of their ancient freedom.

Their popular assembly met no more to make laws or to decide the policy of the State. The king acted as he chose, without asking their advice or consent. Over Goths as well as Romans, though under different forms, Theoderic reigned as a despot—a just and merciful despot, indeed, but a despot nevertheless. Although, as we have said, the two nations were governed in the main according to their own laws, Theoderic issued a brief code of his own, which so far as its provisions extended was binding both on Romans and Goths. This code was chiefly founded on the law of the Roman Empire, but many points in it are plainly of Theoderic's own devising. No offences, we can well believe, were so hateful to the Gothic king's justice-loving soul as the taking of bribes by judges and the bringing of false accusations of crime. The first of these, under the Roman law, had been punished by transportation to an island and confiscation of property. Theoderic (who significantly makes it the subject of the very first paragraph of his edict) decreed that the penalty should be death. The emperors had already -punished the false accuser with death; in the new law he is ordered to be burnt alive. On the other hand, some of Theoderic's alterations of the Roman code are on the side of mercy. The later emperors had enacted that when a man was condemned for any crime, his property should be forfeited to the State, unless he had parents or children. Theoderic ordained that if the condemned man had relatives as far as the third degree their right to inheritance should be undisturbed.

The Ostrogoths sometimes murmured over the loss of their freedom; perhaps they may sometimes have been indignant at the severity with which the king punished all lawlessness on their part, all insulting or oppressive conduct towards their Italian fellow-subjects. But they never rebelled, though as the only armed people in the kingdom they had every opportunity of doing so successfully. If they blamed the king for taking away their liberties, they could not help seeing that he was no selfish tyrant, but a ruler who laboured zealously and wisely for the common good of all. If he was stern to wrong-doers, they knew that he did not neglect to honour and reward faithful service; and they had learned to value the blessings of ordered and settled life too well to think of overthrowing the sovereign to whose firmness and sagacity their enjoyment of these blessings was due.

Theoderic did not, as has sometimes been thought, endeavour to unite the Goths and the Romans into one nation. Perhaps he may have hoped that such a union would at some time be realized under his successors. But in his own day he was content that the two peoples should live together in mutual friendship and respect, each of them being charged with its own special function in the commonwealth. The Goths were to undertake the defence of the country from attack, the maintenance of order, and the execution of the law; the Romans were to labour for the development of art and science; while in the cultivation of the soil both nations were to take their part. So long as Theoderic lived this ideal seems to have been in a great degree realized.

It is no wonder that Theoderic became the subject of many fabulous stones, and that tradition represented his reign as having been almost a kingdom of heaven upon earth. Even before the sixth century closed, men told in Italy nearly the same story that was told in England respecting the days of Alfred— how the great king had so made righteousness to prevail in his realm that gold pieces could be left exposed on the highway for a year and a day without being stolen. Many of his sayings were quoted as proverbs in the land, and anecdotes were related to show how, like Solomon in the matter of the two mothers and their infants, Theoderic had displayed in the judgment seat his wonderful insight into human nature. But it was not in Italy or amongst the Goths that his legendary fame reached its highest point. The whole Teutonic race regarded his glory as their own, and his imagined deeds were the theme of popular songs in all the German lands. The story of "Dietrich of Bern" (the High German way of pronouncing Theoderic of Verona) is indeed, as told in the poems, very different from the history of the real Theoderic. He is described as the vassal of Attila and the foe of Ermanaric, who is partly confounded with Odovacar; and in some of the songs "Dietrich" is even represented as vanquished, and as a fugitive or a captive. But amid all this strange distortion of the history, the character of the legendary Dietrich is essentially that of the Gothic king. A lover of peace and justice, he never takes the sword save unwillingly and at the call of duty; but when he is once prevailed upon to fight there is none more fearless and more terrible than he. The traditions embodied in popular poetry are generally wildly confused with regard to the order of events, but the accounts they give of the characters of famous men are often wonderfully true. Probably it is not without good reason that the German songs have confounded Odovacar with the cruel and treacherous Ermanaric.

The reign of Theoderic is perhaps the finest example in all history of what is called a "beneficent despotism." No freer system of government could under the circumstances have produced such wonderful results; perhaps with a freer system Theoderic could not have established or maintained his kingdom at all. But the efficiency of the government depended wholly on the wisdom and energy of one man, and it might easily have been foreseen that grave troubles would arise when the sceptre passed into weaker hands. For this reason a great historian has described Theoderic's whole policy as "a blunder of genius," and we can hardly deny that this harsh and exaggerated judgment has in it something of truth. Even the great king himself, in the last three years of his life, when his marvellous vigour of mind had been impaired by age, found himself involved in perplexities with which he was unable to deal. But the sad story of the mistakes that tarnished the lustre of a glorious reign must be reserved for a future chapter.

XVIII: THEODERIC AND HIS FOREIGN NEIGHBOURS

The more Italy prospered under Theoderic's wise and kindly rule, the more she became a tempting prize to the ambition of foreign kings. Theoderic knew this well; and he knew besides that the military strength of his kingdom was after all only small. The Ostrogothic army was far inferior in numbers to that of the Franks alone; and if it should happen that the kings of Europe should discover his weakness, and should band themselves together for an united attack upon the kingdom, there was little hope that he would be able to resist them by force of arms. It would have been of no avail for him to labour for the well-being of his subjects, if a foreign conqueror were to overrun the land, and bring to ruin the fabric of order and prosperity which he had raised. And if even if he could have been sure of vanquishing every foe that came against him in the field, he knew that the success of his noble plans was only possible so long as he could ensure the continuance of peace. Famous warrior though he had been in earlier days, no visions of military glory blinded his perception of what was his kingdom's one overwhelming need.

The great aim of Theoderic's foreign policy was therefore to attach all the Teutonic kings to himself by ties of friendship, and to make them look up to him as a superior, with whom it was unwise to quarrel. He connected his family by marriage with nearly every royal house in Europe. His sister was given in marriage to Thrasamund, king of the Vandals, and his niece to the Thuringian king, Ermanfrid. One of his daughters became the wife of Alaric of Toulouse, and another was married to Sigismund, the heir, and afterwards the successor of Gundobad, king of the Burgunds. The mother of these princesses, who does not seem to have been regarded as Theoderic's lawful wife, was dead, and he married Audafleda, the sister of Clovis.

It may be mentioned here that Audafleda had only one child, a daughter named Amalaswintha. The idea of hereditary succession to the throne was now beginning to be much more fully recognized among the Teutonic peoples than it had been anciently, and Amalaswintha was therefore regarded as heiress of the kingdom. When Amalaswintha grew up to womanhood, the question who should be her husband was a very important one, for it practically involved the succession to the kingdom. If her father had bestowed her on a prince of any other royal house, the Ostrogoths would have felt that they were sold into the hands of a foreign nation; and if he had chosen one of his own generals, or some Roman noble, he would have excited jealousies that would very likely have proved dangerous. However, Theoderic found a way out of the difficulty that seems to have satisfied every one. At the court of the Visigoth king there was an Amaling prince named Eutharic, the great-grandson of that King Thorismund, after whose death the throne of the Ostrogoth had remained vacant for forty years, until their Hunnish masters allowed them to choose a king once more. Now according to the new-fashioned principle of inheritance, this Eutharic had a better right to be king than Theoderic himself, and when the latter died there would very likely be a party ready to support his claim. So Theoderic prudently invited this prince into Italy, and by marrying him to Amalaswintha united the two branches of the Amaling stock. Eutharic was entrusted with important offices in the kingdom, and he seems to have been a man of some vigour and capacity for government. His liberality and magnificence won him many friends among the Romans, though the Catholic writers say he was a bigoted Arian, and not at all disposed to follow his father-in-law's policy of toleration. However, Eutharic died a few years before Theoderic, leaving a son named Athalaric, who while yet an infant was proclaimed king of Italy.

It was Theoderic's wish that the Teutonic peoples of Europe should form a sort of league, bound together by the brotherhood of race, and by the family connections of their kings. The Ostrogoths of course were to be at the head of the league, and enlightened by the traditions of Roman statesmanship which they inherited as possessors of the Western empire, were to lead the kindred peoples along the path of civilization. Like all Theoderic's schemes, this magnificent plan could only be worked by a man of genius. But while the man of genius lived it was wonderfully successful. The kings of the other Teutonic peoples—Franks, Visigoths, Vandals, and the rest—looked up with respect to the sovereign of Rome; they sought his mediation in their quarrels, and allowed him to write to them in the tone of a superior. If they did not always follow the counsels which he gave, they at least received them with abundant professions of deference and gratitude.

But notwithstanding Theoderic's love of peace, the annals of his reign include two great foreign wars— one with Constantinople, the other with the Franks — which together occupied about five years.

The war with the Eastern empire began in this way. Theoderic had been endeavouring to secure his northeastern frontier, which, as he knew from the success of his own invasion, was the weakest point of his kingdom. In order to make himself safe against any possible designs on the part of the emperor, he cultivated the friendship of the petty chiefs who ruled in the neighbourhood of the old dividing line between the two empires. Amongst these was a certain Mundo the Hun, a descendant, it was said, of Attila. He was a sort of brigand captain, who had assumed the title of king somewhere in the district now known as Servia. The Gepids, who were still inhabiting the neighbourhood of the river Save, refused Theoderic's offers of alliance, and made an attack upon his territories. In the year 504 Theoderic sent an army against the Gepids, under a commander named Pitzia, who soon captured their chief fortress of Sirmium, and compelled their king Thrasaric to acknowledge himself Theoderic's vassal. Just at the same time, the emperor Anastasius, having heard that Mundo had been committing depredations on the neighbouring lands of the empire, sent against him his general Sabinianus. The imperial troops, assisted by the Bulgars—this famous nation is now for the first time mentioned in history—had almost succeeded in compelling Mundo to surrender, when Pitzia appeared in defence of his master's ally, and inflicted on the emperor's general a crushing defeat. Amongst the Goths who specially distinguished themselves in this campaign was a young officer named Thulwin, who afterwards became one of Theoderic's closest friends.

By way of revenge for this discomfiture, Anastasius caused his fleet to ravage the south of Italy. Theo-deric was at first unprepared to defend himself against this attack, but he soon succeeded in forming a naval force which compelled Anastasius to leave him unmolested. After the year 508 the peace between Anastasius and Theoderic was not again broken, and under the succeeding emperor, Justin, the relations between Constantinople and Ravenna were still more friendly.

Before Theoderic had done with this quarrel, he found himself drawn into another, the consequences of which were of much greater importance. This time his adversary was the king of the Franks.

The rapidly growing power of Clovis, and his evident unscrupulousness and ambition, had long been regarded by Theoderic with well-founded alarm. In the year 496 Clovis had gained a decisive victory over the Alamans, the German nation from whom in modern French all Germans have received the name of Allemands. Theoderic sent a letter to the conqueror, offering him his congratulations, but earnestly entreating him to deal mercifully with the vanquished. Although Clovis might make a show of receiving these exhortations respectfully, he paid little attention to them in practice, and Theoderic granted to the persecuted Alamans a new home in the northern part of his own dominions—in Rhaetia, or what is now known as Southern Bavaria. Clovis pursued his career of conquest; in a few years he had subdued the Burgunds, and was threatening to bring the combined armies of Franks and Burgunds to the subjugation of the Visigoths.

Theoderic laboured earnestly to prevent the outbreak of war between Clovis and Alaric. To the former he wrote "as a father and as a friend," exhorting him not to engage in a fratricidal conflict the result of which was uncertain, and which could bring him no true glory; and he added that if Clovis declared war he should consider the act as an insult to himself. To Alaric, on the other hand, he laid stress on the danger of rushing unprepared into the struggle, and urged him to make every honourable concession, and not to draw the sword until the efforts which he himself was making to bring Clovis to reason should have proved unavailing.

But it was all in vain that Theoderic exerted his powers of persuasion. The Prankish king was bent on war. Alaric, indeed, was only too willing to yield, but he soon saw that no concession would save him. We have already related the sad story of the war of the year 507—how the Visigothic king was compelled by his generals to risk a battle without waiting for Theoderic's promised aid, and how the result was the death of Alaric and the conquest of his Gaulish dominions by the Franks.

It was the war with Anastasius that prevented Theoderic from intervening in time to save Alaric from ruin. As soon as peace was concluded with the emperor, in June, 508, an Ostrogothic army, led by the Count Ibba, Theoderic's principal general, entered Southern Gaul. Before very long Ibba had gained a decisive victory over the Franks and Burgunds, and in the following year Clovis was glad to make a treaty of peace, in which he acknowledged the infant Amalaric (the son of Alaric) as sovereign, not only of Spain, but of a considerable tract of country in the south-east of Gaul, including the great cities of Aries and Narbonne. The greater part of Provence, east of the Rhone, was added by Theoderic to his own dominions.

Theoderic now assumed the government of the Visigothic kingdom, as the guardian of his infant grandson. An illegitimate half-brother of Amalaric endeavoured to make himself king, but after a struggle of about a year he was defeated and put to death. Theoderic committed the management of the Spanish dominions to one of his generals, named Theudis, who however collected a native army, and became so powerful that his master was reluctantly obliged to allow him practically to assume the position of a tributary king. Still, this extension of his empire carried with it an increase of respect amongst foreign sovereigns, and his nominal lordship over Spain was maintained without cost.

In the year 523 Theoderic made another addition to the territory of his kingdom. It was a military conquest, and yet it was won without striking a blow. This apparently contradictory statement is easily explained. Sigismund, king of the Burgunds, prompted by the malice of his second wife, had murdered his own son, the grandson of Theoderic. Thulwin, the general of Theoderic, marched to Lyons with an Ostrogothic army, to inflict punishment on the guilty king. When he arrived, however, Sigismund had already been captured by the sons of Clovis and put to death; and the new king, Godemar, who was carrying on the war with the Franks, eagerly offered to resign to Theoderic the southern half of his kingdom as the price of peace. Thulwin therefore returned in triumph, having secured all the substantial fruits of a victory without the cost of a single life.

The vessel which conveyed Thulwin home was wrecked by a fearful storm in full view of the port where Theoderic was waiting to welcome his friend. Thulwin, taking his only child in his arms, sprang into a boat, and rowed for the shore. The spectators of his struggles thought it almost impossible that the boat could live, and the old king's anguish was so great that he could with difficulty be restrained from plunging into the sea in a hopeless attempt at rescue. The crew of the ship all perished in their efforts to reach the land. But Thulwin's strength and skill enabled him to gain the shore in safety, and Theoderic ran to embrace him, shedding tears of joy for his escape. It was perhaps the last happy moment that the old king enjoyed in his life.

XIX: THEODERIC'S EVIL DAYS

Happy would it have been for Theoderic if he had died in the beginning of the year 523, instead of living three years longer. Till that time he had succeeded in all his undertakings; he possessed the respect and affection of the great mass of his subjects; and he had never committed any great mistake, or shown himself unfaithful to the noble ideal of justice and mercy which he had set himself to realize. In the last three years of his life all this was changed. He discovered, or was made to believe, that those in whom he had most implicitly trusted were conspiring for his ruin. His mind, worn by age and by the cares of his laborious reign, became a prey to universal suspicion, which impelled him to rash and violent deeds strangely at variance with the whole spirit of his reign. The benefactor of Italy died full of remorse and shame for the acts of folly and wrong which had gone so far to undo the work of thirty toilsome years.

The beginning of trouble was early in the year 523, when Cyprian, one of the king's chief ministers, informed Theoderic, then at Verona, that Albinus, a wealthy Roman noble and a senator, was guilty of entertaining a treasonable correspondence with the emperor at Constantinople. A court, composed of the ministers and the principal senators was assembled in the royal palace to hear the case. Albinus was confronted with his accuser, and denied the charge. Amongst those who were present was Boethius, of whose wealth and influence, as well as his fame as a philosopher and a man of science, we have already spoken. On hearing the accusations against Albinus, Boethius lifted up his voice with the words: "My lord the king, the charge is false. If Albinus be guilty, so am I, and so is every other member of the senate!"

But instead of protecting Albinus, as Boethius expected it would, this emphatic declaration only drew down suspicion upon himself Witness after witness, all of them members of the senate, came forward, and brought what seemed to be clear proof that not only Albinus, but Boethius also, had been plotting against his sovereign. The accused were captured at Pavia, and thrown into prison. The written testimony of the witnesses was sent to Rome, and laid before the senate, who unanimously condemned Boethius to death, without allowing him to answer for himself or to cross-question his accusers. What became of Albinus history does not say..

Boethius was not put to death at once, but was kept nearly a year in prison. After his condemnation he wrote that famous book The Consolation of Philosophy, which is the only one of all his works that still finds readers. It is not exactly a literary masterpiece, but as a book written from the heart, as the record of the meditations by which a brave and high-minded man consoled himself when, fallen suddenly from the height of wealth and power to the lowest abyss of misery, he was looking forward to an ignominious death, it has a deep interest, and will always be counted among the world's classics. It has been translated into every language in

Europe; and amongst the English translators have been King Alfred, Chaucer, and, we are told, Queen Elizabeth.

Whether Boethius was really guilty of treason will never be known for certain. He says himself that the evidence on which he was condemned consisted partly of forged letters; but his words imply that his own conduct had given some ground for suspicion. It seems most likely that he had been drawn into some correspondence with Constantinople inconsistent with his duty to his king, but that his enemies had resorted to falsehood and forgery to strengthen their case against him. One of the charges, it seems, was that he had tried to compass the king's death by witchcraft; in those days a very likely accusation to be brought against the most learned man of science of the age.

It is worth notice that Boethius himself, though smarting under the injustice of his sentence, does not omit to bear testimony to the love of righteousness shown by the king in earlier days, and to record the indignation which he always showed at any act of oppression on the part of his Gothic ministers.

After the death of Boethius, his father-in-law, the aged Symmachus, was sent for to Ravenna, and executed, apparently without a trial, and for no other reason than that it was feared that he would conspire to avenge his relative. The wild panic which possessed Theoderic's mind is shown by his issuing an edict forbidding all Romans, under heavy penalties, to carry or possess arms.

Even the policy of religious liberty, which Theoderic had regarded as one of the proudest glories of his reign, was now to be abandoned. This change was provoked by the conduct of the court of Constantinople, which in the year 524 decreed that the Arian churches throughout the empire should be taken from their rightful owners and consecrated afresh for Catholic use. The news filled Theoderic with the fiercest indignation. He sent for the Pope, John the First, and compelled him at once to set out for Constantinople as his ambassador, to demand from the emperor the restoration of his Arian subjects to their former rights.

Pope John was received by the emperor with the profoundest demonstrations of respect. It is even said that Justin submitted to the ceremony of a second coronation, by way of testifying his reverence for the head of the Christian Church. The pope was well assured that if he returned to Italy without having accomplished his errand his life would be forfeited; and so, against his will, he achieved the distinction of being the only Roman pontiff who ever pleaded with a Catholic monarch for the toleration of heretics. He represented to the emperor the danger which would be incurred by himself and the church of Italy if the request were refused. Justin was constrained to yield. The edict was repealed; the Arian churches were given back to their original possessors. Theoderic's demands were fully complied with, except in one point; the Arians whom fear or interest had induced to join the Catholic Church were not to be allowed to apostatise back again.

The pope returned to Italy to announce the success of his embassy. But Theoderic had been informed— whether truly or falsely we cannot tell—that his strangely chosen messenger had taken advantage of his visit to Constantinople to betray to the emperor the weakness of the kingdom, and to urge him to attempt an invasion. The pope was thrown into prison, where he died in May, 526; and the king, feeling now that the whole Catholic Church had become his enemy, promulgated a decree that the orthodox worship should be suppressed, and that the churches should on a given day be transferred to Arian hands. But before the edict could be carried into effect Theoderic was dead.

It was in August, 526, he was seized with his fatal illness. A story, which may or may not be true, ascribes this sickness to the terrors of a guilty conscience. It is said that when seated at supper he fancied that he discovered in the head of a large fish that had been placed on the table a likeness to Symmachus, and rushed from the room exclaiming that the face of the murdered senator was looking at him with eyes full of hatred and revenge. He then took to his bed, complaining of deadly cold which nothing could remove. His frenzied delusion passed away, but the self-reproach that had caused it continued, and he expressed to his physician, his bitter repentance for the murders of Symmachus and Boethius.

When Theoderic knew that his end was near, he sent for his Gothic generals and the Roman ministers of state, that they might bid him farewell and receive his last commands. He appointed his grandson Athalaric, a boy of ten years old, as the heir of the kingdom, and the child's mother Amalaswintha, as regent during his minority. The chiefs of the army and the state took, in Theoderic's presence, a solemn oath of fidelity to Amalaswintha and Athalaric; and then the dying king talked with them long and earnestly of the policy that was to be followed in the government of Italy when he should be no more. He urged them to endeavour to maintain friendship with the emperor, to forget their jealousies of race and creed, and to labour unitedly for the common welfare of the people. Above all, he charged them to be faithful to those great principles of equal justice to all, of strict obedience to law, which at heart he had always loved, even though, amid the infirmities of age and blinded by panic terror, he had for a moment let them slip. He further directed that the government of the Visigoth kingdom should be placed unreservedly in the hands of Amalaric, who was now grown up to manhood, and no longer needed a guardian.

On the thirtieth of August Theoderic died. His remains, enclosed in a coffin of porphyry, were placed in a vast circular tomb of white marble at Ravenna, which afterwards became the church of Santa Maria della Rotonda, and still remains entire, though no longer used for worship. A century or two after Theoderic's death, when the Goths had been driven out of Italy and the Catholics were once more supreme, the tomb was robbed of its contents. The porphyry coffin was found at the door of a neighbouring monastery. What became of the body was unknown, but a discovery made some thirty years ago may, it has been supposed, possibly throw some light upon the question. In the year 1854 some labourers who were excavating a dock, one or two hundred yards from the tomb of Theoderic, came upon a skeleton in golden armour, with large jewels in the helmet and the hilt of the sword. The place was an ancient cemetery, but the body had evidently not been regularly buried; it had just been thrust into the earth in as hurried a manner as possible. The workmen had intended to keep their lucky find to themselves, but the secret leaked out, and came to the knowledge of the authorities. The men were arrested, and made a full confession; but of the golden armour there was nothing left but a few pieces of the cuirass; all the rest had been melted up and sold.

Now, who was the warrior or prince whose body had the strange fate of being buried in golden and jewelled armour, and yet not in a stately sepulchre, but in a shallow trench dug in a common graveyard? Some have thought that it was Odovacar; but it seems more likely that it was Odovacar's conqueror. If the skeleton found in 1854 was, indeed, that of Theoderic, it is plain that those who plundered the tomb of the Arian king were moved only by religious hate, and not by selfish greed, or they would have stolen the gold and jewels instead of burying them with their owner. How fierce was the hatred felt by pious churchmen for Theoderic's memory we may learn from the dialogues of the famous pope, Gregory the Great, who tells how, at the moment of the heretic monarch's death, a saintly hermit beheld in a vision his soul dragged by the victims of his persecutions, and cast into the mouth of the volcano of Lipari.

Here ends the story of Theoderic the Great. To estimate his character aright we must look not at those last sad three years, when, with a mind weakened by age and stung into fury by the treachery of trusted friends, he stained by deeds of cruelty and wrong the glory of a great career, but at the thirty years which he spent in unselfish labour for the welfare of his people. If we so judge him, we shall surely assign to him a place among the noblest men who ever wore a crown. Perhaps Alfred of England—different as the two were in many ways —is of all the kings known to history the one with whom Theoderic may most fitly be compared; and it would be hard to say which was the greater man.

XX: A QUEEN'S TROUBLES

The Ostrogoths must have thought it a strange thing that the kingdom over which the great Theoderic had so long reigned should now be governed by a woman in the name of a child. Never before had this nation of warriors humbled itself by submitting to female rule, and scarcely ever had it acknowledged an infant as its king. In the old days of freedom the custom had been, whenever their king died and left no heir old enough to lead the army to battle or preside in the assembly, for the people to choose as his successor the ablest man amongst the kindred of the royal house. Although there was no man living who could remember those good old times, the history of the nation was still familiar through the popular songs; and there were those who talked of going back to the ancient rule, and placing the crown on the head of Thulwin, Theoderic's most honoured general, and the husband of an Amaling princess.

But Thulwin was faithful to the memory of his beloved master, and, instead of falling in with the schemes suggested to him, used all his influence to persuade the Goths to submit loyally to Athalaric and his mother. Cassiodorus wrote him a grateful letter in the young king's name, conferring on him the rank of Patrician, and loading him with praises for his generous conduct. He compared Thulwin to a famous hero of the past named Gesimund, whom, being the adopted son of a king, the people wished to raise to the throne, to the neglect of the infant heir, but who refused the choice, and served the Amaling line with a faithfulness that "was the theme of song throughout the world, and would be remembered as long as the Gothic name should last."

There was no other man in the kingdom whose claims were powerful enough to weigh against the reverence that was felt for Theoderic's memory; and although the Goths might privately sneer or lament over the altered condition of affairs, they joined their fellow-subjects in taking the oath of allegiance to Athalaric and his mother. Perhaps some of them may have been reconciled to the new government by the thought that under the weak rule of a woman they would have more opportunity to oppress their Roman fellow-subjects than had been allowed them in the past.

If this was their hope, it was doomed to be disappointed. Amalaswintha herself was far more a Roman than a Goth. She had not, indeed, forgotten her native language; but she spoke Greek and Latin equally well; and took delight in literature and science. Her chosen friends were all Romans. Cassiodorus, who seems to have retired for a while into private life while Theoderic was playing the part of an oppressor, again assumed the office of chief minister of state, and his letters still remain to show us what sort of policy was followed. All acts of outrage on the part of Goths were rigorously inquired into and severely punished; the laws with regard to worship were altered in favour of the Catholics; the confiscated estates of Boethius and Symmachus were restored to their children; Roman officials were promoted and rewarded; and special exemptions from taxation were freely granted to the provincials. It is said that during the whole of her reign Amalaswintha never punished a single Roman either with death or loss of property.

But if these measures secured for the queen the goodwill of the Romans, they excited bitter resentment in the minds of her own people. The Goths in Theoderic's reign had sometimes complained that the Romans got too much favour; but they knew in their hearts that their king aimed at nothing but equal justice. But now they could make the same complaint with only too good reason.

What they thought worst of all was the way in which Amalaswintha was bringing up her son. Instead of having him taught to ride and fence, and letting him join in the sports of the young nobles; she kept him closely to his books, and out of school hours made him spend his time in the company of three aged Goths, "the most intelligent and well-mannered"—which means, of course, the most like Romans—that she was able to find. The Gothic warriors said that Athalaric was being educated to be a sickly, useless bookworm, unfit to bear the fatigues or face the dangers of war, and despising his own people as ignorant barbarians.

One day it happened that Athalaric had done something wrong, and his mother had beaten him. The boy went crying into the men's room, and the Goths who were in attendance soon got to know what was the matter. "What a shame!" one of them said, when Athalaric had told his story; "it is plain that what she wants is to kill the child as soon as she can, so that she can marry a second husband, and share the kingdom with him." Many angry speeches were made, and it was agreed that a deputation should be sent to expostulate with the queen on her conduct.

Accordingly a number of the chief Gothic nobles demanded an audience of Amalaswintha. When they were admitted into her presence their spokesman said: "We have come, O queen, to tell you that we consider that the way in which you are training up our young king is altogether wrong. A Gothic king does not want book-learning; he needs to know how to fight, and, as your father often used to say, unless the art of war was learned in youth it never would be learned at all. He never allowed Gothic boys to be sent to school; it was his maxim that a boy who had trembled at the schoolmaster's rod would never face an enemy's sword. Look at his own example. There never was a wiser or a more powerful king than Theoderic, and yet he knew nothing of book-learning, not even by hearsay. Therefore, O queen, we demand that you send these schoolmasters about their business, and let your son be brought up as befits a king of the Goths, among companions of his own age."

No doubt it was true that Amalaswintha's way of educating her son was not altogether the right one. If Theoderic had had the training of an heir to his kingdom he would have taken care that the boy should be taught to excel in all manly exercises, and to display the courage and endurance which his people above all things demanded in their king. But, at the same time, he knew the worth of Roman learning, and though he may have thought it best that the sons of his Gothic warriors should have little to do with books, he would not have allowed the future king of Goths and Romans to grow up in barbarian ignorance.

Amalaswintha was bitterly indignant at the imperious demands of the Gothic chiefs, but she knew it was of no use to resist. She sullenly told them that they should have their own way; she gave up the young king to their management, and promised to interfere no further with his education.

The result was what might have been expected. The poor boy, suddenly set free from his mother's strict control, and with no one else to exercise wholesome restraint over him, fell under the influence of vicious companions, and spent all his time in drunkenness and dissipation. It was soon evident to every one that his health was ruined by his excesses, and that he would not live to the age of manhood.

But Amalaswintha's concessions availed her nothing. The continued insolence of the Gothic nobles made her life a burden. Her commands were seldom obeyed, and the kingdom soon fell into utter disorder.

At length she determined to abandon Italy, and wrote to the emperor Justinian, asking if he would give her a home in Constantinople. The emperor, who was eagerly looking out for an opportunity to make Italy his own, readily consented, and had a palace splendidly furnished for her at Dyrrhachinm (Durazzo) on the Greek side of the Adriatic, when it was agreed that she should live until arrangements could be made for her to take up her abode in Constantinople.

Amalaswintha sent over to Dyrrhachium a ship containing 40,000 pounds weight of gold, and made all preparations for leaving the country. But before she took this decisive step, she determined to make one desperate effort to regain her lost power.

The opposition to Amalaswintha's government was led by three Gothic nobles who were so powerful that she felt that if they could only be got rid of she could rule the kingdom as she chose. She managed to send these three men to different parts of the country, under the pretence of employing them for the defence of the frontiers, and took means to have them assassinated. In case the plot should fail, she had a ship in readiness to take her over the Adriatic at a moment's notice.

But the news came that her three dreaded enemies were dead, and Amalaswintha abandoned her purpose of flight. It is supposed that, one of the victims of this shameful murder was no other than Thulwin, the dear friend of Amalaswintha's father, the loyal servant who had preferred his duty to his master's house to the temptation of placing the crown on his own head.

For a while it seemed as if Amalaswintha had gained her object. The opposition party among the Goths were thoroughly frightened, and she reigned over Italy as an absolute sovereign. But her triumph did not last long.

Justinian was resolved by one means or other to make himself master of Italy. When he learned that Amalaswintha had abandoned her intention of going to live at Constantinople, he had to devise another plan, and found in one of the queen's own relatives a tool by which he hoped to accomplish his end.

This was Theodahad, the son of Theoderic's sister Amalafrida by her first husband. He was a man somewhat advanced in years, greatly celebrated for his learning, being well acquainted with Latin literature, and as well with the writings of Plato and the Holy Scriptures. Unfortunately he was still more celebrated for his cowardice and his avarice. Nearly all the land in the province of Tuscany belonged to him, but he was always scheming to lay hold of some "Naboth's vineyard" that lay near to his own property. More than once Theoderic had compelled him to give back his ill-gotten gains, and just at this very time Amalaswintha's judges were examining into fresh charges of extortion brought against him by the people of his province. Theodahad knew very well that the case would go against him, and he hated the queen with the bitterest hatred.

With the intention of having his revenge, and adding to his own wealth at the same time, Theodahad contrived to let Justinian know that he was ready— for a sufficient bribe—to deliver up Tuscany into the emperor's hands. Just then Justinian was sending over an embassy, partly to Amalaswintha and partly to the pope, and he instructed his ambassadors to see Theodahad secretly, and try to bargain with him for the proposed treason. The price which the traitor asked was the permission to live in Constantinople, the rank of senator, and—most important of all—a large sum of money paid down.

Meanwhile, however, the ambassadors had been negotiating with the queen. They laid before her a long list of wrongs which the empire had suffered from the Goths, and claimed that reparation should be made. One of the principal demands was that the Goths should surrender to the emperor the town of Lilybaeum in Sicily. This was a place which King Theoderic had given as a present to his sister Amalafrida when she married the Vandal king. Now that Justinian, through his general Belisarius, had subdued the Vandals (with the very good will of the Ostrogoths, who had their own wrongs to avenge), he claimed that Lilybaeum belonged to him as the conqueror; but the Goths had taken possession of the place and would not give it up.

Amalaswintha laid these demands before her ministers, and by their advice wrote a very dignified letter to Justinian, respectfully acknowledging that Athalaric was the emperor's vassal, but refusing to yield to his unjust claims, and suggesting that it would be more worthy of a great sovereign to show kindness to "an orphan boy" than to try to pick a quarrel with him over trifles. After having publicly returned to the ambassador this queenly answer, the crafty woman sent for him privately, and made a solemn promise, which was to be kept strictly secret, that she would hand over the kingdom to Justinian as soon as the needful arrangements could be made.

The ambassadors returned to Constantinople. Justinian was delighted with their report; he had secured "two strings to his bow," and felt no doubt that Italy would soon be his. He determined to lose no time in following up his advantage and despatched a certain Peter of Thessalonica, a famous professor of eloquence at Constantinople, to Italy for the purpose of making both the queen and her cousin bind themselves by oath to fulfil their respective parts in the compact. It is said that the Empress Theodora, whose jealousy had been excited by the accounts of Amalaswintha's beauty and accomplishments, gave Peter private instructions of her own to manage matters so that the Gothic queen should never come to Constantinople.

Before Peter had arrived at Ravenna, towards the end of 534, important events had taken place. On October 3rd, Athalaric died of consumption. His mother continued to rule the kingdom in her own name, but she felt that her position was full of peril. The Goths had submitted unwillingly enough to a female regent; there was little hope that they would tolerate anything so unheard of as a female sovereign.

Much as the cowardly Theodahad was hated and despised, he was the next heir to the crown, and with their new-fashioned ideas about hereditary succession it was likely that the Goths would choose him as their king. Amalaswintha was resolved not to be set aside: if she meant to resign her kingdom in favour of Justinian it must be "for valuable consideration," and to be dethroned by the Goths would be ruin to all her prospects.

In her desperate extremity she hit upon a strange plan, which no doubt she thought wonderfully cunning, though it turned out to be the height of folly. She invited Theodahad to Ravenna, and exhausted all her eloquence in protestations of the utmost friendship and respect for the man whom above all others she detested, and whom she knew to be her bitterest enemy. She assured her dear cousin that it had caused her great pain to have to treat him with apparent unkindness, but it had all been done for his own good. Knowing that her poor boy had not many years to live, she had been anxious that Theodahad should be his successor, but she had seen that his course of conduct was prejudicing his future subjects against him, and endangering his prospect of being acknowledged as king. She had, therefore, felt it her duty to interpose, and she congratulated him that by his obedience to her commands he had saved his imperilled popularity, so that she could now venture to associate him with herself in the kingdom. Not that she proposed to make him her equal in power: she would avail herself of his valuable advice, he should have the title of king, and share equally in the outward honours and the revenues of royalty, but he must take an oath to leave the actual government of the kingdom entirely in her hands.

Of course Theodahad could not for a moment be deceived by Amalaswintha's absurdly transparent pretences of friendship, but it is hardly necessary to say that he professed to be deeply touched by the discovery that his dear sister, whom he had always profoundly esteemed, even when he imagined her to be his enemy, had after all only been dissembling her love, and with the best possible motives. He gratefully accepted her offer of the kingly title, and bound himself by the strongest oaths never to attempt to make himself king otherwise than in name. But so far from intending to keep his oath, he was all the while thinking how he could make himself independent of Amalaswintha, and inwardly vowing that he would some day be revenged upon her for all the humiliations she had made him suffer. In the game of mutual imposture which these two were playing, the daughter of Theoderic was no match for her antagonist. She fully believed that Theodahad had been deceived by her clever acting, and had been converted from an enemy into a humble and grateful friend.

So Amalaswintha and Theodahad were solemnly proclaimed king and queen of Italy, and each of them sent to Justinian a letter (drawn up by Cassiodorus, and still preserved in the collection of his despatches) informing the emperor that Athalaric was dead, that Amalaswintha had succeeded him in the kingdom, and had associated "her brother" Theodahad with herself. The queen was full of praises of her brother's learning and virtues, and Theodahad for his part was full of gratitude for the kindness of" his sister and sovereign"; and both letters abounded in expressions of respect for the emperor, and asked his continued protection of the kingdom.

To the senate also Amalaswintha and Theodahad wrote letters in the same strain of mutual flattery.

Only a few weeks later the faithless Theodahad had openly allied himself with Amalaswintha's enemies, the relatives and partisans of the three murdered chiefs. The men who had been employed in the murder were put to death, and the queen herself was imprisoned on an island in the lake of Bolsena, about sixty miles northwest of Rome.

Through his ambassador Peter, who now arrived in Italy, the emperor expressed to Theodahad his displeasure at what had happened, and his intention to act as Amalaswintha's protector. But not long after the avengers of the blood of Thulwin and his companions found admission to the island castle, and the imprisoned queen was strangled in her bath.

Amalaswintha's cruel fate was after all the fruit of her own deeds, and we cannot regard her with the unqualified pity due to an innocent sufferer. But her temptations were assuredly great. Surrounded throughout her reign by conspiracy and treason, involved in perplexities from which there seemed no escape, it was rather from weakness than from wickedness that she allowed herself to resort to those acts of violence and treachery of which she afterwards met the just reward.

Theodahad zealously protested to the emperor's ambassador that he had nothing to do with the murder; but the honours which he bestowed on the men who perpetrated the deed showed plainly that he had at least connived at it. The real history of the crime will never be fully known. It is said on good authority that Peter, who was professedly the agent of the emperor, but secretly also the agent of the wicked empress Theodora, managed to persuade his mistress that Amalaswintha's death had been brought about by his own contrivance, and was rewarded by her with high office in consequence. The correspondence between the empress and Theodahad's wife Gudelina contains some mysterious allusions, which have been supposed to show that these two women had conspired together to have Amalaswintha murdered. It is possible enough: in that evil time there were few among the great ones of the earth who were free from hideous suspicions, which were often certainties, of being concerned in plots for the assassination of their enemies.

Although Justinian had himself no hand in procuring the queen's death, yet no event could have been more fortunate for his schemes. It gave him, what he had long desired, a good excuse for a war of conquest against the Goths. To profess himself the avenger of the murdered daughter of Theoderic was to assume a character which commanded sympathy not only from all the Romans of Italy, but even from many of the Goths themselves, who were still loyal to the memory of their great hero, and were filled with loathing for the treachery and cowardice of Theodahad. The weakness of Italy, divided into hostile parties, with its military system fallen into decay through years of feeble government, invited attack; and the emperor was conscious of the strength which he possessed, not so much in the numbers of his army as in the talents and energy of his general Belisarius, "in himself a host."

And so in the year 535, Justinian declared a war which he vowed should continue until the Gothic power in Italy was annihilated. He kept his promise; but the struggle was harder and longer than he dreamed. It was not until twenty years had passed that the sword was sheathed, and Italy became a part of the dominions of the Eastern empire.

XXI: AN UNKINGLY KING

Justinian's design of conquering Italy was a bold one, for the military power of the empire had sunk so low that the number of men that could be placed in the field scarcely amounted to more than ten thousand. It is true that they were commanded by Belisarius, whose skill had just been shown in the brilliant campaign that crushed the Vandals, and who (so many modern writers have judged) was one of the greatest generals of all time. But it was only the distracted state of Italy, and the helpless weakness of the Gothic king, that gave to the project of conquest any chance of success. It was necessary to act at once, lest the opportunity should be lost; and yet caution was equally needed, for the consequences of failure were terrible.

The sagacity of Justinian was equal to the emergency. First of all, he wrote to the king of the Franks announcing that having been deeply wronged by the Goths, he was about to march against them to reconquer the portion of his dominions which they had usurped, and calling upon his fellow Catholics to lend him their support in a religious war for the expulsion of the Arian heretics. Having obtained a promise of aid from the Franks, he proceeded to make his first attack in a way that involved little risk, and yet would be likely to terrify Theodahad into surrender.

It was determined that Belisarius, with seven thousand five hundred men, should take shipping under pretence of going to Carthage, and should land, as if in passing, in Sicily. If he saw reason to believe that the island could be occupied without trouble he was to do so; if not, he was to sail away to Africa without letting it be known what his designs had been. At the same time the Gepid Mundus was sent to make an attack on the undefended possessions of the Goths on the east side of the Adriatic.

Both parts of the scheme succeeded perfectly. Mundus entered Dalmatia, and obtained possession of the chief city, Salona, without resistance. Belisarius found that the people of Sicily were eager to be freed from Gothic rule. He soon captured Catana; Syracuse opened its gates to him; and the only city that gave him any trouble was Palermo, which was strongly fortified, and was held by an important Gothic garrison. Belisarius called on the Goths to surrender, but, trusting to the strength of their walls, they paid no attention to his demand. The stratagem by which he is said to have gained possession of the city was a strange one. Anchoring his ships in the harbour, close to the city wall, he had boat-loads of archers hoisted up to the tops of the masts. When the besieged found that they were assailed with volleys of arrows out of the air, they were terribly frightened, and at once surrendered. Whether this curious story be true or not, there is no doubt that in a few weeks Belisarius received the submission of the whole island almost without the loss of a man. The Goths never forgave the Sicilians for their ingratitude in so joyfully welcoming the change of masters. It was not long before the visits of the imperial tax gatherers made the islanders feel that the position of subjects of the empire had its palpable disadvantages. Notwithstanding the outbreak of hostilities, the ambassador Peter still continued in communication with Theodahad, and made it his business to stimulate, by cunningly dropped hints, the anxiety which the events of Dalmatia and Sicily had excited in the king's mind. In this endeavour he was perfectly successful. The poor wretch was soon brought into such an agony of terror that he could hardly believe he was not already a prisoner of war, or—what was still worse—at the head of his army, and forced to expose himself to mortal danger. Peter had therefore very little difficulty in inducing Theodahad to agree to all his demands; and a secret agreement was drawn up, which Peter undertook to submit for the approval of the emperor. The conditions stipulated were: "That the emperor should retain possession of Sicily; that Theodahad should pay a tribute of 3 cwt. of gold every year, and supply three thousand Gothic soldiers whenever required; that no senator or Catholic priest should be punished with death or confiscation without the emperor's leave; that the emperor should have the appointment of patricians and senators; that no one should be allowed to shout, 'Long live Theodahad,' but only 'Long live Justinian and Theodahad;' and that no statue of Theodahad should be erected unless accompanied by one of Justinian, which was always to occupy the place of honour at the right hand."

Having obtained Theodahad's consent to this agreement, Peter set out for Constantinople, no doubt thinking that he had made an excellent bargain. As soon as he was out of sight, however, it occurred to Theodahad that possibly the emperor would not approve of the conditions, and that in that case the war would have to go on after all. Tormented by this terrible thought, he hastily despatched a messenger to overtake the ambassador, and entreat him to come back at once. Peter obeyed the summons with a good deal of vexation, for his natural conclusion was that the king, showing for the moment something more like a manly spirit, had repented of his bargain, and that the whole process of coaxing and intimidation would have to be gone through again.

As soon as Peter appeared in the royal presence, Theodahad eagerly asked whether it was quite certain that the emperor would accept the offered terms, and if not, what would be the result. The answer confirmed his worst fears. "I cannot fight," he said; "if it really came to that, I would rather resign my crown, provided the emperor would give me an estate worth twelve hundred pounds weight of gold a year." Peter then persuaded him to put this proposal into the form of a letter addressed to Justinian, but it was agreed that the ambassador should not deliver the letter, or drop any hint about any further offers, until he had tried his best to induce Justinian to accept the treaty as at first drawn up. Himself the most faithless of men, Theodahad had yet the folly to think that the ambassador would keep this absurd promise, at the sacrifice of his duty to his master, and at the risk of his own head. Of course when he got to Constantinople Peter told the whole story. Justinian accepted Theodahad's surrender of the kingdom, and! wrote him a letter complimenting him on his wise' decision, and promising him not merely the estate he asked for, but the highest honours which could be bestowed on a subject of the empire.

The trusty Peter, accompanied by a certain Athanasius, was sent over to Italy to receive Theodahad's formal abdication, and to assign to him the lands for which he had bargained; Belisarius was ordered to go from Sicily to Rome to take possession of the Italian kingdom.

But when Peter arrived in Italy he found that Theodahad's mood of abject humility had given place to one of insolent defiance. The cause of this change was some news which had come from Dalmatia. A strong body of Goths had made an attack on the imperial general Mundus at Salona; a battle had taken place without any decisive result, but Mundus and his son were killed. This event was to many superstitious people rather a cause for satisfaction than for regret. A pretended prophecy of the Sibyl had been for some time much quoted, which said that when Africa was subdued the world and its offspring would perish. After the conquest of the Vandal kingdom by Belisarius, many persons feared that the end of the world was at hand. But as mundus is the Latin for "world," it was generally thought the death of the Gepid general and his son had fulfilled the prophecy, and that the threatened calamity was no longer to be apprehended.

The emperor's armies very soon compelled the Gothic generals to retire from Dalmatia in confusion. But in the meantime the news of a Gothic victory had turned Theodahad's weak head, and Peter and Athanasius were received with mockery and insult, and were even threatened with death. They tried then to negotiate with the Gothic nobles, to whom they had brought separate letters from Justinian; but the chiefs refused to listen to any proposals which did not come through their king. The upshot of the matter was that the ambassadors were thrown into prison, and Justinian saw that Italy would have to be conquered by force of arms.

It was about April, 536, when Belisarius crossed the Straits of Messina to begin the work of subduing the Gothic kingdom. As soon as he landed at Reggio he was met by Ebermund, Theodahad's son-in-law, who had been entrusted with the defences of the southern coast, but who at once deserted to the enemy with all his followers. Belisarius reported the fact to Constantinople, and the traitor was rewarded by Justinian with the title of Patrician and many other marks of honour.

The imperial troops met with no resistance until they came under the walls of Naples. The Gothic soldiers occupying the outworks of the city were soon dislodged, and Belisarius summoned the town itself to surrender. Although a party among the citizens desired to shake off the Gothic yoke, the governing officers and the great mass of the people were determined to resist. Belisarius offered the most honourable and easy terms, but after long negotiations he was compelled to commence the siege.

The inhabitants succeeded in communicating with Theodahad, whom they implored to send them an army of relief without delay. The story goes that when the king received this message he consulted a Jewish sorcerer, asking him what the result of the struggle would be. The Jew directed him to take thirty hogs, and to place them in three different styes, ten of them to represent the Romans, ten the Goths, and ten the imperial troops. He was to keep them without food for a given time, and then to go and see what had happened to them. The result was that the hogs which stood for the emperor's soldiers were all found alive and little the worse, but half the "Romans" and nearly all the "Goths" had died, the few which survived being in a very wretched condition. Theodahad, if we are to believe the tale, accepted the omen as meaning that the Gothic cause was fated to defeat, and pleaded that as his excuse for sending no help to the faithful and unfortunate garrison of Naples.

The city, however, was strongly fortified and well provisioned, and, although the besiegers had stopped up the aqueduct, the inhabitants were able to obtain a sufficient supply of water from springs within the walls. After twenty days, Belisarius had made so little progress that he was on the point of determining to raise the siege and push forward towards Rome. Just at that moment, however, a welcome discovery was made. One of the soldiers, an Asiatic barbarian named Paucaris, who was prowling idly about, took a fancy to see how far he could walk along the aqueduct, entering at the point where Belisarius had broken it open. He managed to go on without difficulty until he was just under the city wall, but there he found that the watercourse passed through a hole in the rock, too narrow for a man to get through. He thought, however, that the hole could easily be widened, and that the tunnel would then afford a means of penetrating into the city.

Paucaris, of course, communicated his discovery to Belisarius, who received it with great delight, and promised the man a handsome reward if his clever plan should result in the capture of the city. A number of men were sent up the aqueduct, furnished with tools suited for scraping away the rock without noise, and before long they had made the opening large enough for a man to pass through in full armour.

All was now ready for the execution of the scheme, but Belisarius wished to give the city one more chance of escaping by a timely surrender or, the miseries of a capture by force of arms. He sent for one of the principal inhabitants, named Stephen, who had before acted as the spokesman of the besieged, and urged upon him to persuade his townsmen to accept the favourable conditions offered. "My plans are now complete," he said, "and in a few days at most Naples must be mine. But I shudder to think what will be its fate if it has to be taken by storm. My soldiers are fierce barbarians; how can I control them when they are inflamed with the pride of victory? Often have I seen a fair city wrapped in flames, and exposed to the cruel rage of a conquering army, and the sight is so horrible that I never wish to behold it again. Go back to your fellow-citizens, tell them what I have said to you, and entreat them to be wise before it is too late."

Stephen saw from his manner that he was uttering no idle threat, and he tried his best to induce his fellow-citizens to yield. But they believed that Belisarius had only renewed his proposals because he was hopeless of capturing the fortress, and they refused to listen. Belisarius had no choice but to carry his plan into effect.

A body of four hundred men was told off for the duty of entering the city by the aqueduct. At first, half of them shrank from the perilous enterprise, but their places were quickly filled by volunteers, and then those who had refused, stung with shame from their cowardice, begged to be allowed to take part in the expedition. So in the dead of night the whole six hundred entered the tunnel, and marched as noiselessly as they could, under the city walls. In order to prevent their movements from being heard by the defenders of the city, a Gothic officer named Bessa was sent by Belisarius to harangue the Goths on the walls in their own language, inviting them to desert to the emperor. The stratagem was successful: the Goths raised such scouts of indignation that no sounds proceeding from below could possibly be noticed.

The six hundred soldiers proceeded along the dried-up watercourse until they came to a large underground chamber, with lofty brick walls and a vaulted roof. Near one corner a few bricks had fallen, and there was a glimpse of blue sky; but there seemed to be no other means of getting out except this hole at the top. The soldiers stood some time considering what was to be done. At length one of them, who was a good climber, threw off his armour, and tying a strong rope round his waist scrambled up the brick wall with his fingers and toes, and succeeded in getting out into the open air. He found himself in a cottage garden in a quiet part of the city. An old woman, the only occupant of the cottage, came to the door. The soldier threatened to kill her if she made a sound. He then tied his rope to an olive tree, and lowered it into the underground chamber, so that his companions were able to climb up with their armour. When they had all emerged, they rushed to the northern wall, which they soon cleared of its defenders, and held until their comrades were able to scale it wdth ladders.

The Goths fought desperately, assisted by a large number of Jews, who had not forgotten the kindness which their race had received from the great Theoderic. But their resistance was unavailing. Before the day was over the city was in the hands of the imperial forces, and then began those scenes of massacre and destruction which Belisarius had foreseen and dreaded. The commander himself used all his efforts to check the rage of his followers: exhorting them to mercy, he rode through the streets of the city, threatening and punishing those who were guilty of outrages. At length his authority prevailed; the soldiers were compelled to abstain from further insults to the citizens, and to restore to their families the women and children whom they had seized as slaves. The townspeople then broke out into fury against the two orators by whose advice they had been led to reject the offered terms of surrender. One of them fell dead of apoplexy: the other was torn in pieces by the mob, and his remains hanged on a gibbet. After this act of vengeance, the streets of Naples assumed once more their accustomed aspect of order and tranquillity.

Belisarius treated his Gothic prisoners kindly, and they enlisted under his standard. Other Gothic forces in the neighbouring territories deserted to the Romans, and the commander was soon able to establish the government of the empire over nearly the whole south of Italy.

While these events were taking place, the Goths in the neighbourhood of Rome waited patiently for Theodahad to take some measures of defence. Their loyalty to the Amaling race had such strange power that it was not until Naples had fallen, and the sovereignty of Justinian had been proclaimed within fifty miles of Rome, that they could bring themselves to believe that their king was a traitor. But now, when all this had happened, and Theodahad still remained inactive, they could doubt no longer.

A great council of the nation was called together at a place called Regeta, some forty miles south of Rome. The chiefs laid before the people their grounds for complaint against the king, and asked what was their will. "Down with Theodahad!"

was the unanimous cry. "Down with the traitor who is buying pardon for his own crimes by delivering his people to destruction!" But who was to succeed him? The time called for a warrior king, and notwithstanding their respect for royal blood, the Goths with one accord chose Witigis, a man of humble origin, but the ablest military leader they possessed.

When Theodahad heard that the Goths had elected a new king, he hastened from Rome intending to take shelter within the walls of Ravenna. King Witigis despatched after him a certain Optahari with orders to bring him back alive or dead. This Optahari had a quarrel of his own against Theodahad: a wealthy and beautiful young lady had been promised to him in marriage, and the king, influenced by a bribe, had compelled her to marry another man. Optahari set out in pursuit of the fugitive, and by riding night and day managed to overtake him before he reached Ravenna. Screaming with fright, the wretched king was thrown on the ground and killed—"like an animal offered in sacrifice," says the contemporary historian.

Such was the end of the most despicable wretch that ever disgraced the Gothic name. It has strangely happened that while we. have no record of the personal appearance of the great Theoderic, the features of his worthless nephew have come down to us on several of his coins. We cannot doubt that the portrait is a faithful one; it expresses too well the mixture of knavery, folly, and cowardice which composed Theodahad's character.

XXII: WITIGIS THE UNREADY

Honest and well-meaning the successor of Theodahad seems to have been, and his valour as a soldier had been proved thirty years before in the war against the Gepids. But he had not the talents which were needed for the supreme command of an army, especially when the adversary was a man like Belisarius. The Goths, however, had unbounded faith in the wisdom as well as in the courage of their new king, and confidently expected that he would very soon drive the imperial troops out of Italy.

But although, as events showed, Witigis was not a very wise or far-seeing man, he had the good sense to perceive that to march against Belisarius forthwith would only be to court destruction. Before he could hope to grapple successfully with such a foe, it was necessary both to restore the discipline of the army, so sadly neglected during two feeble reigns, and to make peace with the Franks, so that the Gothic soldiers engaged in the north might be made available for the struggle against the forces of the emperor. Witigis called an assembly of the Goths at Rome, and, addressing them as "fellow soldiers," he explained to them the reasons for delay. The people listened to his speech with feelings of disappointment, but they deferred to his judgment, and made no protest when he proposed to leave Rome garrisoned with four thousand men, and to betake himself with the bulk of the army to Ravenna.

This part of the king's plan was a terrible mistake. If the Goths had occupied Rome in force, Belisarius would not have dared to attack them with his small army: he would have had to wait for reinforcements, and Witigis would have gained the delay which he required. The foolish flight to Ravenna, instead of postponing the conflict, only hastened it, and threw an immense advantage into the enemy's hand. Although Witigis knew how little the fidelity of the Roman people was to be trusted, he could not see that to leave the city guarded only by four thousand men, was simply to ensure its fall. Nor did he realize how terrible a calamity, if it did happen, the loss of Rome would be; how it would embolden the whole Italian people to declare themselves on the emperor's side, and how it would weigh down the hearts of the Goths with a sense of the hopelessness of the struggle.

And so the fatal resolution was taken. Before leaving Rome Witigis compelled the Pope Silverius and the senators to swear an oath of eternal fidelity to himself; and in order to ensure, as he thought, the observance of the oath he took with him a number of the senators as hostages. An officer of tried courage and skill, named Leudahari, was placed in command of the four thousand; and then the king and his army marched away to Ravenna.

Although Witigis had been chosen king by the unanimous voice of the people, he could not help remembering that he was not of Amaling blood, and he lived in dread of a conspiracy on behalf of the two persons of the ancient line who might be regarded as entitled to the throne. One of these was Theudagisal, the son of Theodahad. The son of a father so greatly detested could not perhaps have been a very dangerous rival, but Witigis, nevertheless, thought it necessary to throw him into prison. It was more reasonably to be feared that plots would be formed in favour of Amalaswintha's young and beautiful daughter, Mataswintha; and, in order to render his claim to the throne secure, Witigis, on his arrival at Ravenna, divorced his own wife and married the princess. He could now claim to be king by hereditary right; in his addresses to the Gothic people he appeals to their loyalty to the house of Theoderic, and some of his coins bear the queen's monogram. But every one knew that Mataswintha had been forced into the marriage against her will; she never concealed her dislike of her husband, and in after years she was with good reason suspected of being in league with his enemies.

One of the earliest acts of Witigis at Ravenna was to call an assembly of the Gothic nobles, for the purpose of obtaining their consent to a proposed treaty of peace with the Franks. The conditions were that the Ostrogoths should give up all their possessions in Gaul to the Franks, and pay them two thousand pounds weight of gold. Witigis himself spoke of this treaty as "a painful necessity," but he assured the nobles that no better terms could be obtained, and after some discussion the proposal was approved. The Franks accepted the bribe, and promised Witigis their assistance in the war. As they did not wish to quarrel with Justinian, they could not themselves appear in the field, but they undertook that their vassals, the kings of the Alamans and the Burgunds, should send troops to fight on the Gothic side.

While King Witigis at Ravenna was busy drilling his soldiers and making his bargain with the Franks, he received the startling news that Belisarius was in Rome. Pope Silverius and the senators had heard of the sad fate that had befallen Naples through its resistance to the imperial army, and determined to save Rome from similar calamities by a timely surrender. Faithless to the oaths which they had sworn to the Goths, they sent an embassy to Belisarius, inviting him to come with all speed to Rome, and promising that the gates should be opened at his approach. Belisarius lost no time in complying with the request. Leaving a garrison of three hundred men at Naples, he set out with his army along "the Latin Way" to Rome.

When the senators received the tidings that Belisarius was coming, they informed the commander of the Gothic garrison of what they had done. The brave Leudahari called his soldiers together, and told them that though thus shamefully betrayed, he was resolved at all hazards to defend the city. But the Goths refused to obey their general, and unaniminously declared that they would abandon Rome, and join the rest of the army at Ravenna.

It was on the 9th of December, 536, that Belisarius entered Rome by the "Asinarian Gate" on the south; and at the same moment the four thousand Goths marched out of the "Flaminian Gate" which led to the great northern road. Leudahari, however, obstinately refused to abandon his post. He remained to be taken prisoner, and was sent, together with the keys of the city, as a token of victory to Justinian.

Belisarius took up his residence in the palace on the Pincian Hill, and at once began to set about the repair of the fortifications, and to procure large supplies of corn from Sicily. The Romans saw these proceedings with dismay, for they showed that the general was preparing to be besieged in Rome. The citizens felt that their treason against Witigis had done them little good, if after all they were to suffer the hardships of a siege, and perhaps—who could tell?—were to fall at last into the hands of the infuriated Goths. The joy with which Belisarius had at first been welcomed now gave place to discontent and gloomy foreboding.

Yet it did not seem as if the danger of a Gothic siege was very close at hand. Witigis remained at Ravenna; and Belisarius ventured to send out detachments of his little army to conquer the province of Tuscany. One of his officers, Bessa the Goth, captured the rock fortress of Narni. Another, named Constantine, marched still further away, and occupied, without resistance from the inhabitants, the cities of Spoleto and Perugia. When Witigis learned that the emperor's troops were in possession of the latter place, nearly half way to Ravenna from Rome, he sent a body of soldiers, under two leaders named Hunila and Pitza, to try to recapture the city. The Goths far outnumbered the soldiers of Constantine, but the battle was long undecided. But in the end the Goths fled in confusion, hotly pursued by the Romans, who left few alive to tell the tale of their defeat. Hunila and Pitza were taken prisoners, and sent at once to Belisarius.

After this disaster, Witigis saw that he must no longer remain inactive. His preparations were not so complete as he had wished, for the soldiers recalled from Gaul had not yet arrived. But even without these, the army which he had collected in the camp at Ravenna numbered 150,000 men, "nearly every one of whom wore a breastplate of steel." With this immense host King Witigis set out along the Flaminian Way, to lay siege to the city which was held by the little garrison of Belisarius.

The king did not stop to attempt the recovery of the captured towns, but hurried forward without pause, eager to stand as soon as possible before the walls of Rome. From time to time the army met with parties of country people who had been turned out of Rome as "useless mouths," and were returning to their northern homes; and as they told how heavily the city was burdened by the presence of the imperial army, Witigis bitterly reproached his own folly in abandoning his capital. Still, he thought that if he could only get Belisarius shut up within the walls his victory was secure. His great anxiety was lest when he arrived at his journey's end he should find that the bird had flown. "Is Belisarius still in Rome?" was the question he impatiently asked of a priest who had left the city a day or two before. "Never fear for that," said the priest with a laugh; "there is not much likelihood of his running away." Perhaps the priest thought that Witigis had more reason to dread Belisarius's remaining where he was than his escape.

The Goths marched on without opposition until they came to the Milvian bridge, which crosses the Tiber about two miles north of Rome; and here they met with an unexpected check. Belisarius had built a gate-tower at the entrance of the bridge, and garrisoned it with a body of soldiers strong enough to render its capture a tedious and costly piece of work. He did not expect to be able to prevent the Goths from crossing the river at all, but he was anxious to gain time, as he was expecting some more troops from Constantinople. Whether the enemy made an attack on the tower, crossed in boats, or marched away to find another bridge, he thought he was sure of several days' delay. In order to make the passage still more troublesome, he determined to place his camp close to the river on the side nearest Rome.

When Witigis saw how the bridge was protected, he was at a loss to know what to do. Most of his officers thought that the best course would be to make an assault on the tower. But it was decided not to attempt any movement until the following morning.

During the night, however, the soldiers in the tower took fright at the immense multitude of the enemy, and abandoned their post. They did not, of course, dare to go in the direction of Rome, but fled into Campania, all except twenty-two, who, being Goths themselves, deserted to their countrymen, and told them what had happened. When morning came, therefore, the Goths had only to batter down the gates, and went over the bridge without meeting any opposition.

The same morning, Belisarius, thinking that the enemy was safe on the other side of the river, had ridden out with a thousand horsemen to choose a suitable place for his camp. Suddenly a fierce shout was heard, and the general's guard found themselves struggling with the van of the Gothic cavalry, who had just crossed the bridge. Belisarius, brave but imprudent, forgetting how much depended on his safety, rushed to the front, and fought like a common soldier. He was mounted on his favourite charger, a beautiful dark-brown horse with a white star on its forehead. The deserters recognized their late general, and the word was hastily passed through the Gothic ranks, "Aim at the horse with the white star." Hardly knowing what was meant, the Goths obeyed the hint, and charged with lances and swords upon the imperial commander. His body-guard gathered round him, and enclosed him within a wall of shields. After a desperate fight, the Goths retired to their camp with the loss of a thousand men.

But now fresh bodies of cavalry came up, and the Romans, who had themselves suffered serious losses, were compelled to have recourse to flight. At the top of a hill, where they had halted for a moment's breathing space, they were overtaken by their pursuers, and the fight was renewed. Valentine, the groom of Belisarius's step-son, fought like a lion, and by his sole prowess succeeded in checking for a moment the advance of the enemy. But it was in vain to resist the overwhelming numbers of the Gothic host, and the Romans were driven close up to the walls of Rome. A few of the fugitives who had outstripped the rest found entrance into the city. They reported that Belisarius was killed, and that the enemy was in close pursuit. The gate was hastily flung to, and when Belisarius and his comrades had crossed the ditch they found themselves shut out In vain the general shouted and threatened; the soldiers on the top of the tower did not recognize his voice, and in the gathering twilight his features, covered with blood and dust as they were, could not be distinguished. It seemed as if in another moment the Goths would have scrambled across the moat and massacred the little band huddled under the walls. A daring stratagem of Belisarius saved himself and his companions from destruction. Drawing up his handful of men in battle array under cover of the darkness, he made a sudden charge upon the Goths, who, thinking that it was a sortie of the forces within the city, were seized with panic, and fled in confusion. The sentinels on the wall reported the flight of the enemy, and Belisarius with his brave little band was now allowed admission. The gate through which he passed was long known as "the gate of Belisarius."

The historian who records the prowess of Belisarius tells also of a hero who on this memorable day distinguished himself no less signally on the other side. It was a certain Wandilhari, appropriately surnamed Wisand (i.e., the Bison), who, pierced with thirteen wounds, was left for dead upon the battle-field. On the third day, his comrades, returning to bury the slain, found Wandilhari still breathing, though unable to speak. When water was poured into his mouth he revived a little, and was carried into the camp. Wandilhari the Bison lived to a great age, and was naturally held in the highest honour by his countrymen for his wonderful display of bravery and endurance.

Weary as Belisarius was with the toils and agitations of this long day, there remained yet much to be done before he could allow himself a moment's rest. His first care was to man the walls, which were thirteen miles in circuit. His little army could not spare soldiers enough for this duty, and he instructed his officers to muster all the able-bodied men in the several quarters of the city, dividing them into bands, some of them to occupy their appointed stations at once, and the others to take their places on the succeeding days and nights. At regular intervals along the walls large fires were to be kept burning during the moonless nights. The Goths remained watching the movements of those upon the wall, and when they saw by the light of the fires that men in civil costume were mingled with the soldiers, one of their chiefs, named Wakis, was sent to harangue the citizens on their treachery. "What madness has seized you, O Romans!" he said, "that you should exchange your valiant protectors for a handful of wretched Greeks, who will never be able to defend you. What did Greece ever send to Italy but play actors and thieves?" No one answered a word, and Wakis returned to the camp.

Belisarius meanwhile was occupied in apportioning to his principal officers the charge of the several gates. Before this task was completed, Bessa the Goth, who had been posted at the Praenestine gate, sent a messenger to say that the gate named after St. Pancrace had been forced, and that the enemy was in possession of the part of the city west of the Tiber. The general was earnestly besought by those about him to make his escape at once by some other gate. He ridiculed the story as absurd, and sent horsemen across the river to make inquiry. They soon returned with the report that all was quiet, and Belisarius gave strict orders to all the officers in command at the gates that they should remain at their posts whatever tidings they might hear from other parts of the city. "Let each man attend to his own duty," he said, "and leave all the rest to me."

From early morning Belisarius had been in ceaseless activity without once tasting food. The intense excitement of the day made him insensible to the calls of hunger and fatigue, and it was not until long after midnight that his wife and friends could prevail on him to interrupt his labours to partake of a scanty meal.

The day which followed was the first day of the longest of all the many sieges which Rome has undergone. It began early in March, 537, and lasted for one year and nine days. Belisarius entered on this great struggle with no fear for its result He foresaw that the vast army of the Goths, badly led and unused to the conduct of a siege, would dwindle away by famine and desertion before the walls of Rome, and that sooner or later the end would be the ruin of the Gothic kingdom, and the establishment of the imperial rule in Italy. The citizens could not understand his cheerful confidence in the face of such fearful odds, and sneered at him as a madman or a boastful Greek. His own soldiers wondered too, but their trust in their well-tried commander could not be shaken.

XXIII: THE YEAR-LONG SIEGE

The story of the long siege of Rome is one continuous record of wonderful patience, resolution, and readiness of resource on the part of Belisarius, and of miserable incompetence on the part of his antagonist. The first thing which King Witigis attempted to do was to enclose Rome with a circle of stockaded camps. But the scale on which these camps were constructed was so ample that even the immense army of the Goths was insufficient to supply men to occupy more than seven of them, which blockaded eight out of the fourteen gates, leaving the six gates on the southern side of the city uninvested. The seven camps, each containing more than thrice the number of men who formed the garrison of Rome, were fortified with as much elaborate care as if they were intended to withstand an assault from an overwhelming force. King Witigis's principle of action was that it is never possible to be too secure.

The next thing which the Goths did was, in imitation of Belisarius's own proceedings at Naples, to destroy the aqueducts that supplied Rome with water. Belisarius did not intend that Rome should be captured as he had taken Naples, and therefore he took care that the underground passages should be solidly walled up. The cutting off of the supply from the aqueducts put an end to the enjoyment of the public baths, the great luxury of Roman life, and the complaints of the citizens were bitter. But with the river flowing through the city, and the wells belonging to private houses, there was not much reason to fear that want of water would compel Belisarius to surrender.

One of the aqueducts, however, had furnished the water-power to the corn-mills, and the consequence of the cutting-off of the stream was that the daily supply of flour could not be doled out to the soldiers and the citizens. Belisarius therefore contrived to have two barges moored just below the Aelian Bridge, near the northern wall of the city, with a water-wheel between them, so that the stream, rushing with force from under the arch of the bridge, should turn the wheel, and so drive the mills which were placed on the barges. The Goths were informed of this device by deserters, and sent floating down the river a quantity of large trunks of trees and bodies of dead Romans, and by this means managed to upset the machinery. However, Belisarius's ingenuity was equal to this occasion also. He caused long iron chains to be drawn across the opening of the bridge, which intercepted everything that came down the stream, and men were employed from time to time to clear away the obstructions which had accumulated. This contrivance served a double purpose, for it prevented the possibility of a night attack being made by boats sailing under the bridge.

After a few days had passed Witigis began to think that the capture of Rome would not prove so easy an undertaking as he had fancied. He therefore determined to see whether Belisarius could be induced to surrender by the offer of honourable conditions. A Gothic chief named Albes, accompanied by several other nobles, was sent into the city with a communication to Belisarius. He found the general surrounded by his staff and the principal senators, and addressed him in a formal speech, bidding him look from the walls at the vast numbers of the besiegers and consider whether it would not be mere foolhardiness to think of resisting them.

Belisarius grimly replied that the question whether resistance was "foolhardiness" or not was his concern and not theirs, and that he did not intend to be guided by the advice which they offered him. Resist he would, and a time would come when the Goths would be glad to hide themselves if they could even in the bramble-bushes. Rome belonged to the emperor; the Gothic intruders who had stolen it had been turned out, and so long as Belisarius lived they should not come back.

After Belisarius had spoken, Albes and his companions looked expectantly at the senators. They had heard from deserters how fiercely some of the principal Romans had talked (in private) about the conduct of Belisarius, and they thought that the appeal made by Albes would call forth such a burst of indignation as would compel the general to yield. But the senators sat pale and trembling, and none of them dared to speak a word except a certain Fidelius, whom Belisarius had made Praetorian Prefect, and who loaded the Goths with abuse.

The envoys went back to the Gothic camp, and were received by Witigis with the eager inquiry, "What sort of a man is Belisarius? Is he going to give way?" They replied with emphasis that the Goths had made a great mistake in thinking they could frighten that man by anything they could say or do. On receiving this report the king hurried on his preparations for taking the city by storm.

The preparations were on a magnificent scale. All the machines which the military engineers of those times were able to devise for the assault on a fortress were constructed in large numbers. There were wooden towers on wheels equal in height to the walls of the city. These were intended to be dragged by oxen close up to the walls, so that the archers on the top could fight on a level with the defenders of the ramparts. Then there were the battering-rams, which consisted of huge beams of wood, each carrying a block of iron at the end and suspended in chains from a wooden framework. The machine moved on four wheels, and was worked from within by fifty men who dragged back the heavy "ram," and then allowed it to swing against the wall. The whole structure was covered with skins to protect the men who were inside. Scaling-ladders, too, were prepared to be used when the soldiers on the wooden towers should have succeeded in clearing a portion of the wall of its defenders; and fascines that is to say, bundles of reeds and brushwood, were made in order to fill up the ditch so as to make a road across it for the machines.

Belisarius for his part was equally busy in organizing the defence. His army had dwindled down to five thousand men, and it cost him a great deal of thought to distribute this little force to the best advantage. The tomb of the great emperor Hadrian, a vast building faced with marble, which stood in the line of the city wall at the western end of the Aelian Bridge, was converted into a fort, and such it has continued to be till this day, when it is known as the Castle of St. Angelo. All round the walls of the city Belisarius mounted those destructive engines which served the Romans as artillery — machines which hurled immense stones and bolts of iron with tremendous velocity and effect.

It was not till the eighteenth day of the siege that the Goths considered themselves ready to begin the attack. As soon as the sun rose the Romans gathered on the northern wall saw with terror the countless host of the enemy approaching with their battering-rams and their siege-towers drawn by oxen. The citizens gave themselves up for lost, but their fears became mixed with indignation when Belisarius, instead of seeming to appreciate the gravity of the situation, actually burst out laughing, and ordered the soldiers not to shoot an arrow till he gave the word. "What might such conduct mean? Was it madness, or worse than madness?" were the questions which one asked of another among the crowd. At last, when the enemy had reached the very edge of the moat, Belisarius took up a bow and aimed at one of the Gothic leaders. The man was clothed in armour, but the arrow hit him in the neck, and he fell to the ground mortally wounded. The Romans, startled out of their discontent, burst into a great cheer, which was renewed when the general again drew his bow with a like result. And then Belisarius gave the signal to the whole army to discharge their arrows, ordering those in his own neighbourhood to aim only at the oxen. In a few moments all the oxen were killed, and the huge machines which they drew were rendered useless. It was easy to see now what Belisarius had been laughing at, and why he had allowed the enemy to come so close before allowing his archers to use their weapons.

When Witigis saw that the attack on the northern side of the city had failed, he determined to direct his efforts to the eastern side—to the neighbourhood of the Prainestine gate, towards which another body of Goths was approaching, also with their siege-towers and battering-rams. But he left a large detachment of his army on the northern side, leaving orders that they should not make any attempt to storm the walls, but should keep up a vigorous discharge of arrows, so that Belisarius might not suspect that the main assault was being attempted elsewhere. Those who were left behind did their best to carry out these instructions, but fighting on the level ground against men posted on the wall they were not able to produce much effect. There was, however, amongst them one famous warrior of noble rank, who found a substitute for the siege-tower in a tall tree, to the top of which he climbed, notwithstanding the weight of his helmet and cuirass, and from that elevated position was able to do much execution amongst the defenders of the ramparts. At last he was hit by a shot from one of the Roman engines. The iron bolt went right through the man's steel-clad body, and pinned him to the tree. His comrades were so much aghast at the sight that they retired to a safe distance out of the way of those terrible machines, and the defenders of that portion of the walls were no more molested.

But now Belisarius received a message to say that the assault on the eastern fortifications had begun. He hastened to the spot, and by a few timely words encouraged his soldiers, who had begun to lose heart when they saw the numbers and equipment of the enemy. Near the Praenestine gate was a space enclosed between the city rampart and an outer wall, where in heathen days were kept the wild beasts intended for the cruel sports of the amphitheatre. The Goths broke through the outer wall, and crowded into the enclosure. The inner wall, they had been truly informed, was much decayed, and they thought it would give them little trouble. But Belisarius directed one of his chief officers to make a sally upon the throng collected between the walls. The unexpected attack threw the Goths into confusion, and they were slaughtered by thousands almost unresisting, thinking only of making their escape by the breach through which they had entered. Then, opening the gate, Belisarius issued with the main body of his army to pursue the fugitives, who imparted their terror to their comrades beyond the outer wall. Soon the besiegers were all in headlong flight, and Belisarius ordered a great fire to be made of their forsaken towers and battering-rams.

What happened else during this eventful day need not be told in detail. It may be mentioned that in their attack on the fort that had been Hadrian's tomb the Goths were nearly winning, until it occurred to the defenders to pull down the statues, and hurl them, whole or in fragments, upon the heads of their assailants. More than one famous work of Greek sculpture has been found in modern times in the moat which surrounds the Castle of St. Angelo; probably many another lies buried there still. The sacrifice of the statues saved the fortress: the besiegers abated the fury of their assault, and then the imperial soldiers, set free by the termination of the fighting in other parts of the city, came up and soon put them to flight.

On all sides the Gothic attack had ended in disaster. Thirty thousand Goths had been slain, and many-thousands wounded, and the towers and the battering-rams were captured and burnt It was far on in the evening when the battle ceased. "The Romans spent the night in singing songs of victory, extolling the fame of Belisarius, and displaying the spoils taken from the slain; the Goths in attending on their wounded comrades, and in wailing for those that were no more."

After this crushing failure no further attempt was made to storm the walls of Rome. Through the remainder of the long siege the aim of Witigis was to compel Belisarius to surrender under pressure of hunger, or to tempt him to squander the lives of his little garrison in fruitless sorties.

Belisarius guessed at once that the Goths, now that their assault had decisively failed, would endeavour to establish an efficient blockade. He, therefore, promptly took measures for economizing the stock of provisions in the city. On the very day after the battle he ordered that the daily rations of food to the soldiers should be reduced to one-half, the diminution being compensated by increased pay in money; and all the women, children, and slaves in the city were sent away to Naples, some of them being conveyed in boats, others travelling on foot along the Appian Way. It would have been to the interest of the Goths to prevent this procession of non-combatants from escaping from Rome; but they were so discouraged by their defeat of yesterday that nothing was done. And so the fugitives all found their way to Naples, whence some of them were removed to the other south Italian towns, and others took refuge in Sicily.

What made Belisarius anxious was that he received no tidings of the additional troops that the emperor had promised to send him. They had sailed from Constantinople about Christmas, but, meeting with stormy weather, had sought shelter on the western coast of Greece, and there they still remained. Belisarius could not understand this strange delay, and wrote a letter to Justinian, telling him that unless aid came speedily Rome must surely fall. The letter concluded with these words: "I know that it is my duty to sacrifice even my life in your service, and therefore no force shall make me abandon this place while I live. But what sort of fame will be yours if you allow Belisarius to come to such an end?"

Justinian was deeply moved by this appeal, and sent peremptory orders to the lagging commanders, Valerian and Martin, that they should push forward with all speed to Rome. He also made vigorous efforts to raise a new army to be sent to the aid of his heroic general. In a few days Belisarius was able to cheer the hearts of his soldiers by reading to them the emperor's letter, announcing that the wished-for reinforcements were on their way.

It was not until twenty-two days after the attempted storm that Valerian and Martin, with sixteen hundred men, arrived in Rome. The Goths had made little use of the delay; indeed they were so discouraged by the failure of their assault that they scarcely attempted to guard the roads leading to Rome from the south, but remained idle in their entrenchments.

By way of revenge for the losses he had sustained, Witigis despatched orders that the senators detained as hostages at Ravenna should be put to death. According to the laws of war these men had forfeited their lives; but the execution of the penalty was as foolish as it was cruel, for the only effect it could have was to embitter the hatred which the Romans felt for their former barbarian masters, and to inspire them with the resolve to fight to the bitter end.

When the sixteen hundred new soldiers had entered Rome, Belisarius ventured to send out skirmishing parties of mounted archers to make attacks upon the Goths. Their tactics were to avoid all close fighting, but simply to discharge their arrows at the enemy, and when their quivers were empty to gallop back to the gates. This mode of combat proved perfectly successful. The little bands did fearful execution with their bows, and the pursuit of the enemy was easily stopped volleys of stones from the engines on the walls. After this manoeuvre had been repeated several times, Witigis thought he had discovered a valuable secret of Roman warfare. It was plain that small bodies of light horse were more easily managed than masses of heavy troops, and afforded the most effective means of inflicting damage upon an enemy. Accordingly, he sent a troop of five hundred cavalry, with orders to take up their position near the Roman fortifications. What happened was that a thousand picked men issued from one of the gates some distance away, and, under cover of the inequalities of the ground, came suddenly on the five hundred Goths, took them in the rear, and left only a few of them alive to return to their camp. King Witigis raved and stormed about their cowardice, and said he would soon find others who would succeed where they had failed. Three days afterwards a second five hundred, chosen for their known bravery out of all the seven camps, were sent to avenge the defeat of their comrades, and, before setting out, were harangued by the king, who bade them act worthily of the fame they had won in former battles. Bravely they may have fought, but they were met by a Roman force of three times their number, and perished almost to a man.

Belisarius wished to continue this method of skirmishing, by which he was able to do the enemy a great deal of mischief with very little loss on his own side. His troops had been thoroughly trained in the art of using the bow on horseback; to the Goths that mode of warfare was quite unfamiliar, so that when it was employed against them they did not know how to meet it. But unfortunately for the Romans, their easily won victories had inspired them with an unwise contempt for the enemy, and they implored Belisarius to lead them in one grand assault on the Gothic camp. He was very unwilling to do this, but the army showed great discontent at his refusal, and the feeling was encouraged by the citizens, who actually assailed the general with reproaches for his want of courage, because he dared not risk a pitched battle with an enemy that outnumbered his own troops more than tenfold. At last Belisarius thought it might be better to yield to the demand than to provoke a mutiny. Perhaps, after all, he thought, just at this moment, when the Romans were full of ardour, and the enemy was disheartened by continued ill-fortune, it might be possible to win a battle even against such overwhelming odds.

It was with grave anxiety that Belisarius led forth his little army against the foe. King Witigis had been informed by deserters of the intended attack, and he marshalled all his troops in battle array, leaving none in the camps but the sick and wounded. His speech to his soldiers, as reported by the Roman historian, was not without dignity. "You know," he said, "that I have always treated you more as friends and fellow-soldiers than as subjects. Some of you may think that I, in so doing, have merely flattered you because I feared the loss of my crown; and you may think that it is from the same motive that I now call on you to put forth all your valour. Such suspicions are natural, and I cannot blame them. But, in truth, I would thankfully lay aside this purple robe today, if I knew that another Goth would wear it in my stead. Whatever ill might happen to myself, it would not be without consolation, if my people did not share in it. But I remember the fate of the Vandals. I seem to see the Goths and their children sold for slaves, their wives abandoned to the insults of the vilest of men, and their queen, the child of Theoderic's daughter, led away whithersoever it might please our enemies. Will you not chose a glorious death rather than safety on such terms? If such be your spirit, you will easily vanquish these few wretched Greeks, to whom you are as far superior in valour as in numbers, and will inflict on them the chastisement they deserve for all the wrongs and insults they have made you suffer."

The result of the battle justified the misgivings of Belisarius. After much hard fighting, the Romans were put to flight, the enemy pursuing them hotly almost to the walls. A few of them succeeded in passing through the gates, and hastily closed them, leaving their comrades gathered in a dense mass between the ditch and the wall. Their spears were broken, and they were so crowded together that they could not use their bows. If the Goths had ventured to cross the ditch they might have massacred their enemies without difficulty; but the soldiers and citizens began to assemble upon the wall, and the besiegers were afraid to pursue their advantage. They retired to their encampment with shouts of exultation over their victory.

The Roman soldiers had received a severe lesson, and never again ventured to distrust the sagacity of their general. Belisarius resumed his plan of skirmishing with mounted archers, and, as before, was nearly always victorious. So passed away the next three months of the siege. The historian Procopius, who was with Belisarius in Rome, has preserved for us many incidents of the conflicts that took place during this period. One of these stories is perhaps worth repeating here. On a certain evening it happened that the Roman soldiers had been worsted in a skirmish, and one of them in his flight fell through a hole into an underground vault, from which he could find no means of escape. He did not dare to cry out, lest he should be heard by the Goths, and so he remained there all the night. The next day a Gothic soldier suffered the same mishap; and the Goth and the Roman, finding themselves prisoners together, became good friends, and agreed that if either of them succeeded in getting out of the trap he would help the other to escape also. They both shouted with all their might, and at last they were heard by a party of Goths, who stooped down to the hole, and called out "Who is there?" "A comrade," the Gothic soldier replied, in his own language; "I fell into this hole this morning, and cannot get out." A rope was lowered into the vault, and there ascended, not the Goth, but the Roman! The Gothic soldiers were stupefied with amazement. "There were two of us," the Roman explained; "your comrade is still below. We knew very well that if he had come out first you would not have troubled yourselves about us." So the rope was let down again, and this time it brought up the Goth, who said that he had given his word that his fellow-prisoner should be set at liberty. The promise was respected, and the Roman soldier was allowed to return to the city, none the worse for his adventure.

About midsummer a certain Euthalius landed at Terracina, sixty-two miles from Rome along the Appian Way, bringing with him the pay which was due to the soldiers. The treasure was conveyed safely into Rome, but at that moment food would have been more welcome than gold; for the besieged people were now beginning to feel the pangs of hunger.

Probably Witigis got to hear that a large sum of money had been brought into Rome, and this may have been what made him think of blockading the southern approaches to the city. It is strange that he should not have done this long before, but he seems to have clung to the hope that the place might be taken by storm. Now, however, he took possession of a point about four miles from Rome, where two lines of aqueducts cross one another twice within a few hundred yards, and he converted the arches of the aqueducts into a fortress, commanding the Appian and the Latin Ways. Here he placed a guard of seven thousand men.

There was now no hope that any further supplies could be imported into the city. The soldiers had still a stock of corn, but all their other provisions were exhausted. The citizens were obliged to feed on the grass and weeds that grew inside the walls. Famine and fever were every day lessening the numbers of the besieged.

Until July was ended, the courage of the defenders was sustained by superstition. For some months past people had quoted a couplet which professed to be a prophecy of the ancient Sibyl, and which said that "when Quintilis (the old name of July) had come, a new emperor would ascend the throne, and Rome should never again fear the Gothic sword." Christians though the Romans were, they still believed in the Sibyl, and eagerly accepted every foolish verse that was uttered in her name. But Quintilis came and went, and still Justinian reigned and still the Goths surrounded Rome.

The last hope of the citizens was gone, and in desperation they went to Belisarius, and begged him to give them arms. "Let us fight for ourselves," they said, "and either conquer or end our miseries by a speedy death." Belisarius ridiculed their demand, and told them that having never learned to fight they would be worse than useless in the field. "But," he added, "I expect in a few days the arrival of the greatest army that the empire has ever mustered. These new troops have already landed in the south of Italy, and will bring with them ample supplies of provisions. I promise you that they will bury the enemy's camp with the multitude of their darts."

This was only an empty boast. There was indeed a rumour that an imperial army was on the way, but Belisarius knew nothing for certain. However, he despatched his secretary Procopius to Naples to see what truth there was in the story, and if it should not be true, to collect what soldiers he could, and to send victuals by sea to relieve the needs of the Romans.

Procopius reached Naples in safety; the expected troops had not yet been heard of, but he was able to get together a band of five hundred men, and to fit out a large number of ships and load them with provisions. Before his preparations were completed, the promised army arrived from Constantinople—not the innumerable host of which Belisarius had boasted, but only about five thousand men. Late in the autumn this body of soldiers arrived at Ostia, at the mouth of the Tiber, half of them having travelled by the Appian Way, and the rest having come by sea in charge of the victualling fleet collected by Procopius.

Meanwhile King Witigis had managed matters so badly that his own army was suffering from want of food. Famine and fever too were rapidly thinning the ranks of the besiegers, and they grew so spiritless that the Romans were able to assume the offensive, and even to intercept the supplies of corn and of cattle on their way to the Gothic camp.

So when the Goths heard that "an immense army" —for this was what rumour called it—was coming to the relief of Rome, they abandoned all hope of victory, and were anxious to treat for peace. Our old friend, Cassiodorus, accompanied by two Gothic chiefs, was sent into the city to try to induce Belisarius to come to terms.

The envoys were admitted into the general's presence, and Cassiodorus began by saying that as the war hitherto had been productive of nothing but misery to either party, it would be to the interest of both if by mutual concession they could arrive at some understanding so as to put an end to the struggle. He proposed that the matter should be discussed, not in set speeches, but in an informal conversation, so that each point should be fully dealt with at the time when it was raised. "Very well," said Belisarius, "there is no objection to that, if only what you have to say is to the purpose." But Cassiodorus could not resist the temptation to make a long speech, in which he argued that the emperor had no justification for the attack he had made upon the Goths. Theoderic had not taken Italy by force from the empire: it had been made over to him by Zeno, on condition of his putting down the tyrant Odovacar. He had fulfilled the condition, and he and his successors had ruled Italy according to Roman law, and with every regard to the welfare of the native inhabitants. It was therefore the duty of the Romans to desist from their unjust encroachments. Let them retire from Italy with the booty they had taken, and leave the Goths to govern their rightful dominions in peace.

All this reasoning was very sound, but it was not likely to make any impression on Belisarius. He replied that Theoderic had been sent to conquer Italy for the empire to which it belonged, and instead of fulfilling his commission he had usurped the throne himself. "I do not see," he added, "much difference between robbery and embezzlement. The country belongs to the emperor, and it is useless to ask me to give it to any one else. If you have any other request to make say on."

"You know very well," answered Cassiodorus, " that we have spoken nothing but the truth. But as a proof of our wish to make every honourable concession, we agree that you shall retain possession of Sicily"—and then, with his accustomed eloquence, he proceeded to favour Belisarius with statistics about the size of the island, and the revenues which it yielded every year, and to enlarge on its importance from a military point of view.

"We are greatly obliged to you," said Belisarius. "In return for so great generosity, we will grant you the possession of the whole of Britain. That is a larger island than Sicily, and it used to belong to us, just as Sicily once belonged to you."

The Goths then suggested that they might give up Naples and the whole south of Italy, and agree to pay a yearly tribute to the emperor. But Belisarius had only one reply: that he had no authority to surrender any of the territories of the empire.

"Well then," said Cassiodorus, "will you agree to a truce for a fixed time, so that we may send ambassadors to Constantinople to negotiate a treaty with the emperor himself?"

Belisarius accepted this proposal, and the envoys went back to their camp.

Several days were spent in settling the conditions of the truce, and in debating what hostages should be given on each side. In the meantime Belisarius had brought the new soldiers, and the cargoes of the provision ships, safely up from Ostia into Rome. The Goths dared not offer any opposition, thinking that if they did so, Belisarius would break off the negotiations.

At length, however, about Christmas, the articles were signed for a truce of three months; the hostages were exchanged, and the Gothic ambassadors set out for Constantinople, accompanied by a Roman escort. Belisarius then sent two thousand soldiers, under the command of a certain John, of whom we shall often hear again, to Alba Fucentia, seventy miles east of Rome. John was instructed to remain quiet so long as the truce was unbroken; but as soon as the Goths committed any act of hostility, he was to ravage the Gothic territories, to carry off the women and children as slaves, and to bring back all the plunder of every kind that he could.

The required pretext was not long wanting. It seems almost incredible that Witigis should have been foolish enough to violate the truce which he had sought with so much eagerness, but the historian tells of three different attempts which he made to surprise the city. One dark night a sentinel, looking out from the watchtower at the Pincian gate, reported that he had seen a sudden flash of light close to the ground a short distance from the wall. His comrades thought he had seen the flaming eyes of a wolf But when, on the following day, Belisarius heard the story, he guessed at once that the Goths, imitating his own stratagem at Naples, were trying to get into the city through an aqueduct, and that what the man had seen was the light of their torches streaming for a moment through a crack in the tunnel. The aqueduct was examined, and there were found in it the droppings of torches and some Gothic lamps. The party of explorers had been stopped by the wall with which Belisarius had blocked up the passage, and they had carried away one of the stones to show to Witigis in proof of the truth of their story. Belisarius placed a guard over the aqueduct, and the Goths made no attempt to enter the city by that means.

On another occasion the Goths had prepared scaling-ladders and torches to make an attack during the hour of the soldier's midday meal, but the plan was discovered, and the assaulting party was dispersed with some loss. The third scheme of Witigis was to bribe two Romans who lived near the part of the wall bordering on the Tiber, to treat the sentinels with drugged wine. When the sentinels had fallen asleep, the Goths were to make their entrance by means of boats and ladders. One of the Romans who had entered into the plot betrayed it to Belisarius; and pointed out his accomplice, who confessed his guilt and was sent to the Gothic camp tied upon an ass and with his nose and ears cut off.

After these events, Belisarius of course considered himself to be no longer bound by the truce, and he sent letters to John ordering him to commence hostilities at once. John was nothing loth to obey; he was the bravest of the brave, but as cruel as he was fearless (John the Sanguinary, he was called in his own day), and the sight of burning farms and strings of weeping captive women and children only filled his heart with brutal joy. With his two thousand horsemen he hurried northward, plundering and destroying all that belonged to Gothic owners, but respecting scrupulously the possessions of the native Italians. An army of Goths, under Wilitheus, the uncle of King Witigis, came to meet him, but the battle resulted in the death of Wilitheus and the slaughter of most of his men. After this victory, John marched forward unopposed to Rimini, on the Adriatic, whither he was invited by the Roman inhabitants. The Gothic garrison, as soon as they heard of his approach, ran away to Ravenna, and John occupied Rimini without a struggle.

While John was at Rimini he received letters from Queen Mataswintha, offering to betray the Goths into his hands and to become his wife. No doubt the proposal included the murder of Witigis, whom she hated with all her heart for having forced her to marry him.

In pressing forward to the Adriatic, John was disobeying Belisarius's orders, which were to assault every fortress that he came to, and if he were unable to capture it then to proceed no further, lest his retreat should be cut off. He thought, however, that when the Goths heard that he had captured Rimini, which was only a day's march from Ravenna, they would at once abandon the siege of Rome. He had calculated rightly. The three months of truce was ended; nothing had been heard from Constantinople; the camp was destitute of provisions, and the city was in a better condition of defence than ever. And when to all these discouraging circumstances there was added the news that Ravenna was threatened by the enemy, Witigis delayed no longer. Early one morning (near the end of March, 538), the sentinels on the walls of Rome reported that the seven Gothic camps had been set on fire, and that the whole army of the besiegers was moving northward along the Flaminian Way.

Belisarius was somewhat taken by surprise at this sudden departure, and felt at first doubtful whether it would not be best to allow the enemy to retreat unmolested. But the fact that the Gothic army would have to cross the Milvian Bridge, two miles from Rome, rendered it possible for an attack on their rear to be successfully made with a small force. Belisarius armed all his soldiers, and, waiting till most of the Goths had crossed the river, he led a furious charge on those that were still on the nearest bank. After some hard fighting, and heavy losses on both sides, the Goths fled in confusion, and many thousands of them perished, some by the swords of their enemies, while others, in their frantic haste to escape, were crushed to death by their comrades, or fell into the river loaded with their armour and were drowned.

So ended the first siege of Rome by the Ostrogoths. Perhaps never in the history of warfare were such splendid advantages of numbers so shamefully thrown away through the incompetence of a general. But in spite of all, the nation continued faithful to the king of its own choice.

XXIV: WITIGIS IN HIDING

Sorely as the Gothic ranks had been thinned by famine, pestilence, and the sword, it was still an enormous army that Witigis led away from the walls of Rome. The joy that Belisarius felt at the raising of the siege was mixed with some anxiety, for the way to Ravenna was through Rimini, where John, still remained with his two thousand horsemen. The general knew the headstrong character of his subordinate, and he feared that John might allow himself to be besieged by the Goths, and that the consequence would be the total destruction of his little force.

To prevent such a calamity Belisarius put one thousand horsemen under two trusty officers, Hildiger and Martin, and commanded them to convey to John his orders to withdraw with his cavalry from Rimini, and to leave the place in charge of a small garrison of foot-soldiers, summoned from the lately taken fortress of Ancona. Belisarius thought that if Witigis found that Rimini contained neither cavalry nor any officers important enough to be valuable prisoners, he would not think it worth while to besiege the place; and even if he did so, John and his horsemen would be able to cause the Goths a great deal of annoyance, and probably to compel them to abandon the siege.

Hildiger and Martin found no difficulty in outstripping the slow march of the Goths. On their way they captured a Gothic post at a place called the Tunnelled Rock (Petra Pertusa), where the road running along a ledge in the side of a precipitous cliff overhanging a deep river-gorge, passes through a tunnel forty feet long, cut through the solid rock in the time of the emperor Vespasian. By way of securing this passage, the two openings had been walled up and provided with gates. The Goths made no attempt at fighting, but took shelter inside their huts at the farther end of the tunnel. So the Romans climbed up to the top of the cliffs, and dislodging huge masses of rock sent them rolling down upon the roofs of the huts. The Gothic soldiers then not only opened the gate, but offered to enter the emperor's service, and the greater part of them accompanied the Roman horsemen on their forward march, while the rest, together with a few Romans, were left behind to guard the tunnel. After this, Hildiger and Martin met with no resistance, and going round by way of Ancona, where they selected from the garrison the required number of infantry, they proceeded to Rimini, and delivered their orders to John. He flatly refused to obey, and the two officers went back to Rome. They left the foot soldiers behind, but taking back with them a few of the garrison of Rimini, who being part of Belisarius's own guard were not subject to John's commands.

Soon afterwards the vast army of the Goths arrived before Rimini, and attempted to storm the walls with the help of a wooden tower on wheels, like those which they had tried to employ in the siege of Rome; but, mindful of their former failure, they contrived that the machine should be propelled by men inside instead of being drawn by oxen. Most of the Romans, when they saw these preparations, gave themselves up for lost; but the energy of John was equal to the need. In the dead of night he issued from the walls with a band of men armed with spades, and dug a deep trench between the siege tower and the walls. So the attack, like every other undertaking managed by King Witigis, resulted in failure and the loss of hundreds of Gothic lives. The Goths therefore determined not to try any more to carry the city by storm, but to starve out the little garrison by a strict blockade—no difficult task, unless, as did not seem likely, Belisarius should be able to send a powerful army to the rescue.

While the Goths were encamped before Rimini, a body of a thousand Romans, at the invitation of the citizens, had entered the great city of Milan. Witigis was greatly enraged to hear of the faithlessness of the Milanese, and sent his nephew Uraias [Wraihya] with a large detachment of his army, to besiege the city, ordering him, when it should be taken, to show no mercy to the traitors. Uraias was joined by ten thousand Burgunds, whom the Prankish king Theudebert had sent in aid of the Goths, and Milan was so closely blockaded that no food could be brought into the city.

Just at this time (about midsummer 538) a new imperial army landed at Ancona, commanded by Narses, the emperor's chamberlain.

This Narses, though he had not had a soldier's education, possessed a great deal of native military genius, and we shall hear how, fourteen years later, his bold and skilful generalship effected the ruin of the Gothic kingdom, and made his master Justinian undisputed sovereign of Italy. But on the present occasion his coming wrought little but mischief to the Roman cause. The truth seems to be that Justinian was beginning to fear least Belisarius's victorious career might end in his aspiring to the diadem of the Western Empire, and that Narses was sent as a sort of spy. Although the emperor's letter to the officers of the army said expressly that Narses was not sent to take the command, but that Belisarius was to be obeyed "in all that tended to the good of the state," there were many who thought this assurance was merely an empty form, and looked to the chamberlain for their orders. Narses for his part continually disapproved of the general's plans, and refused to carry them out. When Belisarius claimed obedience, the chamberlain coolly answered that he considered that the proposed course was not "for the good of the state," and therefore neither he nor the officers were bound to agree to it. It is easy to see how dangerous such a state of things would be, in the presence of an enemy immensely superior in numbers.

Belisarius, however, did not know the temper in which Narses had come, and he advanced with all his army to meet him, congratulating himself on so large an addition to his forces. The two leaders met at Firmium, a town near the Adriatic shore, a day's march south of Ancona, and a great council of war was held to decide on the plan of operations to be adopted. The question debated was whether the first step should be to relieve the garrison of Rimini, or to make an attack on the fortress of Auximum, which was held by four thousand Goths commanded by Wisand.

The general feeling was that it would be highly dangerous to leave Auximum in Gothic hands. It seemed likely that if they did so, the Romans would be taken in the rear by Wisand while they were engaged with the great army of Witigis. "Let us first reduce Auximum," urged several speakers, "and then proceed to the relief of Rimini. If in the meantime Rimini is taken, the fault will not be ours, but John's, because if he had obeyed orders he would not be there at all." Now Narses was a great friend of John, and he pleaded his cause so eloquently, showing how the capture of the two thousand and their commander would raise the courage of the Goths, that Belisarius decided to run the risk of an immediate march against the besiegers. He divided his army into three parts, sending the largest division, under Hildiger, by sea, with orders to anchor in front of Rimini at the same time that the second division, under Martin, arrived by the road along the coast. Belisarius himself, accompanied by Narses, marched through the mountains, passing Rimini at the distance of a two days journey, so that he could bear down upon the besiegers from the north. His object was to frighten the Goths by the sight of an enemy approaching them from three sides at once. In this he was successful. A Gothic foraging party, surprised by the troops of Belisarius, fled to the camp with the news that an enormous army was advancing from the north; the same night the camp-fires of Martin's division were descried eight miles away to the south; and the rising sun shone on the sails of a Roman fleet in the offing.

In a few hours the whole army of the Goths was in headlong flight towards Ravenna, leaving in the camp the sick and wounded, and not a little of their property, to become the plunder of the soldiers of Hildiger. About noon Belisarius arrived, and when he saw the pale and wasted forms of John and his companions, he told John that he ought to be very thankful to Hildiger. "Not to Hildiger," John replied gloomily, "but to Narses." Belisarius understood what his answer meant, and he knew that he had made a life-long enemy.

Thwarted as he continually was by Narses and John, Belisarius succeeding in capturing the strong fortresses of Urbinum and Urbs Vetus (Orvieto). But the dissensions between the generals caused the loss of Milan. Belisarius had sent a large body of troops, under Martin and an officer of Gothic birth named Wilihari, to the rescue of the beleaguered city, but the officers remained idle for months encamped on the south bank of the Po, and at length wrote to Belisarius asking for aid, as they dared not cross the river, being so enormously outnumbered by the Goths and Burgunds, and Belisarius wrote ordering John and Justin to march for the deliverance of Milan, but they refused to obey any orders but those of Narses. At last—early in the year 539—he was constrained to humble himself to entreat Narses to give the necessary commands. The chamberlain consented; but it was too late. Before the order could be executed Milan had fallen.

When the city was suffering the direst extremity of famine, the Gothic chief called upon the garrison to surrender, promising that if they did so their lives should be spared. The Roman commander, Mun-dila (himself, like so many other "Roman" officers of the time, a Goth by birth) insisted that the besiegers should pledge themselves to spare the lives of the citizens as well. But the Goths, according to the orders given to them by their king, were bent on having a terrible revenge upon the Milanese for their betrayal, and refused the demand. Then the brave Mundila, addressing the remnant of his thousand men, called upon them to prefer a glorious death to a dishonoured life, and to follow him in a desperate charge upon the enemy. But the soldiers did not share his heroic courage. They accepted the offered terms, and saved their own lives, leaving the hapless citizens to their fate.

The Goths used their victory like the worst of savages. All the men in the city were killed (three hundred thousand, we are told, but the number seems incredible); the women were given as slaves to the Burgunds, and Milan was levelled with the ground. The surrounding cities, fearing a similar fate, hastened to offer their submission, and without any further bloodshed the Goths were once more masters of the province of Liguria.

The Roman generals, Martin and Wilihari, who had allowed Milan to perish before their eyes without striking a blow for its defence, returned to Rome. Belisarius had set out with all his army towards the Adriatic coast, intending to lay siege to Auximum, and on the journey heard the grievous news of Milan. In bitterness of heart he wrote to Justinian, telling him the whole story of what had happened, and doubtless asking for the punishment of those whose fault had caused the disaster. The emperor, however, contented himself with ordering Narses to return at once to Constantinople, and formally appointing Belisarius to the supreme command of the army of Italy. Belisarius seems to have thought Wilihari more to blame than his colleague, and we read that he never permitted him to see his face again.

The dreary story of the remainder of the year 539 need not here be told in detail. From May to December Belisarius was besieging Auximum, near the Adriatic, and his lieutenants were besieging Faesulae, close to Florence. The brave garrison of Auximum suffered cruel hardships, but were encouraged by continual promises of immediate help from Ravenna. The help never came; Witigis could not make up his mind to exchange the safety of his fortress for the risks of a conflict in the open field. At last, when Faesulae had fallen, and the army which had captured it came with their prisoners to the camp of Belisarius, the resolution of the famished defenders of Auximum broke down. They not only surrendered the city, but they were so hopeless of Gothic freedom under a king like Witigis that they actually I took service in the Roman ranks. And so four thousand valiant soldiers passed over from the side of Witigis to that of the emperor.

While these two sieges were going on, King Theudebert of the Franks, with a hundred thousand men, crossed the Alps into North Italy. The Goths, thinking he came to help them, made no preparations for defence, and fled in great confusion when their supposed friends suddenly made a fierce attack on their camp. Upon this the Romans naturally expected that the Franks would take their side, but they fell into the same trap as their enemies had done. King Theudebert's object was merely to enrich himself by robbery. After impartially plundering both camps and ravaging the country, he went back to his kingdom laden with booty; but he had lost so many men by disease that he had little reason to congratulate himself on the results of his treacherous conduct.

What miseries the Italian country people suffered during this terrible year will never be fully known. Fifty thousand peasants died of famine in the province of Picenum alone. The historian Procopius describes in vivid language the ghastly scenes of which he was an eye-witness. The victims of hunger, he tells us, first grew deadly pale, then livid, and finally black, "like the charred remains of torches."

Their eyes had the wild glare of insanity. It was rumoured that some had yielded to the temptation to save their own lives by feeding on human flesh. Thousands were seen lying dead on the ground, their hands still clutching the grass which they had been trying to pull up for food. The bodies lay unburied, but the birds disdained to touch them, for there was no flesh left upon the bones.

It is a horrible picture; but it helps us to understand in some degree what is really meant by the "famines" that are so often mentioned in passing as incidents in the wars of the centuries to which our story relates.

XXV: THE GOTHS LOSE RAVENNA

Belisarius was now master of the whole of Italy, except Ravenna itself and the northern provinces which form what is now called Lombardy. As soon as the siege of Auximum was ended, he marched with all his army to blockade the fortress capital in which King Witigis had taken refuge.

That Ravenna would fall sooner or later was certain. No doubt the great army of Goths who still remained within the walls might, if they had had an efficient general, have sallied forth and overwhelmed the besiegers with their superior numbers. But with Witigis for their commander nothing of the sort was to be feared; and Belisarius had captured the supplies of corn which were being brought to the city down the Po, while the Roman war-ships in the Adriatic prevented any provisions from being imported by sea. And just at this time the storehouses of corn in Ravenna were consumed by fire, through the treachery, it was said, of Queen Mataswintha. The king's nephew, Uraias, the captor of Milan, had set out with four thousand men to attack the besiegers, but nearly all his soldiers deserted to the enemy, and he was obliged to go back again into Liguria, and to leave Ravenna to its fate.

It seemed, therefore, that the game was nearly ended. But the calculations of Belisarius were disturbed by the arrival of ambassadors from Justinian, empowered to offer the Goths liberal terms of peace. Witigis was to remain king of the country north of the Po, and to retain half the royal treasure. The Goths, as well they might be, were delighted with the proposal, but they suspected that it might be only a trap, and, therefore, they refused to agree to it unless Belisarius would assure them in writing that he considered himself bound by the treaty. Belisarius, however, had set his heart on leading Witigis, as he had before led the Vandal king, a prisoner to Constantinople, and he was greatly mortified that he was to be robbed of his prize at the very moment when it was ready to fall into his hands. If the emperor chose to make peace on the proposed conditions, he could not prevent him from doing so, but at least he would be no party to the transaction. However, as an obstinate resistance on his part might seem disloyal to his master, he called a council of his officers, and asked their opinion. They unanimously declared their conviction that there was no use in carrying on the war further, and that it was best to make peace on the emperor's terms. Belisarius made them all sign a document expressing this conclusion, so that it might afterwards be seen that the responsibility for what he considered a foolish act did not rest with himself.

But in the meantime the Goths had been holding a council, and had come to a very strange decision. If Belisarius would have signed the treaty they could have trusted him, but in the honesty of Justinian they had no faith; and they feared that if Ravenna were surrendered the emperor would order them to be carried away to Constantinople or to Asia Minor. They therefore determined to offer the kingdom of Italy to Belisarius himself. The messengers who conveyed this proposal to the imperial general took with them a letter from Witigis, who was now tired of a kingship which he was unable to make a reality, and who entreated his conqueror to yield to the desire of the Goths.

Perhaps Belisarius may have entertained some thoughts of availing himself of the opportunity of making himself sovereign of the West. But his oath of allegiance to Justinian stood in the way, and the enterprise would besides have been full of perils. However, he saw that to pretend to agree to the Gothic proposal would be a means of obtaining the surrender of Ravenna. He therefore called a council of his officers, together with the emperor's ambassadors, and informed them that he had a plan by which he was confident of being able to save the whole of Italy for the empire, and to carry off Witigis and the Gothic nobles, with all their treasure, to Constantinople. "Supposing," he said, "that this plan should be successful, will you consider me justified in setting aside the emperor's instructions?" They all thought that such an achievement would be worthy of the highest praise. Belisarius then sent word to the Goths that he accepted their offer; and ambassadors were sent from Ravenna to the Roman camp with the request that he would swear that the garrison and citizens should suffer no injury, and that he would reign impartially over the Goths and the Italians.

Belisarius readily took the required oath, so far as it related to Ravenna, but as to his assumption of the kingship he said that he must first confer personally with Witigis and the nobles. The ambassadors made no difficulty in that point, for they thought it impossible that he could mean to draw back from an undertaking so gratifying to his own ambition.

So Belisarius, accompanied by the Gothic envoys, entered Ravenna with his army; and at the same time the Roman fleet, laden with provisions, landed at the port of Classis, and food was distributed to the hungry people. The Romans were heartily welcomed by the inhabitants of the city; but when the Gothic women saw the small-statured, mean-looking men (Huns, perhaps, for the most part) who followed Belisarius, they assailed their countrymen with shouts of derision, and even spat in their faces, for allowing themselves to be beaten by such foes. Belisarius faithfully kept his promise to allow no plundering of private property, but he took possession of the treasure stored up in the palace, and Witigis and some of his chief nobles were kept in honourable captivity until they could be conveyed to Constantinople. The Goths whose homes were south of the Po were permitted to return to their farms.

For some time Belisarius allowed it to be believed that he was going to accept the purple. By and by, however, he received from the emperor the command to return at once to Constantinople. The motive for this order was partly that Justinian had heard that the conduct of his general looked as if he were dallying with the thought of usurping the crown of Italy, and partly that the king of Persia had declared his intention of invading the empire. The Goths heard that Belisarius had been recalled, but took it for granted that he would disregard the summons. When, however, they found that he was actually making preparations for departure, they perceived that they had been imposed upon. Their attention then turned to the two Gothic generals who still held out in the north—Uraias the nephew of Witigis, and Hildibad. First, a deputation of Gothic nobles waited on Uraias at Pavia urging him to accept the crown. He refused the offer, saying that his regard for his uncle forbad him to occupy the throne during his uncle's lifetime, and, besides, that he thought that his relationship to one who had been so unfortunate a commander would prevent him from winning the confidence of the army. He recommended them, howev- however, to choose Hildibad, who was then in command at Verona, and who was a nephew of Theudis, king of the Visigoths.

Hildibad accordingly was sent for to Pavia, and was there invested with the purple robe and hailed as king. But before many days had passed away he began to doubt whether the Goths had done wisely in choosing him as king, and whether he himself had been wise in accepting their choice. Calling together a great assembly of the people, he urged them to make one last effort to persuade Belisarius to assume the diadem.

Accordingly, ambassadors were sent to Ravenna to try to induce Belisarius to change his mind. They reproached him in bitter, but not undeserved, terms with his breach of faith: they taunted him with want of spirit in "choosing to be a slave when he might be a king; "but it was all to no purpose. He replied that he was resolved never to assume the title of king or emperor so long as Justinian lived.

So Hildibad was confirmed in his new dignity, and Belisarius set out to present himself, with his Gothic prisoners and the spoils of the palace of Ravenna, before his imperial master. It was in June, 540, that he arrived at Constantinople—just after the empire had suffered a humiliating blow in the capture of Antioch by the Persian king. All the more welcome to Justinian and his subjects were the evidences of the Italian victories; but his jealousy of Belisarius was not set at rest, and he made no movement to offer the conqueror the honours of a Roman triumph. The enthusiasm of the people, however, made amends for the emperor's neglect. Whenever Belisarius appeared in public the streets were thronged with citizens eager to gaze upon their favourite hero, and to testify their admiration of him by shouts of applause.

Belisarius was now only thirty-five years of age, but he had reached the highest point of his fame. His secretary, Procopius, has chosen this moment to introduce his description of the great general's person and character. He tells us that Belisarius was tall and of well-proportioned frame, and in countenance handsome beyond all men. He was "as perfectly accessible and as unassuming in manner as if he had been some very poor and undistinguished man." His soldiers loved him for his sympathy in all their troubles, and his unequalled generosity in rewarding their deeds of bravery. And yet his discipline was very rigorous; he never tolerated any outrages upon the country people, nor any pillage or wanton destruction of crops, and the provisions required by his army were always paid for at liberal prices. His private life was stainlessly pure, and no one ever saw him excited by wine. His presence of mind was wonderful; no emergency ever took him by surprise. In danger he was cheerful and self-possessed he was the bravest of the brave, yet he never neglected any needful precaution. As he was never cast down by adversity, so he was never inflated by success, nor tempted to relax even for a moment the stern simplicity of his manner of life.

Such is the portrait which is drawn of this great man by one who had lived in close intimacy with him. It is a picture which leaves out all the shadows, and the character of Belisarius was not without grave faults. But in what Procopius says of his excellencies there seems to be very little exaggeration. Pity that so noble a man should have laboured for so unworthy an end as that of crushing a heroic nation out of existence, and subjecting Italy to the rapacious misgovernment of the Eastern Empire.

But though the task was unworthy of Belisarius, the success which he had thus far attained is a proof of his wonderful genius. If he had been allowed to return to Italy at once, a few more months would probably have seen the end of the struggle. Justinian, however, thought that the work which had been carried so far might safely be left to inferior hands to finish. It was a great mistake, the result of which, as we shall see, was that the struggle lasted on for twelve more years. The Goths were conquered at last, but at an immense cost of treasure and of human lives that might all have been spared had Justinian been wise in time.

Belisarius's two royal prisoners had no reason to complain of their treatment. King Witigis was made a "Patrician;" he lived in inglorious luxury at Constantinople for two more years, and then died, unlamented by his young widow—still only about twenty-two—who immediately became the wife of the emperor's nephew Germanus.

XXVI: NEW GOTHIC VICTORIES

The emperor thought that the conquest of Italy was now as good as complete, and he at once proceeded to turn his new acquisition to practical account. Justinian's notion of government was the extortion of money, to be spent in keeping up the splendour of his court, and in building magnificent churches, palaces, and fortresses all over the empire. Although he thought himself a great lover of justice, and took immense pains in reducing the Roman laws to a scientific system, he did very little to ensure the laws being justly administered in his dominions. Whether his subjects were prosperous or not was a secondary matter; the one great thing was that they should pay their taxes regularly. His revenue officers were allowed to oppress the people as they liked, and to enrich themselves with ill-gotten gains, if only they did not fail to send plenty of money to Constantinople. His policy was as shortsighted and foolish as it was wicked; a policy of "killing the goose that laid the golden eggs." As Theoderic had so well seen, the only lasting way to enrich the treasury of the state is to labour for the prosperity of the subjects. Justinian can hardly have been wholly blind to this truth, but his thought seems to have been that expressed in the famous words, "After me the deluge." While he lived the empire was outwardly brilliant and glorious: it was his successors that had to suffer the penalty which his recklessness had deserved.

The first thing that Justinian did after Belisarius's return was to send to Ravenna the most energetic and unscrupulous of his revenue officers, a certain Alexander, whom the people at Constantinople had spitefully nicknamed "Scissors," because, they said, he could clip a gold coin and leave it as round as it was before. This man seems to have been entrusted with almost absolute authority over the government of Italy, and he used his power to oppress all classes alike—not only the native Italians and the Goths who had submitted to the empire, but even the soldiers, whom he cheated out of their pay and punished by heavy fines for trifling or imaginary offences.

It is easy to guess what happened. The Goths who had accepted Roman rule were driven to revolt, and betook themselves to the camp of their native king. The Roman soldiers were unwilling to fight, and many of them deserted to the enemy. In a few months the little band under Hildibad had become a powerful army.

Justinian had appointed no commander-in-chief in the place of Belisarius; the generals in Italy were all equal in authority. They were too jealous of one another, and too intent on enriching themselves by the plunder of the people, to attempt any united movement against the Goths. One of them, however, who happened to be in Venetia with a large portion of the army, ventured to make an attack on Hildibad near Treviso, but was defeated and lost nearly all his men.

The Goths were greatly elated by this victory, and for a time they were full of enthusiastic devotion to their king. But Hildibad forfeited the affection of his people by causing the assassination of Uraias, the very man to whom he owed his kingdom.

He did not deny the deed, but pretended that he had detected Uraias in a plot to betray the nation to the Romans. Every one knew, however, that the real motive of the crime was that Hildibad's queen had been insulted by the wife of Uraias. The Goths did not attempt to depose Hildibad, because they felt that his bravery and ability made him indispensable; but their loyalty to him had received a fatal shock, and they no longer cared to obey him. One day, as the king reclined at the dinner table, in the presence of all his great nobles, a Gepid soldier, who had a private wrong to avenge, came behind him and smote off his head with his broadsword. Bitterly as the Goths had condemned Hildibad's shameful deed, they knew his value as a leader, and his death caused them for a while to lose all heart and hope.

During this time of discouragement, the Rugians, one of the smaller Gothic peoples, who had joined themselves to the Ostrogoths without mixing with them, took advantage of the opportunity to set up one of their own nobles, named Eraric, as "King of the Goths." The Ostrogoths did not like this, but they were so much in need of a leader that they were content to obey even the Rugian, if only he had shown himself a capable man. But Eraric simply remained inactive; and it was found out afterwards that he had been trying to make a bargain with Justinian for the betrayal of Italy.

The Gothic garrison of Treviso was commanded by a nephew of Hildibad, a young man of about twenty-five, whose name was Totila. After Eraric had been on the throne three or four months, without making any movement against the Romans, the Goths became impatient, and sent a deputation to offer the crown to Totila. He informed the delegates (so, at least, we are told) that he had entered into an agreement with the imperial general Constantian, to surrender the city and the army on a certain day. "But," he added, "if Eraric is put to death before the date fixed for the surrender, I am willing to accept the kingdom." Whether this story be true or not, it is certain that Eraric was soon afterwards assassinated, and Totila became king.

If Totila did indeed obtain his throne by breaking his pledged word and by instigating an assassination, the beginning of his reign contrasts strangely with his after history. His character was marked by a chivalrous sense of honour, and a magnanimity towards his enemies which, in that age, were rare indeed. One or two of his recorded actions, indeed, seem unworthy of the man's noble nature; but we must remember that his life has been written by no friend or countryman, but by a foreigner and an enemy, who nevertheless could not refrain from expressing with emphasis the admiration he felt for the uprightness and the humanity of this "barbarian."

It should be mentioned here that Totila seems on becoming king to have changed his name to Baduila. Or possibly the latter may have been his real name, and Totila only a nickname. At any rate he was known to his countryman by both names, though Baduila is the only one which appears on his coins. However, in history he is always called Totila; the other name would have been unknown to us but for the coins and a solitary mention in Jordanes.

When Justinian heard how the imperial cause in Italy was being ruined through the inaction of the generals, he wrote to them in such severe terms that they felt something must be done. So they all gathered together (eleven there seem to have been) at Ravenna, and devised plans for making a combined movement against the Goths. They determined to begin with an attack on Verona; but their cowardice and blundering caused the scheme to fail, and they marched southwards in all haste as far as Faventia. Here they were overtaken by Totila, and a battle took place. Although the Goths had only five thousand men, while the Romans had twelve thousand, Totila was victorious; the imperial army was completely dispersed, with a great loss both in slain and in prisoners. Another battle in the valley of Mucella (Mugello) had a similar ending, and Totila led his army into the south, capturing one city after another, and making the farmers pay into his treasury both the rents due to their landlords and the taxes that were due to the emperor. In other respects, however, he treated the people with so much kindness that he won a great deal of goodwill from those who had suffered from the lawless behaviour of the Roman armies. At last, in the summer of 542, he encamped before Naples, which a certain Conon was holding for the emperor, with a garrison of one thousand men.

The emperor's army in Italy was in a state of general mutiny on account of pay being in arrear, so that the generals could hardly have done anything for the relief of Naples even if they had wished. But apparently they were only too glad of the excuse for remaining inactive in the fortified cities. Justinian, however, sent a considerable land and sea force from Constantinople, but its commanders were no match for the genius of Totila. The fleet was defeated, and the most important of the leaders of the expedition, Demetrius, was paraded in front of the walls with a halter round his neck, and made to harangue the garrison and the citizens, in order to persuade them to surrender. The Gothic king himself also made a speech to the besieged, promising that if they would yield neither soldier nor citizen should be any the worse for their submission.

The temptation was strong, for the defenders were hard pressed by famine and disease; but the garrison was unwilling to seem false to their sovereign, and begged that thirty days' truce might be allowed them. If no help came from the emperor within that time, they promised to surrender. Totila astonished the messengers by his reply. "By all means," he said; "I grant you three months' delay, if you choose to take it." And he undertook to make no attempt to storm the city during that time. He knew that the defenders would find it hard to struggle with the famine for even one month longer. Totila's calm confidence made them feel that the hope of succour was vain indeed; and a few days afterwards the gates were opened.

As soon as Totila entered the city, he saw from the appearance of the inhabitants that they had suffered terribly from famine. He had had, like Procopius, the opportunity of observing the effects of hunger on the human frame, and he knew that if those who were enfeebled by long privation were at once freely supplied with food they were likely to be killed by plenty. With a thoughtful kindness which, as Procopius says, "could neither have been expected from an enemy nor from a barbarian," he ordered that every person in the city should receive a daily ration of food, at first very small, but gradually increased until the danger had ceased to exist. Then, and not before, he allowed the city gates to be thrown open, and proclaimed that the inhabitants were free to go or to remain as they chose.

Conon and most of his soldiers were placed on board ships, and informed that they were at liberty to sail to any port they preferred. They were ashamed to go to Constantinople, and tried to make for Rome. The wind, however, was contrary, and they were obliged to remain at Naples. Naturally they felt very uneasy, for they thought that after Totila had given them one fair chance of escape, he would now consider himself entitled to treat them as prisoners.

But the "barbarian's" generosity again surpassed expectation. Sending for Conon, he assured him that he and his companions might consider themselves as among friends; that until it was possible for them to sail the Gothic markets were open to them, and that he would do everything he could to ensure their comfort. As, however, the wind continued unfavourable, Totila at length recommended them to make the journey by land, and actually provided them with beasts of burden, money for travelling expenses, and a Gothic escort. He did all this, though he knew that Conon and his men were going to increase the garrison of the city to which it was his intention shortly to lay siege. Certainly he had given his kingly word that the soldiers should be allowed to march away "whither they pleased;" but it is seldom that any conqueror has observed a capitulation in this splendid fashion, either before or since. Even more rigorously than Belisarius himself, Totila repressed all acts of outrage on the part of his army. No matter who was the offender, the penalty was death. One officer of high rank, and very popular among his comrades, had committed a crime of this kind, and had been placed under arrest. The chiefs of the army implored Totila to spare the man's life. The king listened courteously and calmly to what they had to say, and then, in grave and earnest tones he expressed his conviction that only so long as the Goths kept themselves pure from injustice could they expect the Divine blessing to rest on their cause. He reminded them how brilliant had been the fortunes of the nation under the righteous rule of Theoderic; how, under Theodahad and his successors, the Goths, forsaking the policy of justice and humanity to which they owed their greatness, had brought themselves to the lowest point of humiliation; and how since they had again begun to act in a nobler spirit their prosperity had returned. Would they, he asked, with this experience before them, insist on making the nation an accomplice in this man's guilt? The Gothic chiefs were unable to resist this reasoning, and the criminal underwent his doom.

"While Totila was behaving in this manner, the Roman generals and their soldiers were plundering the property of those who were subject to their sway, and indulging without restraint in every kind of insolence and excess." We are quoting Procopius, who points out with indignant eloquence the contrast between the "civilized" Romans and their "barbarian" foe. In Rome itself the citizens were bitterly regretting their change of masters. Totila knew of the existence of this feeling, and resolved to work upon it. First he sent a letter to the senate, charging them, if they repented of the crime and folly of their treason against the Goths, to earn their pardon by a voluntary surrender of the city. It is strange that the imperialist commander should have allowed such a letter to be delivered at all; however, he would not permit the senate to return any answer.

A few days passed, and one morning it was found that placards, signed with Totila's name, had been nailed up during the night in all the most frequented parts of the city. They announced that the Goths would shortly march to the capture of Rome, and contained a solemn declaration that no harm should be done to the citizens. The officers of the imperial army tried in vain to find out who had put up these placards, but it was suspected that it must have been done by the Arian clergy, who were therefore banished from the city.

Soon afterwards the emperor Justinian received a letter, signed by all his generals in Italy, expressing their opinion that the imperial cause in that country was hopeless, and that, the attempt to oppose the victorious progress of the Goths had better be abandoned. Very unwillingly the emperor had to yield to the conviction that his Italian dominions could be preserved only by the help of the great general who, four years before, had all but crushed the Gothic monarchy, and whose premature recall was now proved to have been a fatal mistake. And so Belisarius received orders to go to Italy to retrieve the disasters which had befallen the imperial arms.

XXVII: THE FAILURE OF BELISARIUS

It was not merely the old suspicion which made Justinian unwilling to send Belisarius to Italy. The great general had recently fallen into disgrace with his imperial master. In the year 542, Justinian had been smitten with plague, and it was said that while he was on what was supposed to be his deathbed Belisarius had formed a plot for the purpose of succeeding him on the throne, to the exclusion of the Empress Theodora. The emperor, however, recovered, and as he believed the accusations against Belisarius, he deprived him of all his honours and of a large part of his property. He also took away from him his famous "household" of soldiers, and sent them away on foreign service. Afterwards Justinian had professed to forgive Belisarius, and had conferred on him the office of "Count of the Imperial Stable." But he still treated him with haughty coldness, and even in making him the offer of the Italian command he seems not to have been able to conceal the distrust which he felt. Belisarius, however, was tired of inaction, and eager to prove his loyalty, and he accepted the appointment with gladness. He even promised, it is said, that he would himself supply all the money which the expedition might cost. Perhaps it was this promise that overcame the avaricious emperor's reluctance to avail himself of the services of the general whom he distrusted.

It was in May, 544, that Belisarius went to take the command of the Italian armies. He remained five years in Italy, and when he at length returned it was with the consciousness of failure: the Gothic power was still unbroken.

How was it that the great general, who a few years before had so brilliantly, with a mere handful of men, wrested Italy from the grasp of the gigantic host of Witigis, was no longer able to contend against a foe whose army was inferior in numbers to his own. The reasons, no doubt, were many. It is possible that the troubles through which he had passed had in some degree broken his spirit and dulled his brain. Something, too, may be set down to the fact that his adversary now was a resolute and skilful youth, and not a feeble and purposeless old man. But there were other causes which were more important still. The Roman soldiers in Italy were thoroughly demoralized by the shameful oppression which they had undergone at the hands of Justinian's governors, and by the spectacle of the sloth and rapacity of their own commanders. Great numbers of them had deserted to Totila, in whose service they might at least be sure of their pay. Those who remained were rather a mob than an army; they professed to be on the emperor's side, because of the opportunity that was allowed them for pillaging and insulting the Italian country people, but in the field they were worse than useless. Then, too, Belisarius had associated with him other commanders with authority nearly equal to his own; and they were little inclined to submit to a chief whom they knew to be under the emperor's frown. His plans were thwarted continually, and he was sometimes obliged to defer to the opinions of his subordinates against his own wiser judgment.

Even under these miserable circumstances Belisarius managed to gain some advantages over the enemy, and to delay for a long time Totila's march to Rome. But when a year had passed he felt that the Goths would never be conquered with such means as he had. He therefore wrote an urgent letter to the emperor, begging him to send to Italy an army worthy of the name, and money for the heavy arrears of pay that were due to the barbarian troops. To show to Justinian emphatically how hopeless he considered the struggle to be without further resources, he left Italy altogether, and waited at Durazzo, on the other side of the Adriatic, until the soldiers should arrive from Constantinople.

While Belisarius was waiting, Rome was once more undergoing the miseries of a close blockade. The commander of the emperor's garrison was Bessa, the Thracian Goth, a man who in the past had shown himself a brave soldier, but whose hard-hearted avarice now added to the wretchedness of the unfortunate Romans. The hardships which the citizens had to endure were a matter of satisfaction to him, for they enabled him to enrich himself by selling, at outrageous prices, the provisions of which he had collected an ample store.

When the senators found that there was little prospect of speedy relief, they determined to try whether they could induce Totila to agree to favourable terms of surrender. They chose as their ambassador a deacon named Pelagius, who had gained great esteem among the people by the generosity with which he had supplied the necessities of the poor during the siege. His instructions were to ask Totila for a truce of a few days, and to promise, if he would agree to their conditions, that at the end of that period the city should be given up, unless an imperial army arrived in the meantime for its relief

Totila received Pelagius with a great appearance of respect and kindness, but said that before they entered into any discussion it must be understood that on three points his mind was firmly made up. "In the first place," said he, "you must not ask me to let the Sicilians go unpunished for their treachery. Secondly, I am resolved that the walls of Rome shall be destroyed. This will be far better for the citizens themselves, because they will then be in no danger of having again to suffer the calamity of a siege. The third point is that I will listen to no proposals for restoring to their former masters the slaves who have taken service in the Gothic army. I have pledged my word to them that they shall be free; if I broke faith towards these unfortunate people, how could you trust in my observing any treaty I made with you? Apart from these three points, however, I am ready to consider favourably any proposition you have to make."

When he heard these words Pelagius lost his temper, and said fiercely that to lay down such conditions of discussion was a gross insult, and that after this he could only regard Totila's show of politeness as a downright mockery. "I came," he said, "as a suppliant; but now I disdain to make any request of you—I will address my prayers to God, whose it is to humble the arrogance of the mighty." And so Pelagius went back to the city with his message undelivered.

Days passed away, and still no succour came. Men were dying of hunger in the city, while the soldiers were well-fed, and their officers still kept up their accustomed luxury. Assembling in a body, the citizens surrounded the house of Bessa, and by their uproar compelled him to come out and listen to their complaints. They besought him either to let them go out of the city, or to supply them with food, or, if he would do neither, to kill them and end their miseries. Bessa replied coolly that to find them food was impossible; to kill them would be wicked, and to let them go would be dangerous. But he ended his speech by saying that he had certain information that Belisarius was speedily coming with a new army. His manner convinced them that he was speaking the truth, and the crowd dispersed without making any attempt at violence.

The news was indeed true. After every possible excuse for delay had been exhausted, Justinian had at last despatched an army to Durazzo. As soon as it arrived, Belisarius embarked with the troops, and after a sail of five days his ships cast anchor in the port of Rome.

But the famine continued to do its fearful work, until at last an incident happened which compelled Bessa to relax his cruel rule. A certain man in the city, worn out by the cries of his five children for bread which he could not give them, at last bade them follow him, saying that he would find them food. He led them through the streets till he came to a bridge over the Tiber, and then, wrapping his cloak round his head, he plunged into the river and was drowned before the eyes of his children and of the crowd. The city rang with cries of indignation against the Roman officers. Bessa perceived that the hungry populace was becoming dangerous. He gave permission that the citizens might go whither they would, and supplied them with money for their journey. All but a very few accepted the offer, but vast numbers of them died of hunger on the way, or fell into the hands of the enemy and were killed.

The first concern of Belisarius was to try to get Rome supplied with provisions. But his plan required the help of Bessa; and Bessa sullenly refused to obey his orders, and the well-laid scheme came to nothing. After this failure Belisarius prepared for an attack on the Gothic camp; and here again he would have succeeded but for the disobedience of his officers. Ten miles from Rome, and half way between the city and the port, Totila had built a wooden bridge across the river, and had erected upon it two towers, which he manned with four hundred of his bravest soldiers. Belisarius, leaving his wife Antonina and his treasures at the port, in charge of one of his officers named Isaac, set out with a fleet of vessels, headed by two fireships, to destroy the obstacle with which Totila sought to prevent his approach. He sent word to Bessa to second his attack by a sally from the gates of Rome, and he strictly charged Isaac on no account to leave his post.

The attack on the bridge was successful: one of the towers took fire, and two hundred Goths perished in the flames. But Bessa did not make the expected sortie; and Isaac, heedless of his orders, foolishly made an attack on a strong body of the enemy, and was defeated and captured.

The news that Isaac was a prisoner was brought to Belisarius in the midst of his victory. He rushed to the conclusion that the port must have been taken, and that his dearly-loved wife was in the hands of the enemy. "For the first time in his life," says Procopius, "he was struck with panic." Leaving unfinished the work he had so brilliantly begun, he hurried back to the port. His wife was safe; but the anguish he had undergone, and the mortification at the failure of his plan, so worked upon him that he fell into an illness, and was for a long time helpless and in danger of his life. And while Belisarius lay on his bed of sickness, the Asinarian gate was opened by the treachery of four sentinels, and Rome fell once more into the hands of the Goths.

It was on the evening of December 17, 546, that Totila and his army passed through the gate. Totila did not feel very sure that the four sentinels were not leading him into a trap, and so he caused his men to remain in a compact body near the gates until daybreak. In the night the news was brought to him that the imperial army and its leaders had fled from the city, and some of his officers urged him to pursue them. "Let them go," he said; "what could we wish for more than for the enemy to run away?"

When morning came it was plain that the report was true. The city was deserted, except for a few soldiers who had taken refuge in the churches, and about five hundred of the citizens. Totila's first act was to repair to the church of St. Peter to give thanks to God for his victory. While he was thus engaged, the deacon Pelagius brought him word that the Goths were slaughtering the unresisting Romans in the streets, and holding the book of the Gospels in his hand, he implored him to remember the Christian law of mercy. "'So, after all, Pelagius," said Totila, with a smile, "you are coming to me as a suppliant." "Yes," was the deacon's answer, "because God has made me your slave. I beseech you, O our master, to spare the lives of your slaves." Totila at once sent out strict orders that there was to be no more violence, but he permitted his soldiers to plunder the city. A great quantity of spoil was taken, especially in the palace occupied by Bessa, who in his hasty flight had had to leave behind him all his ill-gotten gains.

Amongst the few once wealthy Romans who remained in the city, and who, it is said, were actually reduced to beg their bread from their conquerors, was Rusticiana, the widow of Boethius. Some of the Goths demanded that she should be put to death, because she had given money to the Roman officers to induce them to destroy the statues of Theoderic. But Totila insisted that the aged lady should be treated with all respect.

On the following day Totila harangued his soldiers on his favourite theme— the importance of justice and mercy, as their only hope of obtaining the blessing of God on their cause. Soon afterwards he sent Pelagius to Constantinople with other envoys to ask Justinian to agree to terms of peace; but the only answer the emperor would give was that Belisarius had full powers to carry on or to end the war as seemed to him best, and that the Goths must treat with him. But we do not find that Totila attempted to open negotiations with Belisarius; probably he knew too well the iron resolution of his great antagonist to entertain any hope of success.

The failure of the mission to Justinian was a great disappointment to Totila; and just about the same time he learned that an expedition which he had sent into the south of Italy had been defeated with great slaughter. Under the exasperation produced by these events, he determined to take his revenge on Rome —to burn down its magnificent buildings, and to "turn the city into a sheep-pasture." Perhaps he would really have disgraced his glorious career by this barbarous deed; but when

Belisarius heard of his intention, he sent a letter to the Gothic king, asking him this pointed question: "Do you choose to appear in history branded as the destroyer of the noblest city in the world, or honoured as its preserver?" The messengers who bore the letter reported that Totila read it over many times, as if he was learning it by heart. After deep consideration, he returned to Belisarius the assurance that Rome should be spared. The incident is honourable alike to each of the two men.

Now that the long siege was over, Totila was able to turn his attention to the other parts of his kingdom, which had been suffering the ravages of the imperial armies. He came to the strange resolve of abandoning Rome altogether, destroying a large part of the walls so that it could no longer be available to the enemy as a fortress; he caused the senators to accompany him on his march, and sent the scanty remnants of the citizens, with their wives and children, away into Campania. Many strange things have happened in the history of Rome, but surely one of the strangest of all is that the vast city, with all its noble buildings still uninjured, should have remained for many weeks without any inhabitants.

At first Totila left behind him the greater part of his army to keep a check on the movements of Belisarius, while he led the remainder into the south of Italy. But before long, for some reason not quite clear, he found it necessary to march with all his available force towards Ravenna, and the neighbourhood of Rome was left unguarded.

And now a rather amusing incident took place. Belisarius hurried up from the port, and meeting with no resistance, took possession of Rome. Of course there was no time to rebuild the fortification properly, but by setting men to work day and night, he managed within three weeks to erect a rough wall in the places where Totila had destroyed the original defences. The inhabitants flocked back to the city, which once more regained something like its accustomed aspect.

When Totila heard what had happened he marched hastily with all his army to Rome. When he arrived Belisan'us had not yet been able to put new gates in the place of those that had been destroyed; but the city was defended with so much spirit that after three furious attempts to take it by storm the Goths were compelled to abandon the undertaking. Hitherto, as Procopius says, the Goths had almost worshipped their young king as a god; but now they angrily reproached him for not having either destroyed Rome or else occupied it himself They did not rise in rebellion against Totila: one of their national virtues was that of faithfulness to their chosen leaders, even when unsuccessful. But their trust in his wisdom and fortune were shaken, and they fought no longer with their old enthusiasm and hopefulness.

Belisarius completed the fortifications of the city, and sent the keys of the new gates to Justinian as an evidence of his success. But although the reoccupation of Rome was a clever exploit, it was more showy than useful, and did not help to bring the end of the war any nearer. After several months more of unprofitable skirmishing, Belisarius felt that the Goths were not to be conquered by a general who had no means of commanding the obedience of his subordinates. Weary of the hopeless struggle, he allowed his wife to go to Constantinople to solicit his recall. Justinian granted the request, and early in the year 549 Belisarius quitted Italy to return to it no more.

His after history does not concern us here, but we may briefly say that he lived sixteen years longer, during which he performed one exploit worthy of his earlier fame, in saving Constantinople from the Huns. Near the end of his life he fell into disgrace once more on account of a suspicion of treason, but he was again restored to favour, and died in the enjoyment of all his wealth and honours. It is hardly needful to mention the idle tale that in old age and blindness Belisarius had to beg his bread from door to door.

XXVIII: THE RUIN OF THE OSTROGOTHS

The departure of Belisarius was soon followed by the loss of Rome. Again, as on the last occasion, it was through treason that the city was delivered into the hands of the Goths. The Isaurian soldiers amongst the garrison were discontented on account of their pay being long in arrear. If we may believe Procopius, they had received nothing from the imperial treasury for several years; though doubtless they had been allowed to make good the deficiency by the plunder of the Italian peasantry. They heard that their four countrymen who in the last siege had opened the Asinarian gate to Totila had received princely rewards for their betrayal, and they resolved to follow the example. Totila readily accepted their proposal, and at the time agreed upon a sudden sound of trumpets was heard, which caused the garrison to hasten to the portion of the walls skirting the river, expecting that a great attack was about to be made from that side. Meanwhile, the Gate of St. Paul, on the northwest, was opened by the Isaurian traitors, and Totila and the vanguard of his army marched into the city. The imperial soldiers fled in all directions through the other gates, but Totila had posted strong bodies of men to intercept their flight, and very few of them escaped the sword.

There was, however, one brave officer amongst the besieged, Paul of Cilicia, who with his four hundred men took refuge in the fortress-tomb of Hadrian, and prepared to hold it against all attacks. But the Goths were wiser than to attempt an assault. They closely surrounded the fortress, and remained quiet, waiting for hunger to do its work. At length the brave four hundred found that they could hold out no longer, and resolved to sally forth in one desperate charge against the foe. Feeling that they were about to rush upon certain destruction, they embraced each other, and "kissed each other with the kiss of those doomed to death;" and then they issued from the gate of the castle, expecting to perish, but determined to sell their lives as dearly as they could. Before, however, they reached the Gothic lines, they were met by a flag of truce, bringing the unlooked-for offer from the Gothic king, that he would either send them unhurt to Constantinople, on condition of laying down their arms and giving their promise never more to fight against the Goths, or, if they chose, he would accept them as soldiers in his own army, on an equal footing with his own countrymen. Brave men as they were, life was sweet, and they hailed with joy the sudden deliverance. At first they asked to be sent to Constantinople; but when they thought of the cold reception they would meet with there, and the dangers of the journey to unarmed men, they came to the conclusion that Totila was a better master to serve than Justinian, and so they agreed to be enrolled in the Gothic ranks. There were also four hundred other soldiers who instead of escaping from the city had taken refuge in the churches, and these too joined themselves to Totila's army.

A few months before these events, Totila had sent an embassy to one of the Prankish kings, asking the hand of his daughter in marriage. The ambassadors not only brought back a refusal, but also a very insulting message. "Tell your master," said king Theudebert, "that we cannot recognize as King of Italy a man who could not keep Rome when he had it, but allowed it to fall into the hands of his enemies." Totila was deeply stung by this taunt, and he resolved to prove to the world that he was not unworthy to be the master of Rome. He carefully restored all the buildings and the portions of the walls that had been destroyed, and sent for the senators who were imprisoned in Campania. The city assumed its old aspect, and for the last time the ancient public games were celebrated in the presence of a sovereign who sat on the throne of the Western Caesars.

Again the Goths were masters in Italy; the scattered remnants of the imperial armies showed little sign of being able to offer any serious resistance. Totila now sent an embassy to Justinian, offering to become his vassal, on "condition of being recognized as the ruler of Italy. If the emperor had consented, perhaps the Gothic monarchy might even yet have established itself, and the whole course of the history of Southern Europe would have been different. But Justinian refused to admit the ambassadors to his presence, and they returned without obtaining any answer.

Totila now set out to fulfil his cherished project of punishing the Sicilians for their faithlessness. Two years were spent in the plunder of the wealthy cities of Sicily, in the conquest of the islands of Sardinia and Corsica; and in victorious invasions of the emperor's domains in Greece.

But amid all these victories, the Goths received tidings that filled them with dismay. Justinian, stirred up to action by the entreaties of Pope Vigilius, had prepared a new expedition which he had placed under the command of his nephew Germanus. One reason why the Goths found this news so disquieting was that the new commander was the husband of their own princess Mataswintha, who, it was reported, was to accompanying him to Italy. The thought of having to fight against a descendant of Theoderic was not a welcome one, and it was greatly to be feared that many of Totila's soldiers might be led by this feeling to desert their standards. Besides this, Germanus had proved himself a very able general, and if he had not the genius of Belisarius he was far better supported than that great commander had been. Justinian had, to every one's surprise, granted immense sums of money for the support of the army, and Germanus himself had contributed largely out of his private fortune. The high pay that was offered had tempted great numbers of Gepids, Herules, Lombards, and other barbarians, to enlist under Germanus, so that the expedition which now threatened the Gothic power was by far the most formidable that Justinian had ever sent into the field.

But it was not fated that Germanus should be the conqueror of Totila. Before he had crossed the Adriatic, he fell sick and died, widely regretted throughout the empire, for he was known as a man of pure and noble character, and there were many who hoped that he would succeed Justinian, and that his accession would be the beginning of happier days for the heavily burdened people.

Shortly after his death Mataswintha bore a son, who was named Germanus like his father. It has been supposed that there was a party among the Goths who desired that this young Germanus might some day be installed as Western Caesar, or "King of Goths and Italians," with the consent and under the protection of the court of Constantinople. However, he seems himself to have had no ambition of that kind. He lived a quiet and honoured life for fifty years, and then became involved in conspiracies, on account of which he and his only child (a daughter) were put to death in the year 604. And so the line of the great Theoderic came to an end.

The question which Justinian had now to consider was, who should be appointed commander of the Italian army in his nephew's place. It was above all things necessary that the new leader should be one whose authority all the other officers would obey without dispute. To raise one of the generals to the supreme command would have been to provoke again the jealousies and the disobedience which had been fatal to the enterprise of Belisarius. Justinian solved the difficulty by offering the headship of the army to the highest official of his court, the chamberlain Narses, the same whose meddling in the Italian war twelve years before, and its unfortunate results, we have already described. He was now seventy-five years of age, and feeble in body; but that he was still vigorous in mind was proved by the event. For it was he who achieved the task which Belisarius, in the prime of his manhood, had failed to accomplish —the ruin of the Gothic nation, and the establishment of the empire in Italy.

When Justinian proposed to Narses that he should assume the command in Italy, he refused to do so except on one condition. He must have unlimited supplies of money, so that he might raise an army absolutely overwhelming in numbers—even the army collected under Germanus seemed to him insufficient —and that when he arrived in Italy he might reconcile the mutinous soldiers and win back the deserters by giving them their full arrears of pay. The emperor knew his aged servant's faithfulness and his wisdom, and he had learned by bitter experience that too much parsimony was a great mistake. The request of Narses was granted, and before long he had arrived at the head of the Adriatic with such an army as had never before been collected in the name of Justinian. The soldiers came from every quarter of the eastern empire, and from many barbarous peoples beyond its bounds. Even distant Persia was represented by a large body of deserters, who served under a grandson of the Persian king.

What Narses at first intended to do was to enter Italy from the north, and march southward along the middle of the peninsula. But here he met with unexpected difficulties. Totila had sent the bulk of his army to Verona, commanded by a general named Teia, who had taken vigorous means to render the invasion impossible by destroying the roads, and making ditches and embankments. Besides this, the Franks were occupying Venetia with a strong force, and they refused to allow the passage of the emperor's army, because—that was the reason they gave—their enemies the Lombards were serving in it. It was plain that if Narses persisted in his original plan he would have to fight not only with the Goths, but with the powerful army of the Franks.

But what else was he to do? He had not ships enough to transport his army by sea; and it seemed impossible to march along the coast, because there were twelve broad rivers to be crossed. A council or war was called, at which one of the generals, John the grandson of Vitalian, suggested a clever plan that solved the difficulty. The army was to travel on foot close to the sea-shore, and the ships and boats were to sail alongside of it, so that when there was a river to be crossed a bridge of boats could be made for the soldiers to pass over.

This ingenious contrivance was adopted, and the army arrived at Ravenna without meeting with any resistance. Here they rested for nine days. During this period of repose, Narses received a letter from the commander of the Gothic garrison at Ariminum, named Usdrila [Austrila?], sneeringly asking whether the Romans meant to hide themselves behind stone walls, and challenging them to come out and fight like men. Narses laughed heartily at this foolish letter, and when his men were sufficiently rested he set out on his march to Ariminum. At the bridge over the river Marecchia there was a skirmish, in which the boastful Usdrila was killed, and his head carried into the Roman camp. Narses did not pause to attempt the capture of Ariminum, but hastened along the Flaminian Way, till he came near to the little town of Taginae (Tadino). Here Totila, who had been joined by the army of Tela, had pitched his camp.

Narses now sent some of his officers to the Gothic king, urging him to surrender, and not to risk a battle against overwhelming numbers. Totila would not hear of submission, and the envoys then requested him to fix a day for the battle. "This day week," he replied. But Narses was not to be deceived by such a simple trick as this, and when on the very next day the Goths came in force to attack the Roman camp they found the enemy expecting them, and were heavily repulsed.

Both sides now prepared themselves for a great pitched battle, and the commanders made speeches to their men to encourage them for the struggle which they felt would decide the fate of Italy. The Goths were terribly cast down by the sight of the vast numbers and the splendid equipment of the Roman army, and all Totila's eloquence was needed to keep them from despair.

"Fellow soldiers," he said, "this is our last struggle. If we win this battle, Justinian's power is crushed, and our freedom is secure. Show yourselves men this day, for to-morrow it will be too late; spare neither your horses nor your arms, for whether victors or vanquished you will never need them more. Remember that there is no safety for you but in victory; to flee is to seek destruction. Let not the multitude of the enemy dismay you; we are a nation fighting for our freedom, for our country, for all that makes life precious; they are a hireling band of Huns and Herules, and people of all races and tongues, divided by ancient hatreds and bound together by no common interest but their pay."

The two armies were now drawn up in battle array. The Romans remained quiet, expecting the Goths to begin the attack. But Totila found it necessary to delay, as a body of two thousand men, on whose help he had counted, had failed to arrive at the appointed time. In order to gain time, he sent messengers to Narses pretending that he wished to treat for peace; but Narses refused to agree for a conference, knowing that the request could only be a stratagem. Meanwhile, in order to distract the attention of his own men, Totila rode in front of the Gothic lines, clothed in golden armour and purple robes, and displayed his skill in horsemanship, galloping round in circles, throwing up his spear and catching it as he rode, and other such feats—"just as if he had been trained for the circus," says Procopius. But about noon the two thousand arrived, and then Totila retired to his tent and changed his dress, while his soldiers took their midday meal. As soon as this was over, he marshalled his men, and made a sudden assault upon the Roman lines, thinking that after his temporary retirement he should take the enemy by surprise. But Narses guessed his intention, and the Romans remained in perfect order, their food being served out to them as they stood in the ranks.

Totila's attack was badly planned : but no skill in generalship would have been of much avail against an enemy so far superior in numbers and in arms. Narses had neglected no means of stimulating the valour of his troops. Before the battle he had ridden through the camp, accompanied by men who bore aloft on their lances collars, bracelets, and horse-trappings of gold, which were to be the prizes of those who distinguished themselves on that day. His barbarian soldiers could understand this language, if they could not understand his spoken words, and barbarians and Romans vied with each other in their eagerness to win the promised rewards. The Goths fought with all the energy of despair, and though the battle went against them from the first, it was not till far on in the night that they were driven from the field. Six thousand of them were killed, in the battle; many thousands more were taken prisoners, and afterwards massacred in cold blood.

After the fight was over, the king of the Goths was making his escape from the battle-field accompanied by two or three of his faithful friends, when Asbad, the chief of the Gepids, rushed at him with his lance, not knowing, in the darkness, who he was. One of the Goths indignantly exclaimed, "Dog! would you kill your own master?" Asbad knew then whom he was attacking, and thrust at Totila with all his strength, but himself fell wounded immediately after. The Goths carried their master as far as Caprae, a village seven miles away, where he shortly afterwards breathed his last. His companions buried him secretly near the village where he died, but his grave was not destined to remain unmolested. A few days after the battle, a Gothic woman betrayed the secret of the king's resting-place to some of the imperial officers. Eager to convince themselves that Totila was really dead, they opened the grave, and found that the woman's story was true. They then committed the body again to the earth, having first despoiled it of its clothing and ornaments, which were afterwards sent to Justinian as evidence that his enemy was no more.

Such was the sad end of this gallant young king, after a reign of eleven years. We cannot, as some have done, call him the greatest of the Goths. He had neither Theoderic's unfailing sagacity nor his genius for command. But he had the same passion for justice, the same lofty ideal of kingship; and though the lustre of his career is dimmed by more than one act of cruel revenge, his character is marked on the whole by a chivalrous high-mindedness to which it would be hard to find a parallel in his own age. There are few personages of history whose adverse fate so irresistibly excites our sympathy as does that of Totila—the Harold Godwin's son, as Theoderic is the Alfred, of Gothic history.

After the disaster of Tadino, the remnant of the Gothic army retired into Northern Italy, and there Teia was chosen king of the Goths. Narses pressed forward to Rome, and after a short siege the city was once more captured—for the fifth time during Justinian's reign. Perhaps never before had the Italian people been so miserable as at this time of so-called Roman victory. The barbarians in the imperial army, we are told "treated as enemies all who came in their way," that is, they murdered and plundered indiscriminately both friend and foe. And the Gothic soldiers who garrisoned the yet uncaptured cities, fired with revengeful passion, and no longer having Totila to restrain them, committed dreadful cruelties upon the unoffending Romans. King Teia himself ordered the murder of three hundred youths of the noblest Roman families, whom Totila had detained as hostages.

"The Gothic kingdom had received its death-blow at the battle of Tadino; but it was not yet dead, and its last struggles were terrible. Teia saw clearly that there was little hope of contending unaided with the mighty army of Narses; he tried hard to induce King Theudebald of the Franks to become his ally, and offered him large sums of money as a bribe. But the Franks were not to be tempted: their game was to wait until the Goths were beaten and the imperial army weakened by the fierce conflict that was coming, and then to try to conquer Italy for themselves.

When Teia found that no Frankish aid was to be hoped for, he marched with all his army to the rescue of Totila's brother Aligern, who was besieged by a strong body of the enemy in the fortress-town of Cumae, where a great part of the Gothic treasure was deposited. Narses with all the imperial army hastened to meet him. Teia wished to delay the unequal combat as long as he could: and he pitched his camp in a strong position near the foot of Vesuvius, protected by a deep and narrow ravine, at the bottom of which flows the river Sarno. The two armies faced each other on opposite sides of the ravine, and harassed each other by volleys of missiles; but Narses could neither dislodge the Goths from their position by force, nor induce them to abandon it by stratagem. The Gothic camp was so placed that it could be kept constantly supplied with provisions by sea; and it was Teia's intention to hold out until—vain hope!— Fortune should in some unknown way declare herself in his favour.

But after two months the admiral of the Gothic fleet turned traitor, and delivered into the hands of the Romans the stores which he was bringing to his countrymen. The Goths now began to feel the pressure of hunger, and were obliged to forsake their impregnable position. At first they betook themselves to the heights of the Mons Lactarius, now Monte Lettere, where they were still secure from attack ; but their hopes of being able to find food proved delusive. But still they scorned the thought of surrender to the Romans, and their only alternative was to risk everything in one desperate assault on the enemy. Sending away their horses, they suddenly rushed on foot upon the astonished Romans. The battle that ensued was terrible. "Not one of Homer's heroes," says Procopius, "ever performed greater miracles of valour than did Tela on that day." After fighting for many hours in the front of his army, he called to his armour-bearer to change his shield, which was heavy with the weight of twelve broken spears. Left for a moment unprotected, he was pierced in the breast by a dart. So fell the last Gothic king of Italy. The Romans cut off his head and displayed it on a pole, to encourage their own soldiers and to dismay their enemies. But even the loss of their king was ineffectual to abate the desperate fury of the Goths; they fought on until the fall of night, and at daybreak they renewed the struggle, which continued till darkness again compelled them to pause. On the third morning, worn out with fatigue and hunger, they felt that it was impossible for them to fight any longer. Their leaders sent ambassadors to Narses to treat for peace; but even then they would not humble themselves to become the subjects of Justinian. All they would promise was that they would never again bear arms against the empire, and this only on condition of being allowed an unmolested passage out of Italy, and of receiving money for the expenses of their journey.

The Roman generals held a council to discuss this proposal; they had had such terrible experience of the desperate valour of the Goths that they decided to accept the conditions. So, in March, 553, the remnant of the defeated army set out on their northward march. What became of them history does not say. Perhaps they may have found a home among the Franks or Alamans; perhaps they may have made their way to the kingdom of the Visigoths in Spain.

But even yet Narses had a hard struggle to undergo before the conquest of Italy was complete. The Gothic garrisons in the cities still offered an obstinate resistance to their besiegers; and while the emperor's generals were occupied with their siege operations, the Franks saw the opportunity for which they had been waiting. In the autumn, accompanied by their half-savage allies, the Alamans, they poured into Italy, to the number of eighty thousand men. The brave Aligern, who had defended Cumse for a whole year, surrendered to the Romans, thinking it better to become the soldier of the empire than the slave of the Franks. Soon afterwards Lucca was taken by the Romans; but the Goths who held the other cities opened their gates to the Franks. The invaders were allowed to march over the whole length of the peninsula to the Straits of Messina, plundering, burning, and massacring as they went. The army of Narses had suffered such heavy losses that it was no match for this mighty horde; and the commander was obliged to remain in humiliating inactivity, leaving the barbarians to roam unchecked over the land.

During the winter, however, the armies of the Franks and Alamans were terribly wasted by plague, and by the effects of their own intemperance; and one of the Alaman leaders had returned to his home beyond the Alps. When the spring came, Narses, who in the meantime had been assiduously drilling his men, prepared himself for a decisive encounter with the foe.

At Casilinum, on the banks of the Vulturno, the two armies met. The Romans were still far inferior in numbers to the enemy; but the skill of their general won the day. The defeat of the Franks was so crushing that they offered no further resistance, and hastily sought their own land. After the battle Narses entered Rome, and for the last time in history, the imperial city beheld the stately ceremonies of a triumphal procession.

In the next twelve months, the towns which had still held out fell one by one into the hands of the Romans. The Goths who had defended them either went into exile or became blended with the surrounding population. The nation of the Ostrogoths was no more.

It is strange to think how different were the fates of the two great Teutonic kingdoms which in the last quarter of the fifth century were planted on Latin soil. After fourteen centuries, the fruits of the conquests of Clovis in Gaul still abide. If we cannot say that the state which he founded still survives, yet in a real sense he may be called the creator of the French nation. The Franks were never driven from Gaul, and though they lost their native tongue, and were absorbed in the greater mass of the people whom they had conquered, the country to this day bears their name. Theoderic was in all ways a greater man than Clovis; and yet the results of his conquest of Italy perished utterly within eighty years. The ruin of the Ostrogoths was the effect of many combined causes. Their numbers from the first were too few to enable them to hold Italy by force. Their Arian heresy, in spite of their noble tolerance in matters of religion, estranged them from the sympathies of their Catholic subjects; and the successors of Theoderic inherited neither his genius nor his lofty aims. But even so, we know not what the result might have been if Justinian had encouraged the Gothic kings to build up in Italy a powerful dominion, tributary to his own sovereignty. He would have been wiser had he adopted such a policy, for the conquest of Italy brought no advantage to the empire sufficient to repay the terrible sacrifices of blood and treasure by which it was bought.

The conqueror Narses was appointed the emperor's "exarch" or governor of Italy. He took up his residence in Theoderic's city of Ravenna; and for just two hundred years he and his successors continued to govern, on behalf of the emperors, as much of the country as was left them by the successive conquests of Lombards and Franks. But with the fortunes and misfortunes of Italy under their rule our story has nothing to do.

XXIX: THE VISIGOTHS AGAIN

We have now to take up again the story of the Visigoths, of whom we have lost sight while following the history of their eastern kinsmen to its tragic close. The Gothic dominion in Spain lasted for a century and a half after the downfall of the Ostrogoths; but only a very meagre outline of its history has come down to us. Our authorities henceforward are nearly all churchmen; and very often they pass over the things which we should most like to know, in order to dwell on matters which we regard as trifles, but which were interesting to themselves because they had some connection with religion.

It has already been mentioned that after the death of Alaric IL, in 507, the great Theoderic constituted himself the guardian of Amalaric, the infant king of the Visigoths, who was his grandson. While Theoderic lived, Spain and the narrow strip of Southern Gaul which had been spared by the Prankish conquests were governed by him in Amalaric's name. The Ostrogoth general, Theudis, who was appointed viceroy in Spain, was, however, practically the king of the country. We are told that he sent his appointed tribute to Ravenna every year, and professed to render obedience to his master's commands. Theoderic was jealous of his power, but did not dare to dismiss him from his office, lest he should revolt to the Franks. He made many attempts to persuade Theudis to visit Italy, but the viceroy was too cunning to fall into the snare.

When Theoderic died Amalaric, then twenty-four years of age, was recognized as sovereign of all the Gothic territories west of the Rhone, and the royal treasure of the Visigoths was sent from Ravenna to Narbonne, where the young king held his court.

Amalaric endeavoured to strengthen his kingdom by marrying into the family of his dangerous neighbours, the kings of the Franks. But this marriage proved to be the cause of his ruin. His queen, Clotilda (Hlothhild), the daughter of Clovis, was a fervent Catholic, like her mother, after whom she had been named. Amalaric had promised to allow her to retain her own religion; but his promise was broken. We need not believe the Frankish historian when he tells us that the queen was cruelly tortured to induce her to change her faith, and that she sent to her brothers a handkerchief stained with her blood, to excite them to avenge her wrongs. But no doubt she did complain that she was not allowed to worship according to her own conscience. A Frankish king was always ready to seize upon a pretext for attacking his weaker neighbours; and King Hildebert, of Paris, with a powerful army, marched against Narbonne. The Goths were defeated, and fled into Spain. The capital was taken, and Hildebert returned home, enriched with the royal treasures, and with the plunder of the Arian churches. Queen Clotilda accompanied her brother, but died before arriving at Paris. Amalaric was murdered in a church at Barcelona, by the orders of Theudis, whom the people elected king in his stead.

About the seventeen years (531-548) during which Theudis reigned in his own name, we have very little information. The two kings of the Franks, Hildebert and Hlothhari (Clotaire), invaded Spain in the year 543, and laid siege to Caesaraugusta, now called Saragossa. A wild story is told, how the citizens, hard pressed by famine, and on the point of surrendering, invoked (heretics though they were) the pray-prayers of the Catholic martyr, Vicentius. Clothed in mourning robes, and carrying the relics of the saint, they marched solemnly round the walls, singing penitential psalms. When the Franks knew what was the meaning of this display, they were seized with superstitious panic, and fled in wild disorder. The story was probably invented to excuse the Frankish defeat. The Goths overtook the flying invaders at the foot of the Pyrenees, and the Frankish army would have been utterly annihilated, if its chiefs had not bribed the Gothic general with large sums of money to allow them to make their escape unmolested through the mountain passes.

Even the Catholics admit that Theudis was a wise and able ruler, and that he followed the great Theoderic's policy of equal justice to his subjects of every creed. When the army of Justinian was making war upon the Vandals, their king Gelimer tried in vain to persuade Theudis to take his part, on the ground of their religious sympathies. Afterwards, however, his own nephew, Hildibad, king of the Ostrogoths, besought his aid in his struggle with the emperor, and Theudis led an army to attack the cities which Belisarius had conquered from the Vandals in Africa. The Goths were beaten with great slaughter, and their king barely escaped with his life. The story told to excuse their ill success is that they were surprised while engaged in worship on the Sunday. They thought that their enemies, being Christians, would observe the day as religiously as themselves, and therefore they were in no fear of attack. This tale would have been more credible if it had been told of Wulfila's converts two centuries before.

Shortly after this event Theudis was murdered in his palace by one of his own soldiers, who pretended to be a lunatic. The dying king expressed bitter remorse for his share in the murder of Amalaric, and begged that the life of his assassin might be spared.

The usurpation of Theudis had broken off the hereditary succession, and the kingdom of the Visigoths became once more an elective one, as it had been in the most ancient days of their history. An elective monarchy, where representative government is unknown, and where the nation is too large to be brought together in a body, must inevitably lead to disputes and civil war. The successor of Theudis was Theudigisel, the general who had led the Goths to victory over the Franks. He proved to be a cruel tyrant, and the whole nation rejoiced when, after a reign of eighteen months, he was murdered by his guests at a banquet in his own palace. The next election was a disputed one. Agila, the king who was chosen by the northern cities, was not acknowledged by the south, and his arbitrary rule soon disgusted even his own supporters. The southern rebellion was headed by Athanagild, who appealed for help to Constantinople. The emperor sent the Patrician Liberius with a powerful army to his assistance. The struggle lasted five years. Agila was defeated, and was put to death by his own soldiers, and then Athanagild became king.

Athanagild's reign of fourteen years was prosperous and peaceful, except for his wars with the dangerous allies whom he invited into the country. The emperor's soldiers seized many of the cities of Spain, and it was found impossible to drive them out.

Like so many other Visigoth kings, Athanagild sought to add security to his kingdom by connecting his family by marriage with the house of Clovis. The consequences were unhappy, as usual; the fate of Athanagild's two daughters is one of the most tragic episodes of Prankish history. The younger of them, Brunihild, was married to King Sigebert of the East Franks. The wedding was celebrated with great pomp, and the fashionable poetaster of the time, Venantius Fortunatus, composed a poem for the occasion. It is a very heathenish sort of performance, though the author was a bishop; it tells how the God of Love wounded the heart of Sigebert with an arrow, and then Venus and her son extol in turn the manly virtues of the bridegroom and the loveliness of the bride. The brother of Sigebert, Chilperic, king of the North-west Franks, sought the hand of Athanagild's elder daughter, Geleswintha, and in spite of her tears and entreaties she was compelled by her parents to accept the unwelcome bridegroom. Both princesses adopted the religion of their husbands. It was not long before Chilperic's affection was estranged from his queen by the wiles of a woman named Fredegunda, and Geleswintha was put to death by his orders. Brunihild stirred up her husband to avenge the murder of her sister. In the war between the two Prankish kingdoms Sigebert died, and Brunihild had a long and stormy reign as queen-mother. She was a woman of masculine energy and wonderful powers of mind, a great ruler, but tyrannical and unscrupulous, and it was said that ten kings and queens lost their lives in the turmoils which she excited. At last she fell into the power of her enemy Fredegunda, who caused her to be tied behind a horse and dragged along the ground until she died. Then her lacerated body was thrown into the flames.

Athanagild did not live to hear of his daughter's miserable end. In the year 567 he died in his palace at Toledo, beloved by his own subjects, and respected by foreign nations. He was the first Visigoth king since Euric who died a natural death; his five predecessors had all come to a violent end—one in battle, and the rest by the hand of assassins.

XXX: LEOVIGILD AND HIS SONS

After Athanagild's death, five months passed before the Goths could agree on the choice of his successor. The dispute, however, was settled without an appeal to the sword. The Gothic parties had learned to dread the danger of civil war, and the different Spanish cities, by way of compromise, withdrew their respective candidates, and agreed to choose a king from Gothic Gaul, now the least influential part of the kingdom. The new king Leuva (Liuba) was a quiet, unambitious man, of whom we hear neither good nor evil, only that he handed over the government of Spain to his brother Leovigild (Liobagilths), preferring for his own part to remain at Narbonne, which thus became for a short space once more the Visigoth capital. In the third year of his reign he died, leaving the kingdom to his brother.

Leovigild was in many ways one of the greatest kings of his time. A bold and skilful general, he subdued the kingdom of the Sueves in the north-west of Spain, wrested from the emperor's soldiers several of the cities which they had occupied, and brought the native inhabitants of the peninsula into complete subjection. He built fortresses and founded cities, established a new system of administration of the kingdom, and made many new laws suited to the altered needs of his people. It was under his firm rule that the Goths and the Romanised natives were taught to feel themselves to be the fellow subjects of one kingdom, and so the process began which ended in the complete blending of the two peoples into one. In the splendour and magnificence of his court, Leovigild far surpassed all his predecessors. He was the first Visigoth king who sat on a raised throne in the assembly of the nobles, and who placed on his coins his own likeness wearing a crown. It will be remembered that Southey, in his poem of "Roderick," in the complete blending speaks of, "The golden pome, the proud array, Of ermine, aureate vests, and jewelry, With all which Leovigild for after kings Left, ostentatious of his power."

The name of Leovigild, however, is best known on account of the tragic story of the rebellion of his eldest son Ermenegild, honoured in later ages as a saint and martyr of the Catholic Church. The cause of trouble was, in this instance as in so many others in Visigoth history, a Prankish marriage. The bride whom Leovigild obtained for his son was Ingunthis, the young daughter of Sigebert and Brunihild, and the wedding was celebrated in Toledo with the splendid ostentation of which the king was so fond. Ermenegild had already received from his father a share in the kingly dignity, and Leovigild hoped that the marriage with a Prankish princess would help to ensure his son's succession to the crown.

But the young daughter of Brunihild belonged of course to the Catholic faith; and Queen Goiswintha (the widow of Athanagild, whom Leovigild had married) was a bigoted Arian. The Prankish historian, Gregory of Tours, tells the story that Goiswintha dragged Ingunthis to the ground by her hair, beat her cruelly, and then forced her to undergo baptism by an Arian priest. Very likely this is pure fiction, but it seems to be true that Queen Goiswintha and her daughter-in-law quarrelled so much that Leovigild, for the sake of peace, was glad to send his son to Seville as ruler of Southern Spain.

Soon afterwards, Ermenegild was persuaded by his wife and his uncle Leander, the Catholic bishop of Seville, to forsake the Church of his fathers. His conversion to the Catholic faith bore no good fruits; he made common cause with the remnant of the imperial army, and headed a rebellion for the purpose of wresting the kingdom out of the hands of his heretic father.

Leovigild tried in vain by entreaties to bring his favourite son to a sense of filial duty. Ermenegild, whether it was through fanaticism or ambition, refused to listen to any of his proposals, and the king was compelled to take up arms for the recovery of his revolted provinces. Before long Ermenegild was shut up in Seville. The siege lasted for two years; at length the city was taken, after the defenders had suffered terribly from famine. The prince escaped to Cordova, but his faithless friends from Constantinople betrayed him to his father for a bribe. Taking refuge in a neighbouring church, he sent to implore Leovigild's mercy. He received a solemn promise that his life should be spared, and then ventured to leave his place of refuge, and threw himself at his father's feet. Leovigild burst into tears, and clasped his son in his arms. But he felt that Ermenegild could no longer be trusted with any share in the government, and he ordered him to lay aside the royal robes, and to take up his abode in Valencia as a private person.

A year had not passed, however, when Leovigild heard that his son had broken his promise to remain at Valencia, and was making his way to Gaul. Before setting out he had placed his wife under the care of the enemies of his country, the Greek officers from Constantinople; and it seems to have been his purpose to get the Franks to help him in another effort to dethrone his father. He was captured at Tarragona by Leovigild's soldiers and thrown into prison. It is related that he was visited in his dungeon time after time by messengers from his father, promising him freedom and restoration to his royal honours if he would only consent to abandon his new faith. But his steadfastness was not to be shaken either by promise or threats. At last, an Arian bishop, who was sent to administer to him the Eucharist, brought back word that Ermenegild had received him with gross insults, calling him the servant of the devil. Transported with passion, Leovigild commanded that his son should be put to death. The sentence was swiftly carried out: an executioner was sent to the prison, and the rebellious prince was killed by a blow with an axe, without any pretence of trial.

It is a repulsive story. On one side, we see a son making war against his father on the professed ground of his duty to the Church; and on the other side, we see a father commanding the murder of his son. The Catholics of Ermenegild's own time and country, to do them justice, seem generally to have regarded his rebellion as a crime. But in later ages, when the circumstances were partly forgotten, his wicked conduct was extolled as an act of the noblest Christian virtue, and his name was placed in the calendar as that of a saint and martyr.

The widowed Ingunthis was treated by the emperor's officers more like a prisoner than a guest, and she tried to make her escape to her relatives in Gaul. She was overtaken in her flight, and with her infant son Athanagild was placed on board a vessel for Constantinople. Ingunthis died on the journey, but her son was delivered into the hands of the emperor, at whose court he remained while he lived. This is the last we hear of any interference of the eastern emperors with the affairs of Gothic Spain.

It is not wonderful that after his son's rebellion Leovigild regarded the Catholic Church as a danger to the State, and that he did some things which are complained of as persecution. But the stories are greatly exaggerated. He did banish several bishops but it is not true that any Catholic suffered martyrdom, in his reign. Leovigild was so far from being a bigot that he was often accused of hypocrisy because he paid religious honour to the shrines of orthodox as well as heretic saints. He soon found that harsh treatment of the heads of their Church was not the way to win over his Catholic subjects; and he tried to effect his object by gentler means. He persuaded the Arian clergy to consent that converted Catholics should be received into their Church without being baptized afresh, and to state the articles of their faith in such a way as to make the differences between them and the orthodox appear as small as possible. The result was that large numbers of Catholics professed to accept the king's religion. But the Arians were still a small minority, and their attachment to their creed was feeble, while the zeal of the Catholics grew daily more and more intense. It was plain that it would be hard for a heretic sovereign to hold the throne of Spain; and when the great king died (in 587) men believed that a great struggle was at hand, which would end only in the overthrow of the Gothic rule.

XXXI: THE GOTHS BECOME CATHOLIC

It had been Leovigild's ambition to found a hereditary dynasty; and with this end in view he had caused his son Reccared to be elected his associate in the kingdom. So when he died there was still a crowned and chosen king in possession of the throne, and it was not necessary even to go through the form of an election.

If Reccared had not already gained the goodwill of his people, very likely his father's far-seeing scheme would have failed. But the young king had distinguished himself as a general, leading the Goths to victory over the Franks, and he had shown wisdom and energy as a ruler. The nation therefore gladly accepted him as sole sovereign after his father's death.

Reccared saw clearly that he was likely to be overmatched in the struggle with the growing power of the Catholic Church. He resolved to convert that power from an enemy into a friend, by himself adopting the religion of the majority of his subjects, and inducing the Goths to follow his example. It is quite possible that he may have been sincerely convinced that the Catholic faith was true; but this change of religious profession was certainly the wisest step he could have taken in the interest of his kingdom.

In order that his conversion might seem to proceed from deliberate inquiry, he called together the bishops of both churches, and invited them to hold in his presence a public discussion of the arguments for their respective creeds. He was anxious, he said, to know the truth, and the result of the debate should determine whether he should accept the Catholic faith, or remain an Arian. The champions on both sides put forth all their eloquence and learning, and when the discussion was ended the king proclaimed his conviction that the orthodox creed was supported by overwhelming evidence of Scripture and miracles; and soon afterwards he was publicly received into the Catholic Church.

The conversion of the king was soon followed by that of the whole nation. At first sight this seems strange; but the Goths had long been losing interest in the distinctive articles of their creed. They had lived surrounded by Catholics, hearing daily of the miracles wrought at the tombs of Catholic saints. They could not help seeing that their church was only an insignificant sect, a small exception to the unity of the Christian world. They could not help being impressed by the fervent faith of their Catholic neighbours. And to these many influences they were all the more open because their divines had taught them to be tolerant in their judgment of those who rejected their creed. In Leovigild's reign a Spanish Goth had horrified the Catholic bishop Gregory of Tours by saying that it was a Christian's duty to treat with respect whatever was revered by others—even by idolaters. It is by a strange accident indeed, that the name Visigoth has given rise to our word bigot, for never was there a nation who so little deserved the reproach of bigotry as the Visigoths of Spain. If their name had become a synonym for religious indifference or lukewarmness, it would have been much more appropriate.

Still, however little the Gothic people knew or cared about the differences between the two churches, Arianism had been for three centuries their national faith, and patriotic pride had kept them faithful to it so far. It was a bold venture on Reccared's part to go over to the foreign church; but he had not miscalculated the power of his popularity. Not only the laity, but even the clergy, including many bishops, speedily followed the king's example.

A great thing had been accomplished. The work which Leovigild had begun — the creation of the modern Spanish nation—would have remained unfinished if his son had not succeeded in removing the barrier of religious differences which hindered the blending of Goths and Spaniards into one people.

The great change, however, was not made altogether without resistance. In Southern Gaul, where Reccared was less known than in Spain, the news of his conversion excited a dangerous rebellion. An Arian bishop, Athaloc, and two Gothic nobles, put themselves at the head of the rebels, and called in the help of the Franks. But Reccared's generals soon restored order; and the people of the province before long professed themselves Catholics. The bishop Athaloc, it was said, died of vexation at the failure of his plans. In Spain, also, there were some insignificant conspiracies prompted by Arian bishops, but they were speedily crushed, and their leaders punished. The king's stepmother, Goiswintha (the same who is said to have treated Ingunthis with such shameful cruelty) had professed herself a convert to the Catholic Church. But in her heart she hated the change, and she was detected in a conspiracy against the king's life. Reccared inflicted no punishment upon Goiswintha, though he banished her accomplices from the kingdom. But soon afterwards she died suddenly, and her death was of course regarded as a divine judgment for her treason.

In May, 589, Reccared summoned to Toledo the bishops of his kingdom, to celebrate the victory of the orthodox faith, and to devise laws for the government of the Church. Sixty-seven bishops presented themselves in obedience to the royal command. The king addressed them on the importance of the work for which they were assembled, and exhorted them to spend three days in prayer and fasting before beginning their deliberations. When the three days were passed, and the bishops again met in council, Reccared opened the proceedings with a speech, setting forth the grounds of his conversion. It is worth notice that he honestly admitted that "earthly motives" had had their share in opening his mind to the arguments which had led him to the true faith. He ended by reading a formal statement of the articles of his faith. This document, after being approved by the assembly, was signed by the king, by his queen Baddo, and by all who were present. The bishops then proceeded to draw up a code of laws settling the constitution of the Church of Spain.

The religious change effected by Reccared was a necessity. But its good results were not unmixed. With the zeal of a new convert, the king lavished wealth and honours upon the Catholic Church, and allowed its clergy to attain a degree of political power that was full of danger to the State. It was not long before the Gothic kings learned the bad lesson of persecuting Jews and heretics.

Reccared himself, however, zealous though he was for his new faith, was no persecutor. He seems to have honestly striven in all things for the welfare of his subjects, and his reign was one of great prosperity. He is praised by historians as a wise lawgiver, and from his time onwards all the new laws that were made were declared binding alike on Goths and Spaniards.

One of the great events of Reccared's reign was the attempt of the Prankish king Guntram to conquer the Gothic domains in Gaul. An army of 60,000 men entered the Narbonnese province, and besieged the city of Carcassonne. Reccared's general Claudius (a Roman, not a Gothic name, it is worth while to note) with a very small force, inflicted on the invaders such a crushing defeat that never again, while the Gothic kingdom lasted, did the Franks attempt any attack upon its Gaulish lands. The Basques, who had given trouble in the earlier part of the reign, were subdued; and the interloping "Greeks," though not driven out of the country, were compelled to confine themselves to their fortresses, so that the last years of Reccared's life were a period of profound peace.

Reccared died in the year 601, having in his last illness given proof of his piety by making public confession of his sins. The Goths honoured his memory by electing to the throne his youthful son Leuva.

XXXII: A PRIEST-RIDDEN KINGDOM

One short chapter will be sufficient for the story of the next seventy years. During that time eleven kings reigned over the Visigoths, but the records of their reigns are scanty, and contain few events of any great interest. The main thing that strikes us in reading the history of this period is the rapid growth of the Church's influence in the government of the kingdom.

Reccared's young son reigned only two years. There was a Gothic noble named Witeric, who had already in Reccared's lifetime headed an unsuccessful rebellion, and had obtained the king's generous pardon. This man, ungrateful for the mercy that had been shown him, now rebelled against Leuva, and succeeded in getting himself acknowledged king-in his stead. The dethroned boy-king, his right hand having been cut off, was thrown into prison, and afterwards put to death.

The seven years of Witeric's reign were unprosperous, and his rule was that of a selfish tyrant. It is said that he wished to restore the Arian religion; however that may be, he seems to have made himself detested by the clergy, as well as by the nobles and the people. In the year 610 he was murdered at a banquet, and his body was buried in unhallowed ground without the rites of the church.

The short reign of his successor, Gundemar, contains no events worth relating; but Sisebut, who was chosen king in 612, was a man about whom we would be glad to know more. He was a successful general, and his victories compelled the Greeks to surrender nearly all their possessions in Spain. Like the Gothic heroes of older days, Theoderic and Totila, he was distinguished for humanity towards the conquered. Many of the Greek prisoners had been sold into slavery by their Gothic captors, and the king purchased their freedom at his own cost. He was also a scholar, and a generous patron of such learning as existed in Spain in his day. Unhappily it has to be added that he was the first Gothic king who ever persecuted the Jews. "Baptism within one year, or scourging, mutilation, banishment, and confiscation of goods;" such was the choice which Sisebut offered to that unhappy people. Thousands of Jews professed to accept the gospel. But the dread of persecution could not make them Christians at heart. The Jews till now had been attached friends of the Goths, the forced conversions under Sisebert changed them into bitter enemies. Those of them who received baptism and attended Christian worship continued in the secrecy of their homes to practise Jewish ritual, and to teach their children to curse their oppressors. The best men of the Spanish Church felt that these persecutions were wrong, and succeeding kings did something to lighten the burdens which Sisebut had imposed. But the mischief was irreparable. The Jews, whether professedly converted or not, had become embittered against the Goths, and when the kingdom was attacked by the Moors they joyfully lent their aid to its assailants.

When Sisebut died in 621, his general, Swinthila, was elected to the throne. According to some writers Swinthila was a son of Reccared. He is remarkable as being the first king who reigned over the whole Spanish peninsula. The Greeks of the empire, whom Sisebut had confined to a small strip of Spain, became in Swinthila's time subjects of the Gothic kingdom, and their soldiers took service in the Gothic armies; and the rebellious Basques were brought to complete submission. Swinthila won the affection of the common people among his subjects. The title given to him was "the Father of the Poor," but he seems to have aimed at limiting the power of the Gothic nobles and the bishops. The discontent of these two classes reached its height when—without asking their sanction—he appointed his son Reccimer the partner of his throne. The nobles, led by Sisenanth, rose in revolt, and obtained the help of the Prankish king, Dagobert, by promising to give him the most valued object among the Gothic royal treasures. This was a golden dish or table, weighing five hundred pounds and richly jewelled, which had been given by Aetius to Thorismund, king of the Visigoths, as part of his share of Attila's spoils in 453. The Franks marched into Spain, and on their approach the Goths who had supported Swinthila abandoned his cause, and Sisenanth was crowned at Saragossa. The Prankish army then returned home, and Dagobert sent ambassadors to claim the price of his assistance. Sisenanth delivered to them the precious object which had been promised, but the Goths were so indignant at the thought of losing this renowned treasure that they took it by force from the ambassadors, and brought it back in triumph to Toledo. Sisenanth dared not oppose himself to the will of his people, and he had to pay Dagobert a large sum in compensation.

The elevation of Sisenanth was a victory of the power of the nobles over that of the king and the commons. But in the end it led to the supremacy of the Church over all three. In order to secure the ecclesiastical sanction for his usurpation, the new king caused a council to be held at Toledo in the year 633. Sixty-nine bishops were present, either in person or by their representatives; and after they had finished their deliberations on the Church questions submitted to them, they formally confirmed the right of Sisenanth to the throne, and declared Swinthila and all his family incapable of holding any office of dignity in the State. The bishops then decreed that in future, whenever a king died, his successor should be chosen by the nobles and the clergy in council; and every man who attempted to rebel against the king so chosen was declared liable to be cut off from the communion of the Church, and to be in danger of eternal destruction. The same terrible penalties were threatened against any king who should endeavour to set aside the new law of election by raising his son to the royal dignity without the sanction of a duly constituted council. It was further enacted that henceforward the clergy should be freed from all taxation.

What became of the discrowned Swinthila and his family is not known. In the fifth year of his reign Sisenanth died at Toledo, and Kindila was chosen as his successor. He too was a mere tool in the hands of the bishops. The only events of his reign worth recording are the decrees of the Church councils that no king should in future be chosen who was not of noble Gothic descent, or who had assumed the dress of a monk. It was also ordained that every future king before his coronation should take an oath to tolerate no heretics or Jews within his realm.

Kindila died in 640, and the assembly of bishops and nobles chose his son Tulga in his stead.

The young Tulga gave promise of being just such a king as the clergy loved; but all the awful threats of the bishops were unavailing to prevent a rebellion among the Gothic nobles. The leader of this rising, Kindaswinth, succeeded in getting Tulga into his power, and by clothing him in a monk's habit rendered him, according to the law passed in the last reign, incapable of sitting on the throne.

The bishops were obliged to submit to Kindaswinth's usurpation. He was a man of great energy and strength of character, and his accession was followed by a reign of terror that compelled both clergy and nobles to feel that they had found a master. Two hundred Goths of the noblest families and five hundred of lower rank were punished with death for conspiring against his throne. Many others were banished, and their goods confiscated, or bestowed on the king's faithful supporters. The heads of the Church were wise enough to bow to the storm, and they sought to win the king's favour by decreeing the penalty of degradation and excommunication against all priests who were guilty of countenancing any conspiracy against his throne. By these measures all opposition was crushed, and the kingdom was brought into a state of order and tranquillity such as had not been known before.

Strange to say, this fierce and energetic sovereign was already nearly eighty years old when he seized the throne. After he had reigned seven years the bishops, doubtless at his own secret suggestion, presented to him a petition that he would abdicate in favour of his son Recceswinth, in order to prevent the tumults which might be expected to arise at his death. Kindaswinth consented joyfully to the request, and his son was crowned in 649, with the assent of the clergy and of the nobles. The aged king, it is said, spent the remaining years of his life in acts of piety and beneficence, and died in 652 at the age of ninety years.

Recceswinth seems to have inherited much of his father's energy without any of his harshness. The oath which he had taken at his coronation contained a clause binding him never to pardon any man who conspired against his throne. One of his first acts after his father's death was to call an assembly of the nobles and the higher clergy of his kingdom, and to ask them to release him from this cruel promise. The council decided that the oath was no longer binding, and enacted that the right of pardoning rebels should be restored to the king. Other important laws for the government of the kingdom were passed by the same assembly; the most important of them was that the property amassed by a king during his reign should not descend to his family, but to the successor who should be chosen by the council of nobles and prelates. For twenty-three years Recceswinth governed his people with such success that the kingdom enjoyed unbroken peace—except for a brief rebellion of the Basques, led by a Gothic noble named Froya. The leader was captured and put to death; but the Basques obtained redress of their grievances, and were thenceforward content to accept the rule of the Gothic king.

But the great reason for which Recceswinth deserves to be remembered is that he carried a step further the work begun by Leovigild and Reccared, of blending Goths and Spaniards into one nation. Till his time intermarriage between the two peoples was forbidden by law. Recceswinth abolished the prohibition; and, following in his father's footsteps, he forbade, under heavy penalties, the use of the Roman law in his dominions. Henceforward Goths and Romans alike were to be judged according to the law-book of the Visigoths.

In the year 672 Recceswinth died, deeply lamented by his people. In the history of the Visigoths a reign of twenty-three years of peace had never been before, and it was not destined ever to be again.

XXXIII: THE STORY OF WAMBA

The history of King Wamba has often been told with many fabulous embellishments; but the simple facts, as they are admitted by sober historians, and as we shall here try to set them forth, are themselves not altogether wanting in the elements of romance.

Round the bed on which the dead Recceswinth lay, in the castle of Gerticos, the nobles and prelates of the Gothic state were assembled for the purpose of choosing his successor. Notwithstanding the long period of calm which the kingdom had enjoyed, signs of coming trouble were plainly visible; and all present felt that there was only one man qualified to guide the State through the perilous times that were at hand. With one voice they declared their choice of Wamba as king of the Goths.

At first Wamba stoutly refused to accept the crown, pleading that he was an old man, and that the burden of the kingly office was more than he could bear. His fellow nobles and the bishops expostulated with him long and earnestly, but he continued to urge them to choose some younger man, who would be equal to the arduous labours which the nation required of its king. At length one of the officers of the royal household exclaimed, brandishing his spear, "Wamba, thou shalt never leave this chamber save as a dead man or as a king!" The Goths echoed the words, and Wamba consented to accept the greatness thus strangely thrust upon him.

On the nineteenth day after Recceswinth's death, Wamba was crowned at Toledo. Throughout the whole of Spain the event was received with unbounded rejoicing; but the old jealousy between the two portions of the kingdom showed itself once more, and before Wamba had been many weeks king he received the news that the Gothic province of Gaul was in open revolt.

The leader of the rebels was a Gothic noble named Hilderic, Governor of Nimes, who bad himself aspired to be chosen king of the Goths. He was supported by Gunhild, Bishop of Maguelonne, and the army which he collected was strengthened by a large body of Jews who had fled from persecution in Spain, and were glad of the opportunity to fight against their oppressors. The Bishop of Nimes, who protested against Hilderic's conduct, was loaded with chains, and his bishopric bestowed on an abbot named Ranimer, who had supported the party of the rebels.

The general whom Wamba sent against the Gaulish rebels was a cunning and unprincipled Greek named Paul. As soon as he arrived at Narbonne, he called the officers of the army together, and after having harangued them on the grievances they had to suffer from the ruling party in Spain, he called upon them to renounce their allegiance to an imbecile old man, who knowing his own weakness had shrunk from accepting the kingship until he was compelled to do so by those who aimed to use him as their tool. The speech produced its desired effect, and when one of the general's accomplices proposed that the army should elect Paul king of the Goths, the whole assembly answered with applause. The decision of the officers was approved by the army; Hilderic and his followers joined themselves to the usurper's party; and after a few weeks Paul was crowned at Narbonne, with a golden crown that Reccared had presented to the church of Gerona.

Wamba was at this time in the Western Pyrenees, fighting with the Basques, whom Paul's emissaries had incited to rebellion. The news was brought to him that his treacherous general was accepted as king by the Gaulish cities and by a large portion of Northeastern Spain. A council of war was called; some of the officers recommended a return to Toledo in order to seek reinforcements; others wished to hasten at once to the encounter with Paul. Wamba's decision was that the subjugation of the Basques must first be complete, and that then the march on Narbonne should be prosecuted without a moment's delay. We are told—perhaps this is an exaggeration —that the Basques were reduced to entire submission in one week. Then Wamba led his forces into the revolted province of Spain, and in a few days all the cities had opened their gates or had been taken by storm. Two of the rebel leaders fell into Wamba's hands at Clausurse, and were sent in chains to Toledo; a third, Wittimer, escaped to Narbonne, to give warning of the approach of the Gothic army. When Paul heard that Wamba was on the way to Narbonne, he retired to Nimes, leaving Narbonne in Wittimer's charge.

Soon afterwards Wamba arrived before the walls of the city, and invited Wittimer to surrender, promising that if he and his comrades would surrender they should suffer no harm. The proposal was scornfully refused, and after a terrible struggle the city was taken by assault. Wittimer took refuge behind the altar of the Virgin, till a soldier threatened to crush him with a huge stone slab. Then he yielded himself up; and he and his companions, loaded with chains, were flogged through the streets of Narbonne.

Wamba then sent a body of thirty thousand men to attack Nimes, while he occupied himself with the capture of the smaller cities. Paul's garrison made a vigorous defence, and after a whole day's fighting the Goths were obliged to send to Wamba for more troops. The next morning ten thousand more men arrived, and the attack began again. Paul tried to persuade his men to risk a battle outside the walls, saying that the Goths had become slothful and cowardly, having enjoyed so many years of peace, and that if once they were met boldly they would soon take to flight. But his eloquence was in vain, and when the assault began it was soon perceived that the Goths were anything but cowards. Paul was assailed with bitter reproaches for his folly in making light of the enemy's prowess. After five hours' hard fighting the gates were burst open, and the troops of Wamba rushed into the city, slaughtering all that came in their way.

Paul and what remained of his army and the citizens took shelter in the great Roman amphitheatre, the splendid ruins of which are still the chief sight at Nimes. They converted the building into a temporary fortress. It was easily defended, but there had been no time for provisioning it, and the people, pressed by hunger, broke out into mutiny. One of Paul's own relatives was seized by the crowd and murdered before the commander's own eyes, and in spite of his commands and entreaties. When Paul saw that he was no longer obeyed as a king, he tore off his royal robes, and flung them aside in the sight of all the people.

On the third day (September 3, 673) the inhabitants, feeling that further resistance was hopeless, sent their bishop Argabad to plead for mercy with Wamba. The king promised that no blood should be shed, but he kept himself free to inflict any other punishments on the rebels. Officers were sent into the city to restore order, and to arrest the ringleaders of the rebellion. Paul was dragged by the hair of the head between two horsemen, and brought into the king's camp. He threw himself at Wamba's feet, and with tears and abject professions of repentance entreated the king to have mercy on him. Wamba scornfully assured him that his life should be spared.

On the third day after the victory Paul and the other rebels were brought up for trial before a court composed of the king and the great officers of the realm. They confessed their guilt, and the tribunal sentenced them to death and to forfeiture of their property. The king, however, refused to break his promise, and ordered that their punishment should be scalping and imprisonment for life.

After restoring peace and settled government in the Gaulish province, Wamba returned to Toledo, which he entered in triumph like an ancient Roman conqueror, followed by a long procession of his captives with shaven heads and bare feet. Paul was adorned in mockery with a crown of leather, fastened on his head with melted pitch.

The next seven years of Wamba's reign were peaceful and prosperous. He ruled firmly and wisely, and though no enemy of the Church, he knew how to keep the priesthood duly in check. He even made a law that in time of war the clergy of all ranks should be bound like other citizens to take up arms for the defence of the country. Wamba also decreed that free birth should no longer be a condition of serving in the army. Gothic warriors of the olden time would have scorned to fight in the same ranks with slaves; but the warlike spirit of the nation was decaying, and military service was now looked upon as an evil necessity, to be avoided if possible.

The events which brought Wamba's reign to an end are strange indeed. On October 14, 680, he fell into a stupor, and continued insensible for many hours. The physicians declared that he was dying, and after the custom of those days he was clothed in a monk's robe, and his head was shaven; for it was believed that those who died in the dress of a religious order were sure to obtain salvation in the next world. After twenty-four hours Wamba recovered consciousness; but when he knew what had been done, he recognized that according to Gothic law the fact that he had worn a monk's robe disqualified him from ruling any longer. So, in the presence of the great officers of the kingdom, he signed a document declaring that he abdicated the throne, and appointing a certain Erwig as his successor. It was afterwards believed that Wamba's mysterious trance was caused by a sleeping draught given to him by Erwig. If so, the nobles of the court must have been sharers in the conspiracy. Although it was quite contrary to Gothic law that a king should name his successor, neither the nobles nor the people offered any protest. Erwig was anointed and crowned by the Archbishop of Toledo, and Wamba retired into a monastery, and there spent the remainder of his life.

XXXIV: THIRTY YEARS OF DECAY

Wamba is the last great man, and his victories the last brilliant exploits, that appear in Gothic history. His fiery energy had for a moment seemed to inspire the state with new life; but the decay of national spirit had gone too far to be arrested. The Visigoths had exchanged their old free constitution for a despotism controlled by bigoted prelates: the poorer freemen had almost all sunk into slavery, and had naturally lost their interest in the welfare of the kingdom; the nobles, corrupted by long peace and fancied security, were sunk in idleness and vice. Henceforward our story tells only of "ruin and the breaking up of laws," which went on unchecked till the day when the kingdom was crushed like a hollow shell in the hands of the Saracen invader.

The accession of Erwig to the throne was not only illegal because he had not been regularly chosen; it was also a breach of the law which provided that the king should always be of pure Gothic blood. His mother, indeed, was a Gothic princess, a cousin of King Kindaswinth; but his father was a Greek of Persian origin, named Artabazes, who had been banished from Constantinople, and had found a home in Spain. Erwig seems to have had all the cunning and the love of intrigue with which the Greeks were so often charged. He had, however, but little courage or force of character, and throughout his reign was little more than a puppet in the hands of his chief counsellor, the fierce and unscrupulous Julian (afterwards called Saint Julian) the Archbishop of Toledo. This archbishop was one of the most remarkable figures of his time. It is to him that we owe our knowledge of the history of Wamba's campaign against Paul; and his book on this subject is perhaps the most brilliant literary work of the seventh century. Its savage exultation over the fallen foe, more befitting a warrior than a churchman, is in accord with all that we know of the writer's character. After having in this book extolled Wamba to the skies as a pattern of a hero and a Christian, he quarrelled with him, and he is supposed to have been the chief inspirer of the conspiracy against him. Himself of Jewish origin, he was the most cruel persecutor of the Jews, and the tyrant of both Church and people.

To prevent any reaction in favour of Wamba, Erwig and Julian caused the council of bishops and nobles to publish again the law which disqualified from high office in the State all who had ever worn a monastic dress. The words in which this decree was expressed are significant indeed. "There are some persons who, having been clothed in the garments of penitence when in peril of death, and having afterwards recovered, have the audacity to claim that their vow is not binding, because it was taken by them in a state of unconsciousness. Let all such reflect that children are baptised without their will or knowledge, yet no man can renounce his baptism without incurring eternal damnation. As it is with baptism, so it is with the monastic vow; and we declare that all who violate it are worthy of the severest punishment, and are incapable of holding any civil dignity." It would have been more honest if the fathers had simply declared that Wamba had forfeited the throne.

Erwig's acts as a lawgiver consisted chiefly in undoing what Wamba had done to strengthen the tottering state. The penalties imposed on those who shirked military service were relaxed; the clergy were no longer required to take their part in the defence of the kingdom; those who had been guilty of rebellion in former reigns were restored to their forfeited dignities and estates; and all the arrears of taxes owing at the end of Erwig's first year were cancelled. The unfortunate Jews, whose misery had been in some small degree lightened in Wamba's reign, were now persecuted more fiercely than ever at the instigation of an archbishop sprung of their own race.

In order to prevent any rebellion on behalf of Wamba's family, Erwig appointed as his successor the late king's nephew, Egica, and gave him his daughter in marriage, making him take an oath that when he came to the throne he would protect his mother-in-law and all the royal family in the possession of all their property. In the year 687 the land was desolated by a great famine, which Erwig's guilty conscience regarded as God's vengeance for his crimes. He took to his bed, and soon afterwards retired to a monastery, where he died in November of the same year.

One of the first acts of Egica after he was anointed king was to call a council of bishops and nobles for the settlement of questions relating to the government. When the council was assembled the king presented himself in the chamber, and kneeling on the floor, implored the prayers of the bishops on his behalf He then retired, after handing to the president a document in which was stated a question of conscience which he desired the fathers to resolve.

The question proposed was the following: "When I married King Erwig's daughter he compelled me to swear that I would always protect his widow and children in the enjoyment of their possessions. But when I was anointed king I took an oath to exercise equal justice towards all my subjects. It is impossible for me to keep both these oaths, for much of the wealth that Erwig left behind him was gained by extortion. In order to secure his throne Erwig reduced many nobles to slavery, and seized their property. They or their heirs now demand restitution. My coronation oath commands me to grant their just claims; the oath I took to Erwig forbids. I pray you, reverend fathers, to tell me what my duty is to do."

The bishops had not much difficulty in deciding. The promise made to the nation, they said, outweighed all merely private engagements. They added, very ingeniously, that as Erwig by appointing Egica his successor, had been the cause of his taking the second oath, he had thereby released him from his former obligations inconsistent with it. In this way Egica succeeded in defeating his predecessor's carefully devised schemes for the interests of his family.

The same council had another piece of business to dispose of One of the theological works of their president, the Archbishop Julian, had been blamed by the pope as not quite orthodox. Julian was not the man to receive correction meekly, and at his prompting the bishops prepared a reply, defending Julian's book, and even hinting that the Holy Father must have read it carelessly. They gained their cause: the new pope withdrew his predecessor's censure.

Two years after this triumph the haughty tyrant of the Spanish Church died, and was succeeded in the archbishopric by a Goth of noble birth, named Sisebert. Before his elevation Sisebert had made a great display of austere piety, but when the object of his ambition was attained he threw off the mask, and lived an openly profane and immoral life. What seems to have shocked his contemporaries more than anything else in his conduct was that he ventured to clothe himself in the "holy robe," which was said to have been given to Saint Hildifuns by the Virgin Mary, and also to ascend the pulpit on which the Virgin had been seen to stand, and which had never since been profaned by human foot.

Archbishop Sisebert was desirous of succeeding to the same power in the state that had been enjoyed by Julian; but Egica was a man of stronger mould than Erwig, and the prelate found himself overmatched. He then formed a conspiracy, in which several of the great nobles were involved, to murder the king, his family, and several of his faithful supporters. The plot was discovered, and Sisebert was condemned—not to death, for the crimes of the clergy were always more lightly punished in Spain than those of other men, but to banishment, excommunication, and the forfeiture of all his property.

In the year 694 the Government was thrown into the wildest panic by the discovery of another plot, in which nearly all the Jews of the kingdom were supposed to be concerned. It is no wonder that they conspired. In the midst of their own miseries— though Egica had somewhat relaxed the persecuting laws—they heard from the people of their own race and faith in Africa that under the Saracen rule the Jews were protected and honoured. Who can blame them if they intrigued with their kinsmen in Africa to bring about a Saracen invasion of Spain?

The numbers and wealth of the Spanish Jews were even yet large enough to render them dangerous enemies of the kingdom; and besides those who professed Judaism there were thousands more whose families had for generations been accounted Christian, but who in secret cherished their ancestral religion, and the bitterest hatred of the Gothic oppressors. The king and the bishops, when the treason of the Jews was revealed, resolved upon nothing less than the entire uprooting of the Jewish faith. It was enacted that all the grown-up Jews should be sold as slaves to Christians, as far off as possible from their original place of abode; and the children at six years of age were to be taken from their parents, to be educated in the Christian religion, and to be married to Christians when they were old enough. The masters to whom the Jews were given were strictly forbidden ever to grant them their liberty unless they underwent baptism.

No one now will doubt the folly any more than the wickedness of these savage proposals. Of course they could not be carried out; but enough was done to make the most peaceably disposed Jew in the kingdom the deadly foe of the Gothic power. Little as we know of the history of the conflict of the Goths with the Saracens, there is proof enough that the help of the Jews contributed not a little to the victory of the invaders.

Three years after the date of this council Egica raised his son Witica to be the sharer of his throne; and in 701 he died, leaving Witica sole ruler.

Although Witica reigned nine years, we know strangely little about him. Later writers have delighted to represent him as a monster of wickedness; but all that is recorded of him on good authority is greatly to his honour. He pardoned and restored to their rank and estates those whom his father had banished or degraded. There were many other wealthy persons whom Egica had compelled to sign documents, acknowledging themselves debtors to the treasury; Witica caused these papers to be publicly burnt It seems that he tried to reform the corruptions of the Church. A writer belonging to the priestly party complains that Sindered, the Archbishop of Toledo, inspired with a zeal for holiness, but not according to knowledge," obeyed the king's orders by continually harassing and persecuting men of high standing among the clergy. It is likely enough (though the statements cannot be traced back beyond the ninth century) that he encouraged the clergy to marry, and that he showed some degree of favor to the Jews – at any rate, that he did not try to carry into effect the insane persecution laws passed in his father's time. Altogether Witica seems to have made him beloved by the people, and hated and feared by the churchmen. It is easy to understand why in later ages he was accused of all sorts of dreadful crimes. The sudden ruin of the kingdom in the first year of his successor could only be accounted for by ascribing it to divine vengeance; and Witica was supposed to have been the great sinner whose wickedness had drawn down the wrath of Heaven.

Witica died in February, 710, leaving two sons not yet come to the age of manhood. It seems that he had named one of these boys as his successor in the kingdom, but the council of nobles and prelates set aside his wishes, and elected to the throne a certain Roderic; a Gothic noble who had had the chief command of the army.

XXXV: THE FALL OF THE VISIGOTHS

Every one has heard of "Roderic, the last of the Goths;" but of the real history of this famous king we know scarcely anything for certain. The romantic story of which he is the hero is the invention of chroniclers who lived many centuries after his death. But we ought not to pass over in silence a story which Scott and Southey in England, and many a poet in other lands, have taken as the theme of their song.

According to this legend, Roderic was the son of Theudefrid, a grandson of King Kindaswinth, and one of the many victims of Witica's tyranny. The cruel king had put out his eyes, and thrown him into prison, where he died. To revenge his father's fate, Roderic raised a rebellion, seized the person of Witica, and having first blinded him, put him to death. Roderic was then crowned king; but Witica's two sons bided their time to avenge their father and to attempt to regain their inheritance.

Their opportunity might have been long in coming if Roderic had not made a more powerful enemy in Count Julian, who in the late king's reign had distinguished himself by a brave defence of Ceuta, the one Gothic fortress in Africa that had not fallen into the hands of the Saracens. Julian, although a kinsman of Witica's, had quietly accepted Roderic's usurpation, and had continued to fight bravely and successfully against the Moors. But when he heard that the new king had dishonoured his daughter, the beautiful Florinda, he resolved to revenge his own wrongs by the betrayal of his country. He sought an interview with the Mohammedan chief, Musa, and counselled him to undertake the conquest of Spain. The success of the undertaking, he said, only too truly, was certain, for the Goths as well as the Spaniards hated the usurper, and would desert his standards when the conflict came.

Musa needed little persuasion. A body of twelve thousand men, led by a Berber chief named Tarik, and accompanied by Julian and the Goths who followed him in his treason, set sail from the African coast, and landed at the place since called "the mountain of Tarik" (Jebel Tarik, Gibraltar).

The Gothic governor of the southern province, Theudemer, was taken by surprise, and wrote to Roderic for aid. The king, who was then fighting the rebellious Basques in the Pyrenees, broke up his camp, and hastened southwards, summoning his army from all parts oi the country to meet him at Cordova. A hundred thousand men—so runs the story—assembled under his banner; but among this great host there were few who were loyal to his crown. The Gothic nobles who had reluctantly submitted to his rule now said among themselves, "Why should we risk our lives in the defence of the usurper? The Moors are only in quest of plunder; when Roderic is beaten they will go home with their booty, and then we can give the throne to whom we will." But Roderic thought that now the country was threatened by an infidel foe his rivals would lay aside their selfish aims, and unite against the common danger.

In this confidence he entrusted the command of the two wings of his army to the sons of Witica.

The great battle took place near Xeres de la Frontera, ten miles north of Cadiz, beside the river Chrysus, now called the Guadalete. Roderic appeared on the field clothed in a purple robe and wearing a jewelled crown. His chariot of ivory was drawn by eight milk-white steeds. It was not until after several days' fighting that the sons of Witica offered their aid to the enemy. Tarik agreed to their conditions, and the battle ended, on July 26, 711, in the utter rout of Roderic's supporters. As to the fate of Roderic himself there are three different stories. Some say that he was slain by Tarik's own hand; others that he was drowned in attempting to cross the river, and that long afterwards his golden shoes, and his horse Orelio, were found in the mud of the stream. The third legend is like that which was afterwards told of Harold of England—how the defeated and wounded king escaped from the battle-field, and lived for many years in a hermitage under a feigned name, devoting himself to prayer and to self-mortification in atonement for his sins. It is this last version that Southey has used in his poem of "Roderick, the Last of the Goths."

Such is the story of Roderic, as it is told by Spanish and Arabic writers of the thirteenth and later centuries. Perhaps it may contain fragments of true history here and there; but what we really know of Roderic's reign is little more than this, that his defeat on the Guadalete was the end of the Gothic kingdom of Spain. Almost unresisted, the conquerors spread over the land, taking possession of city after city, until "the green flag of the Prophet waved from the towers of the royal palace of Toledo."

XXXVI: CONCLUSION

The Visigoths were never driven out of Spain as the Ostrogoths were driven out of Italy. They remained to become, like the older inhabitants of the country, subjects of the Moors. Under the Mohammedan dominion the two Christian peoples, drawn together by their common hatred of the infidel, and by their common aspirations after freedom, became finally one nation. The story of the Goths merges now into the story of Spain.

Yet even through the seven centuries of Moorish dominion the descendants of the native Spaniards continued to look up to the descendants of the Goths as to their natural leaders and chiefs. After the battle on the Guadalete the Goth Theudemer, the former viceroy of Southern Spain under Roderic, betook himself with a small band of men to the eastern coast, and there defended himself so valiantly that the conquerors allowed him to establish a tributary Christian kingdom in Murcia, where he reigned until his death. Afterwards the Moors broke the treaty which they had made with him, and the "land of Theudemer," as the Arabic writers call it, was joined to the Mohammedan dominions. In the far north-west, the Christians of the Asturias maintained their independence under a succession of Gothic chiefs, to whom the later kings of Spain were proud to trace their ancestry. In all the uprisings of the Christians against the Moors, and in the last great struggle which ended in the overthrow of the infidel rule, men with Gothic names appear as leaders and champions. But for the Gothic element in the Spanish people the chivalry of Castile would never have been, and Spain might even yet have remained under Mohammedan rule. To this day the noble families of Spain boast, if not always with reason, of the purity of their Gothic blood.

For the last traces of the Goths as a separate people, speaking their own language, we must, however, look not to Spain, but far away to the east of Europe. At the end of the fourth century, when the empire of Ermanaric fell under the yoke of the Huns, a small remnant of the Ostrogoths found shelter from the savage invaders in the Crimea, and in this remote corner of Europe they preserved their existence as a nation for more than a thousand years. Early in the fifth century they were converted to Catholic Christianity, and their bishops long continued to take part in general councils of the church. In the year 1562 a traveller from Belgium, named Busbek, met with two ambassadors sent by this little nation to Constantinople, and wrote down a long list of words belonging to their language. Of course many of these words were greatly corrupted, and some of them are not Gothic at all, but borrowed from the laneuasres of the surrounding nations. But still the list makes it quite clear that the language spoken by this Crimean people must originally have been the same with that used by Wulfila in his translation of the Bible. Nearly two hundred years later—about 1750—a charitable Jesuit of Vienna, named Mondorf, ransomed a prisoner from the Turkish galleys, and learned from him that he came from the Crimea, and that his native language bore some resemblance to German. It is possible that Mondorf was not mistaken, and (strange as it seems to think of it!) that the language of Wulfila was actually surviving, in some corrupted shape, only a century and a half ago. Mondorfs ransomed captive knew nothing about Christianity, but said that his countrymen worshipped an ancient tree. Until the eighteenth century the Crimea was still called Gothia, at least in the official documents of the Greek Church; but the name is now gone out of use, and, so far as we know, the Gothic language is wholly extinct.

So ends the story of the once mighty nation of the Goths. Many other peoples that have played as famous a part in history have passed away; but they have left behind them abundant monuments of their ancient greatness. With the Goths it has been otherwise. They have bequeathed to the world no treasures of literature, no masterpieces of art, no splendid buildings. They have left no conspicuous impress on the manners or the institutions of any modern European people. The other great Teutonic nations that overran the Roman Empire have their memorial in the modern names of the countries which they conquered. The Franks have given their name to France, the Burgunds to Burgundy, the Langobards to Lombardy, and the Vandals to Andalusia. But of the conquests and dominion of the Goths not even such slight record remains.

Yet though the Goths have passed away, leaving behind them so little to show what once they were, their memory can never die. History cannot forget the people whose valour shook the decaying Roman Empire to its fall, and prepared the way for the rise of a worthier civilization on the ruins of the old. In their work of destruction they succeeded; whenever they tried to build up they failed. But it is something to have attempted nobly; and, for all the sadness of its ending, the history is not wholly inglorious that records the saintly heroism of Wulfila, the chivalrous magnanimity of Totila, and the wise and beneficent statesmanship of Theoderic.

THE END

Made in the USA
Monee, IL
22 July 2021